dai

daughters

A STORY OF FIVE GENERATIONS

BHARATI RAY

~

Translated by Madhuchhanda Karlekar

Foreword by **AMARTYA SEN**

PENGUIN BOOKS

PENGUIN BOOKS
Published by the Penguin Group
Penguin Books India Pvt. Ltd, 11 Community Centre, Panchsheel Park, New Delhi 110 017, India
Penguin Group (USA) Inc., 375 Hudson Street, New York, New York 10014, USA
Penguin Group (Canada), 90 Eglinton Avenue East, Suite 700, Toronto, Ontario, M4P 2Y3, Canada (a division of Pearson Penguin Canada Inc.)
Penguin Books Ltd, 80 Strand, London WC2R 0RL, England
Penguin Ireland, 25 St Stephen's Green, Dublin 2, Ireland (a division of Penguin Books Ltd)
Penguin Group (Australia), 250 Camberwell Road, Camberwell, Victoria 3124, Australia (a division of Pearson Australia Group Pty Ltd)
Penguin Group (NZ), 67 Apollo Drive, Rosedale, North Shore 0632, New Zealand (a division of Pearson New Zealand Ltd)
Penguin Group (South Africa) (Pty) Ltd, 24 Sturdee Avenue, Rosebank, Johannesburg 2196, South Africa

Penguin Books Ltd, Registered Offices: 80 Strand, London WC2R 0RL, England

First published in Bengali as *Ekaal Sekaal* by Ananda Publishers 2008
First published in English by Penguin Books India 2011

Copyright © Bharati Ray 2011
Translation copyright © Madhuchhanda Karlekar 2011
Foreword copyright © Amartya Sen 2008 and 2011

10 9 8 7 6 5 4 3 2 1

ISBN 9780143416487

Typeset in Adobe Garamond by InoSoft Systems, Noida
Printed at Gopsons Printers, Noida

For Kabir

CONTENTS

MA

ME

KHUKU

FOREWORD

Writing good social history in a style that is readable is not an easy thing. Presenting family annals in an organized way is equally tough. But combining the two in a balanced manner, weaving family history in with the larger narrative of social change, is a well-nigh impossible task. That Bharati Ray has conquered this high and difficult terrain with such consummate skill is indeed cause for wonder. Of course, for those who already know Bharati, this new—and arduous—achievement of hers will come as no surprise. Since I have been well acquainted with her from our student days, the uniqueness of her new book has not astonished me. But the lucid brilliance with which she tells her story, relating events and incidents to illumine the wider social panorama of changing times, has an invaluable merit which I wish to proclaim in no uncertain terms.

Though Bharati's work may be compared to climbing an inhospitable mountain, the subject of her book is far removed from any tortuous landscape. There is no lack of entertainment in the situations she describes. Even those who are not constantly on the lookout for weighty wisdom, who have no objection to gaining pleasure from a straightforward story, engagingly told, will enjoy this book immensely. If some knowledge of social developments is gained in the process, that would be a bonus.

Of the five generations Bharati deals with, the first person we meet is her mother's grandmother, Shailabala. Eager to be educated, undoubtedly meritorious, Shailabala is thwarted by the conservative values of her marital home. As times change and society evolves, fields of opportunity increase for subsequent generations. Bharati belongs to the fourth generation. When I saw her in Presidency College, amidst work or at her hilarious best in a circle of friends, I didn't think of her as being particularly disadvantaged. But circumstances became even more favourable for her daughters—of the fifth generation.

In this story of five generations, the main characters are always women. As we learn of their life stories, narrated in vivid detail one after another, we simultaneously gather a clear picture of the progress being made regarding a particular aspect of Bengali society. Here we see the progress happening gradually. Of course, not all Bengali women have been similarly benefited. There is no dearth of disadvantages—social, political or economic—in their lives, particularly among the poor. I know that Bharati has always been eager to work towards removing these disadvantages from the time she was a student. She has long been working for social progress beyond her own immediate circle; and marks of this larger perspective are evident in different ways in many parts of her book.

The person who arranged for Shailabala's childhood marriage into a highly conservative family was none other than her father. Although Shailabala's life was full of suppressed contradictions, nevertheless, she remained deeply and immeasurably devoted to this very father. This is a commonly noted aspect of the socially handicapped. All too often we see that those who suffer most from the effects of social inequality will not blame the patriarchs who are most responsible for their sorry state; thereby, the unequal conditions are further perpetrated. Many such thoughts come to mind as we read through this book. Without marring the beauty of her narrative, Bharati has brought up many such issues in a simple way, to provide food for thought for the reader. In describing her own book, Bharati has said, 'It is a personal story, a family story as seen mirrored through my own life.' The reader will see how current events can be presented with simple, good taste; and with it they will also see how very ordinary events can sometimes reveal some bigger truths.

I have no doubt that readers will find much to enjoy and much to think about in this beautiful and well-conceived book. Before I end this short introduction, I congratulate Bharati once again.

AMARTYA SEN

BEFORE I BEGIN

In most parts of India, family histories are traced through the male line. Bengal is no exception. But I have chosen to break with tradition and tell my story of five generations via the female line. Apart from research on a few scattered matrilineal societies that still survive in different parts of the world, such an attempt has probably not been made. My focus on mothers and daughters operates within the patriarchal joint family structure. There are grandmothers on the fathers' side of course, but chiefly the subjects are the grandmothers on the mothers' side. In Bengali joint families, a father's mother had a huge role to play in the upbringing of granddaughters; in the way they were nurtured and socialized, the values they imbibed. By contrast, the mother's mother whom one visited only on occasion, was someone who indulged and spoilt. As a short-term visitor, you did not expect to be scolded much in her home. Normally, therefore, the father's mother would be expected to have a much greater influence than the mother's mother. But it cannot be denied that a powerful yet invisible chain of values, hopes, aspirations were bequeathed from mother to daughter. Not everything of course, but definitely some. In a sense, my story deals with how this stream operates through generations.

The setting is a middle-class Bengali home—not in villages but small towns and cities. The five generations are: my mother's grandmother, my grandmother, my mother, me and finally my eldest daughter Khuku. The time span is from the late nineteenth century to the early years of the twenty-first. How much change has there been during this period of more than a hundred years? Or has there not been much basic change at all? What has been the nature of this change, if any? The moving picture of life may capture just half of reality, and fail to capture the other half.

I relate the story of five ordinary women. A few of them might exhibit some exceptional traits—life itself is so full of variety—but by and large, they are indeed ordinary. They set no new standards of achievement and have no list of outstanding contributions to boast of. They were born, they gave birth and spent their lives—or will spend their lives—in joy and sorrow, tiffs and piques, with honour or humiliation, fulfilment and despair, gain and loss, like other average women. Many of their experiences may be similar to your own, many of you may feel that you have seen such faces in your own homes, or still see them today. Many aspects will feel all too familiar, many sentiments may match your own exactly.

This story would have been better written by my mother. She was right in the middle of the five generations. She was the one who observed the others from close. I had requested her to write it but she laughed it off, saying, 'Who would be interested in ordinary women like us? Who would want to read such a book? I haven't done anything extraordinary to write an autobiography.' I wanted to make her understand that the high achievers, whether they were men or women, would always find a place in history books. But if ordinary men and women, who make up our society, who form the majority of people, don't write about themselves, how will future generations know about them? Do ordinary people have no history? No life to lead? No problems to solve? If future generations know nothing of them, by what standards will they measure their own actions? How will they make progress, or work for change? How will they refashion their own lives? Ordinary human beings are our real inheritors. Our life experiences are our chief inheritance. My mother heard me out, but continued laughing!

She is no more. I can't beg and cajole her now. So I have written the story of five generations myself. I don't have all the details, but I do know a substantial amount. The first woman in my story is my mother's grandmother whom I had known. Even in earlier times, not many people were lucky enough to see five generations. Girls were married off at a very young age; they produced children while they themselves were little girls. These days, marriage and child-bearing age have been pushed back. Even till the 1960s, there were many who had seen their great-grandmothers. When I was born my great-grandmother had just reached middle age. This was possible because she gave birth to my grandmother when she was only fifteen years old—her third child and first daughter. My grandmother was fourteen when she gave birth to my mother, her first child. My mother was nineteen when she gave birth to me—her firstborn. And I was twenty-six when my daughter Khuku was born. My great-grandmother was only forty-eight years old when I was born. A half century of rapid change. *Tempus fugit!*

This is a personal story, a family story. Therefore there is nothing impersonal about it. There is no analysis of world events, no re-evaluation of history. This is merely an idle looking back at the past and glancing into the future. Just words strewn before you at will. A story purely, and nothing more. But true, nonetheless.

BHARATI RAY
Kolkata
November 2009

SUNDAR-MA

THE HOUSE ON HANUMAN ROAD

My great-grandmother was no beauty, but to all of us, the children in the family, she was Sundar-ma—pretty Ma. In Bengal, it is common practice to affectionately call the elder generation by fancy names—Sundar-ma, Moni-ma (jewel mother), Kaka-moni (jewel uncle), and so on. Our Sundar-ma was large and dark and very plainly, very unfashionably, dressed—coarse white khaddar sari, khaddar chemise, no blouse. A slim gold chain hung around her neck, on her left wrist was the customary iron bangle, plain, with no gold trimmings, and a thin gold bangle adorned each of her wrists. She was unattractive and her manners unrefined. The image of the idealized Bengali housewife of old, a cultural stereotype that shines like a beacon in our collective memory 'decked in a fine Dhaka sari, red sindur dot on her forehead', or at least 'a red-bordered white sari over her head'—Sundar-ma was nothing like that. Quite the opposite, in fact. She was of heavy body, coarse dress, plain speech, rough gait; her head was unveiled, her brow devoid of a vermilion bindi and the ubiquitous bunch of keys did not dangle from her sari's train. Sundar-ma was entirely lacking in what we might call grace. What she did possess, however, was strength of spirit, tej, a quality rare in her time as well as in ours. It didn't draw you close to her but it inspired awe. Such was Sundar-ma, the first of the five daughters in this story. Her name, Shailabala Sen.

When I think of Sundar-ma, the first image that comes to my mind is of our house at 48 Hanuman Road in New Delhi; the house, so I've been told, I was born in. I have such warm and tender memories of that place: an immense two-storeyed mansion skirted by large verandas in front and rear and surrounded by lush, sprawling gardens. Tall trees provided shade in the front garden and close to the house on the right hand stood a tree that soared beyond the second floor. I can see that tree even now; I need to only close my eyes.

After you crossed the front garden and climbed up five steps, you would reach a large, white marble veranda. The first room to the left was Dadamoshai's—my great-grandfather's—huge dispensary and consultation room. To the right was the drawing room, almost as large. It had heavy chintz-covered sofas with carved mahogany armrests. In front of them was an arrangement of four medium-sized tables. There were no peg tables like we have nowadays. An air cooler stood in one corner. In another corner was a large carpet made for an Indian-style seating arrangement; with several bolsters encased in covers with Rajasthani mirror-work and Gujarati stitches randomly strewn around. All expensive things, but not necessarily of high aesthetic value.

Behind these two large rooms were four or five medium to small rooms on either side. Kitchen, pantry, dining room to the left plus two other rooms stacked with books, files, papers and documents of all sorts. You could call it an office-cum-library. In one room was a large table with two chairs facing each other; in the other room were glass-fronted cabinets filled with medical textbooks and foreign journals. The five rooms to the right were for guests and for Dadamoshai's nephews and their families. They led to a wide veranda enclosed with an ornamental railing. Further up was a tiled courtyard.

On one side of the veranda, a marble staircase led to the second floor.

The rooms upstairs were mostly bedrooms. Above the dispensary was Dadamoshai's bedroom, with a dressing room attached. Two large mahogany closets and a dresser took up all the space. Next came the room for all kinds of extras—quilts, blankets, bedding, warm clothes. The smallest room was Dadamoshai's personal puja room adorned with photographs of his guru, Anandamoyee Ma. On the right, above the drawing room, was the gigantic central living room. Beds were laid out there from end to end for children and grandchildren to sleep. There was a gigantic almirah in that room—not to talk about it will leave my story incomplete. It was essentially a linen cupboard, stacked with pillows, sheets, counterpanes and so on. But we children valued it more as an ideal place to hide. We would creep into it and close the doors; cover ourselves with quilts and cushions and lie very still. It was difficult for anyone to find us, particularly when we played 'Dark Room'. Unfortunately, after a few rounds of the game, the secret hiding place became common knowledge and lost its charm.

Adjoining the inner room was a walled terrace where we would sit and enjoy the evening breeze or sleep on moist mats on hot summer nights. Sleeping under the open sky on summer nights is an old custom in Delhi. From a corner of the terrace, a wrought iron spiral staircase led to the third floor on which there was a single room, the rest being another open expanse of terrace, surrounded by railings.

Behind the house, a little over half an acre of land was planted with fruits and vegetables. Custard apple, melon, papaya, malta, jujube, cherry, guava and seasonal fruits of all sorts hung from the trees. We gorged on them in the late afternoons. Seasonal vegetables too grew in abundance—cauliflower, cabbage, carrot, radish, pea, tomato, okra, aubergine, pumpkin, potato, bottle gourd, spinach and coriander. There was also a greenhouse in one corner where exotic flowers bloomed. Just outside it, a creeper laden with bunches of white and pink malati flowers swung from a bower made of bamboo strips. I had named the flowers madhumalati, for they were like honey, mild and pleasing to the senses. On the other side of the archway, opposite the greenhouse, was a two-roomed annexe in a corner of the garden. Dadamoshai had built it for the exclusive use of Anandamoyee Ma. In another corner were the garages and servicemen's quarters.

A big attraction of the house was its location near Connaught Circus and Jantar Mantar, right next to the Hanumanji temple. When I visited 48 Hanuman Road recently, I saw a sad, dilapidated old place, still standing as mute testimony of the past. My eyes started smarting with tears. I addressed the house in the eloquent words of the poet Rabindranath Tagore, 'Speak, O speak!'

I stood outside the gate for a long, long time. Suddenly, the Hanumanji temple did seem to speak out. I heard the bells tolling for the puja. I saw in my mind's eye the prayer lamps being waved before the image for the evening ritual, felt the warmth of the fire. And all at once half a century seemed to vanish. I was a little girl in a frock again, walking through the Hanumanji fair which was held every Tuesday on the temple grounds. It still is, I am told. People came with their wares from nearby villages. Folks in colourful clothing laid out their goods for sale—cane baskets of all shapes and sizes, clay dolls, cooking utensils—ladles, tongs—tasty snacks, hot, sweet and sour. Freshly cooked jalebis were piled high on tables, as were the boxes of a fluffy pink sweet we called burir chul, old woman's hair (I never asked what its real name was), which melted in the mouth. Sohan halwa I couldn't afford to buy, so I simply looked at it greedily. There were then those big, hot samosas, crisp-fried namkeens, an assortment of dalmut, and best of all, the salty-spicy-powdery churan, my favourite. Streams of eager and happy customers crowded the fair and sales were brisk. The most popular items were the oil-filled clay lamps, the golden marigolds and the shallow clay bowls of peda, a sweet made from highly condensed milk—all essential offerings for the presiding deity. But my attention was fixed on one special corner where glass bangles glittered in their multicoloured splendour. The light on the matching bead necklaces sparkled; not any one colour, but rainbow-hued. I bought some bangles, wore them, and broke them. I was sad when they shattered but bought new ones the following week. They cost so little—five to ten paise a dozen. I haven't worn glass bangles for many years now. Perhaps I should start. But Sundar-ma is no more. Who will buy me bangles from the Hanumanji fair? It is no fun buying them with one's own money. And there is no one who will gift them to me. No Sundar-ma to gently press my fingers with her soft hands and slip them on.

The first time I saw Sundar-ma was in Delhi. I, Ma and my younger sister Tapati boarded the Delhi-Kalka Mail from Howrah station and took our seats in the inter-class (what is today called the second-class category by the Railways) ladies' compartment. We were visiting Ma's rich relatives in the capital. What a thrill! It was a hot and stuffy journey with people packed close, women chatting loudly in Hindi, children bawling and creating a racket, but none of this bothered us one bit. Ma had packed luchi, alu dom, and home-made sandesh in a large aluminium tiffin carrier. We ate heartily and slept peacefully all night, spent the next day bubbling with excitement and finally reached Delhi.

Date: August 1945. Time: well past late evening. World War II had just come to an end. The English and their allies had defeated the Japanese–German axis powers. The sky was awash with blazing searchlights. Not in search of enemy aircraft but to proudly declare to the world the mighty prowess of Great Britain. They splashed it across the sky—V for Victory! V for the Victors! So the British had won, had they? But we had been chanting a different rhyme till only the other day!

Do—Re—Mi—Fa—So—La—Ti
The Japs are on a bombing spree!
Inside each bomb, a cobra snake!
The British holler, heaven's sake!

I don't know who penned those lines or where we children picked up the silly rhyme. I've no memory of these details now. The author probably felt closer to the Japanese as fellow Asians than to the British. He must have been pleased when the Japanese bombed Imphal, Manipur and even Kolkata; he never suspected that atom bombs, spewing poison a zillion times more deadly than a cobra's, would be dropped on Hiroshima and Nagasaki. Who could imagine then that the price for those horrendous war games would have to be paid by thousands upon thousands of Japanese for generations to come? That the one vile act would mushroom through time as the ever-present threat of a nuclear holocaust affecting all mankind! Wars and bombs never resolve any conflict; they engender greater enmity and hate.

At that time I, a little girl being reared in various small towns of Bengal, did not think of these things. I only raised my eyes up to the sky and gazed in wonder at the brilliant lights as we drove to the house on Hanuman Road. I was half asleep by the time we finally arrived. Sundar-ma was waiting for us at the door. Ma bent down and touched her feet. All Sundar-ma said was, 'Come.' I was disappointed. There we were, the three of us, at the end of a long and arduous journey. Ma was visiting for the first time after her marriage and with two daughters in tow. Was this all the welcome she was to get? No hugs or kisses, no voices raised in excitement, not even a faint smile; just 'Come'? Was this the Sundar-ma my mother had talked so much about? My heart sank. However, Sundar-ma did escort us upstairs to the central room. I fell asleep the minute I hit the fluffy white family bed. Ma must have cleaned us up and changed our clothes but I don't remember. I caught sight of the big veranda though, and fell asleep with the thought that my sister and I could have a great skipping race there the next morning.

The race didn't happen. For early next morning I heard Ma's younger brother Ashok, who was my age, loudly reciting a poem by Hemachandra Bandhopadhyay: 'Sleep no more, open your eyes and see . . .' Didi-ma, my grandmother, who was visiting her own mother at the time, had brought her youngest son along. Ma, Didi-ma and Sundar-ma planned to spend some time together. Ashok's nickname was Bachchu. He didn't like the name at all because his friends teased him about it. So I called him Mamu, not Bachchu-mama. He was always delighted to see me—for the first one or two minutes, that is. Then we started arguing about something or the other. That morning at breakfast he provoked a huge argument with this question: who has more courage, boys or girls? Mamu said, 'Boys.' 'Girls!' I screamed. 'Okay, prove it.' Breakfast uneaten, we rushed off to prove each other wrong, ignoring Ma and

Didi-ma's shouts: 'You children—finish your food first!' Mamu led me to the downstairs veranda. He dragged a heavy bench to the top of the marble steps leading down to the garden. Panting with excitement and strain, he placed a chair on the bench, climbed on top of it and jumped down to the ground below. 'See how brave we boys are!' I immediately placed a three-legged stool on top of the chair. It started wobbling. But eager to prove I had more courage than boys, I got up on that stool and promptly fell down. I hit my forehead on a corner of the bench and blood gushed out. It hurt and frightened me at the same time. Could there be so much blood in one's forehead? I didn't cry, in case it proved my cowardice. When I touch my forehead today, I can still feel the long scar right in the centre. It serves as an identity mark for me; it's noted in my passport. Ma picked me up that day, a big eleven-year-old girl, and laid me down on the bed upstairs. Sundar-ma remarked, as she applied medicine on my wound and soothed me down with a cold compress, 'Never wage a war on a man. If you have to, watch your step.'

SUNDAR-MA'S CHILDHOOD AND MARRIAGE

That much loved house on Hanuman Road was not Sundar-ma's birthplace. She was born in Bogurha, though her father's ancestral home was in a village called Kalia in Jessore district, then part of East Bengal, now of Bangladesh.

Her father's name was Pyareshankar Das Gupta. Her mother Sukhadasundari Devi was a zamindar's daughter from Kashiani, a village in the Faridpur district. Though no one knows the exact date when Sundar-ma was born, it was probably 1882. The conch shells that greet the birth of a male child remained silent for her. Yet, Shailabala was not a neglected child. But first, a little bit about her family.

Several generations ago, Ramballav, an ancestor of Sundar-ma, used to work as an office clerk for the zamindar of Boral. Having gained his employer's favour, Ramballav sought permission to build his home in Kalia. In those days Kalia was mainly an overgrown forest. The zamindar bequeathed the land with a few simple words: 'You want it? It's yours.' Ramballav cleared the area and built a house of his own. Umashankar, one of Ramballav's descendants, was Pyareshankar's father. Umashankar was a scholar of Sanskrit as well as a kaviraj, an Ayurvedic physician. In those days many such physicians used to run their own medical schools; Umashankar too ran a training school of his own. The curriculum for students of Ayurveda comprised primarily grammar, poetic literature, Kapila's ancient Sankhya philosophy, the two classic Ayurveda texts by Charaka and Susruta, the *Charak Samhita* and the *Susrut Samhita* and a few other Sanskrit texts. Learning Sanskrit was critical to qualifying as a kaviraj since all the relevant texts, particularly the Atharva Veda, the foundation of kaviraji medicine, were written in that language. The other essential part of the curriculum was field training on medicinal herbs. Students would roam the forests, collect roots and plants and learn how to prepare a variety of medicines with them: some needed to be ground to a paste while others had to be boiled to extract the juices. These medicines were extremely efficacious.

Of course, if the need arose, medicines for certain diseases were also bought from Ayurveda shops in the market.

Most conscientious kaviraji doctors did not take any fees in those days. The novelist Tarashankar Bandhopadhyay has written of this tradition in great detail in his novel *Arogya Niketan*. The protagonist of his novel is 'Moshai' kaviraj, scion of a long line of healers and worshippers of Lord Krishna. Healing the sick was their religion, their way of worshipping the divine. They were adept at diagnosis and medication and they never sold their knowledge. Tarashankar says that his 'Moshai' is based on a real person. Much like Moshai, Umashankar practised kaviraji well into old age. Even when he was bent over and his feet trembled, his granddaughters-in-law would lead him by the hand to his customary seat: a broad pallet bed covered with a worn, white sheet that had lost its pristine hue. Umashankar was not a rich man. His patients would take a holy dip after they were cured and send him farm produce by way of gratitude—usually half a maund, about twenty kilograms, of paddy or rice, plenty of fresh vegetables, some fruits, a pitcher of milk and fresh clarified butter. These came along with sun-dried lentil balls, home-made condiments, mango preserves, as well as cleaned and husked spices for the kitchen. These goods were sufficient for his family's daily meals. His personal needs were few, his ambitions none. He lived simply, and the principles of kaviraji ruled his life as well as profession.

Umashankar's son Pyareshankar was, however, cast in a different mould. He carried within his soul the seeds of rebellion which later manifested in his politics, his religion, even in his everyday behaviour. Pyareshankar refused to pursue the family tradition and opted for the Western system of medicine. Ignoring his father's frowns, he joined a medical college. After passing, he settled in Bogurha, soon established a roaring practice and gained great respect. Pyareshankar maintained a huge joint family of relatives, both close and distant. It is said that a maund of rice was cooked daily to feed them. His gatekeeper Bachchu Singh alone ate a seer, about one kilogram, of rice every day. His house in Bogurha stands to this day, occupied now by a Vaishnav family. It is a large mansion surrounded by three bighas of land. The outer quarters are two storeys high and the inner quarters are single-storeyed. The grounds are of red earth, as in Santiniketan, and the river Karotowa flows nearby.

As long as Pyareshankar lived, his household observed none of the rituals that are considered traditionally Hindu. He was Westernized, a rationalist in the imported British tradition and in his heart a follower of the Brahmo leader Keshab Chandra Sen. He did finally adopt the Brahmo religion towards the end of his life. Many kinds of people constantly visited his house but the saffron-clad monks were not among them. The routine Hindu festivals like Lakshmi puja, Saraswati puja or Shasthi puja were never observed. In those days, little girls would wake up early in the morning, make little clay models of Lord Shiva and pray to them. No girl in Pyareshankar's house ever did that. Pyareshankar's wife Sukhadasundari was from East Bengal where women were particularly keen on observing special fasts and rituals throughout the year. Yet she could not introduce these practices in Pyareshankar's home, or perhaps she did not want to, knowing how her husband felt about such matters.

Pyareshankar was in many ways a unique man—stubborn and strongly principled. He was once invited to his in-laws' place in Faridpur. On the way he had to cross a river. After he was ferried across, he paid the boatman a rupee. His brother-in-law and the others who had come to receive him began to accost the boatman. 'A whole rupee to cross such a narrow strip of water? Is this a joke, you rascal? How dare you cheat our son-in-law!' In an instant, they cut off the Muslim boatman's beard. Pyareshankar was so offended that he took the very same boat back. There was no way he could accept the hospitality of those who had insulted and abused the boatman.

On another occasion, Pyareshankar had gone to see a patient in some village. The patient's little daughter was sweet and gentle and Pyareshankar was quite taken with her. As he was leaving, a well-wisher remarked, 'Doctor-babu, since you like the little girl so much, why don't you make her a part of your home?' Pyareshankar replied simply, 'Very well, I will.' He blessed the girl with the money he had received as fees and shortly after, married her to his second son Benoyshankar.

In matters such as this, his wife Sukhadasundari was just as impulsive. It was she who arranged her older son's marriage. She was having a bath at the Boro Kalia river when she saw a cute little girl. On asking she was told that the girl was the daughter of a teacher, Khirode Master, and of suitable lineage. On returning home, she announced that she would bring home the girl as her eldest son's bride. Soon after she did just that. Unfortunately, Sukhadasundari did not get a chance to mould the girl in the way she wanted. She died soon after, still in the full flush of youth, decked up in all her fine jewellery and the vermilion bright on her forehead. Sukhadasundari had made no mistake: the little girl was as efficient as she was pretty; and large-hearted too. Benoyshankar's children readily admit that it was their aunt who brought them up, not their mother. That is how things worked then. The smooth functioning of a joint family depended mostly on its women, particularly on the ginni, the seniormost among them. If you could love your brother-in-law's or your sister-in-law's children as much as you loved your own, the family would be peaceful.

Although he lost his wife fairly early in life, it did not occur to Pyareshankar to remarry. He became passionately involved in the politics of the swadeshi movement. This movement had begun as a protest against Lord Curzon's proposal to split the state of Bengal into two. Pyareshankar joined the Congress Party and soon set up a store for locally made cotton goods. He hung a placard in Bengali outside the store which said:

> Whenever you have things to buy,
> Remember your poor Motherland's cry

For Pyareshankar, just opening the shop was not enough. Convinced that buyers would throng there if he were personally present, he often neglected his medical practice to supervise activities in the shop. It soon became an obsession with him.

His second son Benoyshankar had his obsessions too, but they were of a different kind. He was greatly fixed on horse-riding. Pyareshankar, who spoilt his son, acquired a pedigree racehorse called Prince from the Calcutta Race Course for him. Young Benoyshankar would, every day, wear black breeches and ride Prince for fourteen miles. How long could a racehorse bear such excessive strain? Prince met an early death—pining for his dear racecourse perhaps. Benoyshankar was devastated. He thought of nothing but his horse night and day. Finally, a Muslim mendicant advised that the family should perform Hindu funeral rites for the dear departed horse. His advice was followed at once. Benoyshankar visited the place where Prince had been buried, fed every horse in the neighbourhood half a seer of chickpeas as part of the funeral observances, and was at last at peace with himself.

Pyareshankar's elder sister Dakshina-thakarun was an outstanding personality. She came back home to her family after she was widowed at the age of twelve. When Pyareshankar grew up, he tried very hard to get her remarried but he failed. While the Widow Remarriage Act had been passed in 1856, the practice was yet to take hold in reality. Dakshina-thakarun thus stayed with her brother Pyareshankar. She was not at all like Mokshada-thakarun, the widowed aunt described in Ashapurna Devi's novel, *Pratham Pratisruti*. She didn't spend her life cooking or making lentil balls and pickles all day. She invited students home and taught them Bengali language and literature. Sometimes she read to them Krittibas's *Ramayana* and Kashiram Das's *Mahabharata*. Even the tuition fee that she charged from the students was unique—for each page studied and explained, students brought her a ripe banana. After every six pages, they brought her a full pot of rossogolla which cost one rupee! Such was the aunt, whose niece Shailabala is the subject of my story.

Shailabala had three brothers and two sisters, none of whom are alive today. Their children and grandchildren are scattered all over India. Some are lawyers, some doctors and others are well-placed executives in multinational companies. One of them, Shatrujitshankar, Benoyshankar's son, proudly declares, 'We are descendants of a kaviraj family. The tree of our knowledge, Sankhya philosophy, provides no proof of the existence of god.' Shatrujit has no interest in someone whose existence cannot be proved or perceived. He has dedicated himself to the service of those who *can* be perceived, human beings. He is not a kaviraj but a doctor—unmatched in his field of specialization: mental illness. He treats patients, he writes books and he studies. In his spare time, he tells me stories that bring the past alive.

Shailabala had very little contact with her maternal family, having lost her mother in childhood, and was always more influenced by her father. Pyareshankar had given her some basic education before he married her off, for which Shailabala remained grateful all her life. In middle-class Bengali families, education for women was not yet the norm, though it was not totally unknown. Kadambini Ganguly and Chandramukhi Bose, Bengal's first BA graduates, were Sundar-ma's contemporaries. Yet, not every girl was allowed to leave home to attend school and college. Many were tutored at home by father, husband or brothers. Swarnakumari of the Tagore family received her first incentive to study from her father; Rokeya Sakhawat Hossain was taught by her elder brother; Kailasabasini Devi's tutor was her husband Durgacharan Gupta; Prasannamayee Devi Chaudhurani was encouraged by her father to dress like a boy and go to the estate manager's office for tuition. Like them, Sundar-ma too studied at home. Of course for her the ceremony of hatey khari, the holding of the first chalk, was never observed. The ceremony was reserved for boys. Sundar-ma had no memory of when she first opened her alphabet book or when she moved on to other primers. What she did remember very well was her sister Indubala's fate. Pyareshankar had allowed Indubala to go to school. On hearing about this, his elder brother came rushing from Jessore and demanded an explanation. 'What is this I hear, Pyare? What evil foreign ways are you trying now? Why do you insist on dragging the family name through dust by sending out a daughter to attend school?' However, his most powerful argument was this: 'Is she your daughter alone? Is she not part of *our* family?' Pyareshankar had always been a bit of a rebel. But faced with this emotional outburst, he lacked the courage to say what he should have: 'She was born in our family but her life is her own. I have put her in school so she can have a chance to enrich that life.' The inevitable happened. Ignoring Indubala's tears, her uncle took her with him to Jessore and got her married.

Pyareshankar did not even think of sending his eldest daughter Shailabala to school. He got her married at the age of eleven to a bright young medical student, Gyanadakanta Sen, who was also from their own village, Kalia. Child marriage was the norm in those days. Families firmly believed that it was best to bring home a little girl who could be easily controlled and moulded before her personality and opinions were fully formed. The girls' parents believed it was their religious duty to give away their daughters early, ideally before they were eight years old. This latter practice, called gouri daan, was considered to be an act of infinite piety. While Pyareshankar, a Brahmo, did not give his daughter away at the age of eight, he did get Shailabala married at a very early age. Since he was so broad-minded, so progressive, so powerful and so strong-willed, why did he not keep her at home for some more years? Why did this exceptionally intelligent girl not get a chance to pursue her studies? Why did he not look for a more suitable family where the in-laws valued education? He was not interested in gaining recognition for piety. Nor could he have cared for the censure of society. Shailabala may have been devoted to her beloved father, but I don't think he did right by her. He failed to rise above the social mores of his times in the case of both his daughters.

Gyanadakanta's family was not affluent. The gifts for her adhivas, traditionally sent by the groom's family for the bride before the wedding, were quite minimal. A bottle of red alta to decorate her feet, soap and hair oil, a little box of face powder, one Benarasi sari, one Benarasi blouse, and two chemises. Also the customary betel leaves and nuts, one medium-sized fish and a few trays of sweetmeats. While Pyareshankar's practice was going great guns at the time, there was no question of him paying any dowry. He did, however, adorn Shailabala in gold from head to toe. She was given a long seven-stranded gold necklace called the Sita haar, gold paisley-shaped ornaments that covered her ears, a gold choker and matching danglers in a peacock design, a ruby-and emerald-studded necklace and chandelier earrings, two thick gold bracelets, a pair of thick gold bangles, two dozen thin gold bangles with a barley and paddy design, a gold comb and floral-design pins for her hair, gold tiara, silver hip-band, silver anklets and elaborate foot decorations called charan padma. I have always wondered what Sundar-ma looked like when she wore all that jewellery, and how she managed to fit it all on her little body. But there is more to getting married than gold ornaments and Benarasi silk. However decked out in finery she might have been, what did Shailabala feel in her heart as she set out for her marital home? We can guess a little of those emotions from Rasasundari Devi's renowned work, *Amar Jiban*, the earliest autobiography written by a Bengali woman, published in 1868.

> I saw some people looking deliriously happy and others in tears. My heart skipped a beat when I saw this . . . for I realized at that moment that my mother would definitely give me away to them. So I jumped on to her lap, clung to her desperately and cried, I beg you Ma, don't let them take me away!

This heart-rending cry must be common to all child brides of all times. Rasasundari Devi was twelve years old when she was married. Shailabala was eleven. She had no mother to cling to at the last minute. She wiped away her tears, took leave of her father and other relatives, and went on her way. She journeyed by boat and then by a palanquin till she finally arrived at her new home.

She found no affectionate mother-in-law or sympathetic relatives. She was dark to begin with and her features were quite plain; she was too young to be blooming with the blush of youth. Though the jewellery she wore dazzled all eyes, they could not stop wagging tongues. 'What have you done, Gyanada's mother? Your son will soon be a doctor and earn piles of money. Is this a suitable bride for him?' Some said, 'Her eyes are too small and she lacks charm.' Some said, 'Fat nose, flat face.' Still others commented, 'They say she's eleven, but she looks nothing less than fourteen or fifteen.' The little girl, who in her father's house had buried her nose in books or played with dolls in her spare time, breathed a heart-rending sigh. She thought to herself, 'When we got our dolls married, dressed my friend's doll as a bride and brought her home, I never thought of whether she was dark or fair, or if her nose was sharp or blunt, her eyes large or small. Am I inferior to a doll then?' She didn't ask this question. But she wondered about this and was sad. The shy diffident thing was plied with plenty of unsolicited advice. 'Remember, this is your real home. You must forget about your rich father now.' Girls are born to serve their in-laws.' Shailabala nodded obediently but said to herself: 'How can I forget my father's home? My father whom I have always adored as a guru. And how can I forget my books?' Never. She sat in her room and studied in secret whenever she could. But spare time was rare. She spent her days much like the other village housewives of her times; her sari drawn over her head like a veil. 'If you're hungry, don't mention it. Never express a wish. Never cry when rebuked. And don't complain if ill—such is the custom in Bengal.' Sundar-ma once read me these words from an article published in 1880 in an old Bengali journal *Somprakash*.

Sundar-ma, the book lover, had opportunity enough later in life to read to her heart's content. But in her early married life, she used to read in secret. If her mother-in-law caught her, she would confiscate the books, shake her by the hair and say, 'You wretch, do you want to become a widow and take my son away?' (It was a popular belief among women then that too much reading caused widowhood.) But Sundar-ma persisted. 'I have no complaints against anyone,' she later said to me. 'Life was like that for all girls. The path for you people is clearer—you must take the lead and take it running.' And when I asked how she negotiated the roads that were closed, Sundar-ma answered: 'I told myself all the time—be patient. Believe in yourself. Hold fast to your resolve and your day will certainly come.'

NEW DELHI: SUNDAR-MA'S HOUSEHOLD

Her day really did come. Gyanadakanta Sen passed his medical exams and left Bengal to earn a living. He went to Simla first and then to Delhi. Shailabala, the child-bride from Jessore, left her in-laws' establishment in her youth and started keeping house on her own in northern India. That was in the year 1912. New Delhi really was new then. The

British rulers had moved their Indian capital from Calcutta to Delhi that very year. Perhaps to teach Bengal a lesson. Curzon's proposed division of Bengal provoked a mighty stir-up. The agitation had one main thrust—be patriotic, boycott British goods. How could the British merchants tolerate that? They may have assumed the ruler's sceptre but had not given up the standard of traders. How dare those Bengali babus defy them? The best thing to do was to transfer the capital to Delhi, once the centre of the Mughal empire. A splendid durbar was held. The emperor George V and Queen Mary arrived in state and inaugurated the new capital. British history is replete with descriptions of that marvellous display of supreme national pride—the Delhi durbar.

The city of Delhi is a peculiar place and, it might be said, quite unique. It has been built, has fallen into ruin, and been rebuilt so many times. Known as Hastinapur in prehistoric times, it was renamed 'Dehli' at some point and some centuries later it became Shahjahanabad where the Emperor Shahjahan built his architectural masterpiece of a fort. His daughter Jahanara ordered the construction of Chandni Chowk; the seat of Mughal culture gradually took shape and became known as Dilli. But how long did that last? The British took over and Dilli became Delhi. It was practically devastated in 1857 during the great revolt. The poet Ghalib's soul cried out: 'Where is Dilli? No longer a city but an army encampment merely. Everything we possessed has been looted. All that remains is our desire to see our old city rebuilt once again.'

Delhi was indeed rebuilt, though not in the Mughal style. The area from where the Mughals ruled became known as Old Delhi. Sir Edwin Lutyens, son-in-law of Viceroy Lord Lytton, arrived in person to plan for New Delhi. An arrogant man, he envisioned Delhi in his mind and restructured it completely along the slopes of Raisina Hill. The Viceroy's House on top of the hill did retain some Mughal influence, but the avenue that stretched from there to India Gate was similar to the Champs Élysées and the Arc de Triomphe of Paris.

It was while this French–English–Mughal baby was growing up that Gyanadakanta Sen came to Delhi to seek his fortune. His timing and skill combined to work magic for his career as a doctor. The city grew fast and so did this young man. He bought a dispensary from an old Bengali doctor and started his private practice. It didn't take time for him to gain fame as a doctor. His income grew rapidly. The sky-high prices of our times were unimaginable in those days so it was possible for him to acquire an acre of land close to Raisina on Hanuman Road. He built a two-storeyed house and the Sen couple moved into their brand new home in 1923.

Very soon the house became a focal point for the huge joint family. In those days if one member of a family, or someone from one's village, became famous or rich, the whole family, nay the whole village, would treat him as their guardian and expect all kinds of help. If they needed money, he was the one to turn to. If they fell sick or faced any kind of trouble, he was always there to help. If someone needed a job, he was approached. Providing food and shelter for four or five people was no great favour to ask. In fact it was taken for granted; as a matter of right. The joint family structure was still very common, particularly in the villages, and so were its ideals. It is true that the changes wrought by colonial rule compelled many to leave their homes in the village alone or with their wives. They no longer lived under the same roof nor did they eat from the same joint kitchen. But in their hearts they identified with the large joint families they had left behind. The strength of that feeling of belonging is something we cannot imagine nowadays. The values of a joint family were so inclusive that not only relatives and neighbours, but many with no ties of blood would assemble there. The mistress of the house was duty-bound to receive them, serve them meals and generally look after them.

Shailabala was mistress of the house on Hanuman Road. What kind of mistress was she? How did she spend her day? This I relate from my own experience. She woke up early and went to the garden. She picked with her own hands the vegetables and fruits that were to be served that day. She brought them to the first-floor balcony and sat down with a bonti. She started cutting up the vegetables on this metal blade, with the wooden piece held firmly under her folded legs in true Bengali style. I watched fascinated as she worked. In our small nuclear family in Calcutta, Ma never needed to cut so many vegetables and she did it very quickly. But for Sundar-ma, every vegetable had to be cut just right depending on how it was to be cooked. One way for shuktoni, a dish of bitter neem or bitter gourd, traditionally eaten as the first course in Bengali cuisine and considered good for the health, round gourds and another way for a thin curry. If someone was ill in the house, vegetables for his stew were cut in large halves in a different style. The same squashes, potatoes, beet, carrots, round gourds, tomatoes, were cut in three or four different shapes, neatly divided and set apart.

There were many mouths to feed every day—a cook, three or four servants, driver and gatekeeper, apart from the children, nephews, nieces, various daughters-in-law, the master of the house and his guests. Every morning a vegetable vendor would stop by and offer his produce, 'Madamji, these are really excellent vegetables. You must take some.' He carried his vegetables in two large baskets strung on two ends of a bamboo rod that he balanced on his shoulders—the way curd sellers in Bengal carry their clay pots. If Sundar-ma needed some vegetables that were not in her garden, she would shout out her orders from upstairs. The fishmonger came daily too, carrying his wares in similar fashion. He weighed the fish and cut it up on a big sharp chopper that he kept wrapped in a piece of white cloth. It was mostly rohu he brought. These days all kinds of fish are available in plenty in Delhi. Better even than those we get in Calcutta. The market where Bengalis shop at Chittaranjan Park sells fresh pabda, parshey and topsey. In Sundar-ma's time, not many middle-class Bengalis lived in Delhi and there was no demand for these gourmet items. But even when other types of fish were available, Sundar-ma always preferred rohu.

The truth is that however grand the appearance of her garden and drawing room, the lifestyle Sundar-ma maintained was quite plain and simple. For breakfast, most days, we had roti, soaked gram and molasses; buttered toast was only occasional. For lunch we had coarse, parboiled rice, dal, a vegetable and a light fish curry. And curd, of course. There was a long white marble shelf in the kitchen where rows of red stone bowls were kept to serve the home-made curd in. If there were extra guests, some more curd would be bought from outside. Sundar-ma would add a bit of milk to the curd to make it go further. That I didn't like. The evening meal was similar, except there was only roti and no rice. No especially tasty dish was cooked. But we had heaps of fruits, especially mangoes. Doctor Dadamoshai's patients would gift him baskets of fruits, trayloads of almonds, currants and sweets. I always eyed the cashew nuts greedily. Sundar-ma would hand me some; I wished I could have some more. I loved cashew nuts, I still do. On Tuesdays, baskets of fruits and sweets arrived from the Hanumanji temple. We ate to our heart's content for the next two days. But what I looked forward to most was Sundar-ma's mango sherbet, sprinkled with fried cumin seed powder. She tucked the mangoes into her coal-fired stove to first burn the skin. Baking them the way we do now can somehow never recreate that flavour. I can still feel Sundar-ma's green mango sherbet, with its unique burnt flavour, on my tongue.

People said Sundar-ma was stingy. Why did she not live in greater style and be a little more lavish when entertaining guests? Of course she could have; there was no shortage of funds. Perhaps she was stingy, I don't know. It could also be that she never understood why people wanted anything in excess of their needs.

As I was saying, Sundar-ma finished her vegetable routine and went off for a bath. She came out in a coarse, red-bordered, hand-woven white cotton sari, the kind called khaddar. This was worn over a thick long-cloth chemise. Her well-oiled hair would be dripping wet and parted down the centre. If she did wear sindur, it could hardly be seen. Cream, powder and perfume were completely dispensed with. She went straight to her books. She read and wrote for the next few hours till it was time for lunch. Sharp at noon she would close her books and go downstairs. People would start drifting in for their midday meal. Down the long wide veranda, piris, low stools, would be placed on the floor and each one would come and sit at his or her assigned place. A bell-metal platter engraved with lotus flower designs would be placed before each person, with a slice of lemon and a bit of salt at one corner of each. On the right of the platter would be a heavy bell-metal tumbler of drinking water. The cook staggered in with huge brass containers of food and placed them before

Sundar-ma. She had a long-handled ladle with which she doled out the dishes. She also apportioned the curd. She herself ate after everyone had finished—a large helping of rice and a small quantity of vegetables. Afterwards she went straight up to the attic on the second floor and spent all afternoon spinning thread on her charkha. *Dhog dhog dhog dhog dhog dhog*, she went at it for hours on end until the clock struck four and it was time to put it away and make that heavenly mango sherbet. Sometimes she made bright red watermelon juice for those who didn't prefer their sherbet so sweet. She poured cool water from a clay pitcher on the water melon juice, topping each glass with crushed ice and a sprinkling of fried cumin seed powder.

After that, it was time for her to survey the guestrooms downstairs. She also visited the workers' family quarters and talked to the women and children about their problems. Some boy who had not been admitted in any school; some girl who needed textbooks; someone's mother who had to be taken to hospital—she listened to all this while she walked around the garden. Birds were eating all the fruits on a particular tree, vegetables were drying on the branches somewhere else. What fertilizers were needed and what trees needed pruning, she discussed every detail with the gardener. When dusk set in, she came up again to bathe and say her prayers—never in Dadamoshai's prayer room; always on the veranda or on the terrace upstairs. Around eight o'clock she came down again to serve us dinner. She also supervised the servants' meal at night. 'Take some more dal, Bahadur. Bai, your child is still very young, you must have another piece of fish.' She spoke in Hindi. After everyone had eaten, she was free to plunge into her own world where books held undisputed sway, apparently lifeless yet so inspiring. She studied till deep into the night. Not for any degree. Not for any high position. Not even in the hope of sending articles to magazines and becoming a writer. She read for the sake of reading. Rabindranath Tagore's Gandhari in his popular poem 'Gandharir Abedan' said, '*Dharmai dharmer shesh*', Dharma is an end unto itself. Sundar-ma believed that knowledge was an end unto itself.

This was Sundar-ma's life more or less, as I saw it. I did not think about it too much then, but now I look back and wonder. Sundar-ma did everything. Calling it 'lifeless' would be unfair and perhaps too harsh a judgement. But, apart from her reading and spinning, she did everything else as a matter of duty. There was dharma in it but no joy, a sense of responsibility but no excitement, it was correct but it wasn't carefree. If she had her heart in what she did, why did I never hear her laugh? She had everything a woman could possibly want. And yet she lived like a hermit in her own home. Did she feel some deep sense of deprivation? No one was privy to what her relationship with her husband was like. There was neither any loving exchange nor any obvious quarrel. In my perception, two individuals, who were polar opposites in temperament, had been bonded through marriage. Gyanadakanta amassed a huge fortune through his life, but can money really satiate one's heart?

I don't know what she did when she was young but in later life, Sundar-ma never touched any money. This is a fact that would go against her ill-repute as a skinflint. Or perhaps contradiction is inherent in human nature. Dadamoshai, after spending all day with his patients, came back with his pockets loaded with cash. He put it all on the table. Sundar-ma never even glanced that way. Her daughters-in-law and other women of the house put the notes into a heavy cash box and locked it in a safe for the night. The next morning they sent the money to the bank. Gyanadakanta could not give Sundar-ma what her heart desired. Nor could her worthy sons or any of her other relatives. While I don't have a clear idea of exactly what she pined for, I do think she had a sense of alienation. She was alone and isolated, forever in search of something that she herself could not put a name to.

SUNDAR-MA'S FAMILY

Sundar-ma entered 48 Hanuman Road when she was in her late thirties—in the full flush of youth by today's reckoning. But in those days, just being twenty was enough for a woman to be considered old. And while Sundar-ma was certainly not an old woman, she was not youthful either. She had borne eight children and already had one granddaughter.

Her first son Nalinikanta was born when she was thirteen. It seems unbelievable now. Thirteen-year-olds these days go to school in their uniforms. They study, play, run around and are naughty. Sundar-ma at thirteen was a little mother who carried her little child around, shy and diffident, following her mother-in-law's orders, accepting her scolding meekly and always keeping her head covered. Two years later, she had another son, Kumudkanta. Another two years, right at the start of the twentieth century, came her first daughter Ushabala. Followed by son Sisir and daughter Santwana. Some years later, came three more sons one after the other—Santosh, Ajit and Ranjit (whose nickname was Lalli). Ushabala was already married and had had her daughter, Kalyani, before her youngest brother Lalli was born. So Sundar-ma came to Hanuman Road with seven children.

All her sons were very successful students. And why wouldn't they be? Sundar-ma was a strict disciplinarian and no luxuries were allowed in her home. It was all duty and nothing else. To me the family seemed to lack any sense of humour—except for one of them, I never saw anyone laugh out loud. Any form of emotional display was absent in all from their very childhood. This is not to say that they never smiled at all. But everyone was generally serious, busy working or talking about their work, with no time for useless chatter or jokes. Sundar-ma taught them to follow a strict routine. They didn't have to be chased to sit with their books; they studied on their own. They sailed easily through every exam and found good jobs in time.

Nalinikanta, the eldest son, passed a tough exam without any trouble and joined the Imperial Service, at that time the highest civil service in India. They say he was a wonderful human being, as was his wife Ila. English culture might not have affected his mother, but it did deeply influence him as well as his wife. The couple lived in grand style. My mother's sister Urmila told me of her visit to her uncle Nalinikanta's house in Rangoon. Ila passed her matriculation exam (in today's parlance, the secondary exam after Class X) with flying colours—after her own son had already passed them. In the context of the time, this was quite remarkable a venture. More so because Ila wanted to study not for any gainful employment but only for the sake of knowledge. She wanted next to sit for her intermediate examination—what we now call the higher secondary—as a private student not affiliated to any school. She chose Calcutta University and went to

Behrampore for the exam. Ila's husband's sister, Usha, and *her* husband Jyotish, lived there. Urmila's parents, in other words. So Ila and Urmila sat side by side at Krishnanath College, Berhampore, to write their exams. After the exam, Ila dragged Urmila off to Rangoon.

Nalinikanta was the accountant general in Rangoon. He lived next door to the governor. There were innumerable rooms, an enormous lawn in front, a beautiful garden full of exotic flowers and a tennis court in the rear where the couple played along with their elite Bengali friends. On weekends, they went rowing on the lakes or to the seaside. Coming from an ordinary middle-class home, Urmila was quite stunned to see all this. Even more amazing was the fact that when they didn't go swimming in the sea, Ila and Nalini would enter the bathroom together for a bath. The bathroom was large enough. But Urmila had never in her life seen two people, particularly a man and a woman, entering a bathroom together and locking the door! No wonder her seventeen-year-old imagination ran riot! In short, Ila and Nalini were happy. They had a lovely family: two daughters, Chitra and Amita; two sons, Bulbul and Siddhartha. But all at once something came over them. Perhaps all that pleasure cloyed them. They became disciples of Sri Aurobindo and the Mother and decided to live in the Aurobindo ashram at Pondicherry. In the meantime, their younger son Siddhartha insisted on becoming a pilot. They asked for the Mother's blessing, which she gave. Siddhartha finished his training, touched his parents' feet and left home for his first solo flight while his parents started out for Pondicherry. The day they reached the ashram, they received news that Siddhartha's plane had crashed and he was dead. Even the gods weep at the loss of a son. Ila wiped away her tears and wrote to her favourite sister-in-law, Ushabala: 'Siddhartha has finished the work Mother had assigned him on this Earth, and has returned to his Mother's lap.' The mother who had borne him surrendered him to his heavenly mother with complete trust. Nalinikanta and she stayed on at the ashram with their other children.

An ashram in name, the place in Pondicherry was more like a little township. Hundreds of people, both Indian and foreign, lived there. They practised meditation, studied and discussed philosophy, did voluntary service and ate simple food together from a common kitchen. There were many language groups represented there; but I think Bengalis were predominant and most influential.

Sundar-ma went to Pondicherry once to visit her son. She didn't like the place or the fact that people prayed to humans there. 'They don't worship god. They worship the Mother. And there's too much show and ceremony.' Sundar-ma's questioning mind did not accept 'The Mother' as an all-pervasive divinity. She returned to Delhi. Her connection with her son and his family became more tenuous over the years. She must have cried after she had lost her eldest son to the ashram, but she never spoke a word about it. Nalini and Ila remained in the ashram all their lives. Their son Bulbul returned to the ashram with an FRCS degree from England; he restricted his knowledge and experience to its precincts alone until his untimely death. Their elder daughter Chitra still teaches yoga at the ashram; Amita, the younger one, lives with Chitra.

Grieving for lost sons was Sundar-ma's fate. Nalinikanta was drawn to the Pondicherry ashram and Kumudkanta to the other world before his time. Kumudkanta was not in the least like his elder brother. He, and his wife, were down-to-earth and family oriented. His family was filled with wonder and pride when he became India's deputy auditor-general when he was only forty. He went to Simla to take up his new post and never returned. A massive heart attack did him in within seconds. When the news reached his parents, they went into their prayer room in complete silence. When Kumudkanta's body was brought to Delhi, it didn't go to Hanuman Road. Sundar-ma didn't want it to. 'What use is it for me to see his soulless body? He is no longer there. You must not weep for what is inevitable. Thus says the Gita.' Yet, did Sundar-ma and Dadamoshai not feel like weeping? Did their hearts not cry out to the heavens above? I could find no entry in Sundar-ma's diary about that day. But on another page, with no mention of the year, she had written about another child who had met an early death.

> Today is the second day of Baisakh. Himadri came to us on this day and brightened our home for two and a half years. He gave us so much joy with his beauty and his intelligence and then he left even before he had completed two and a half years. A child of god left for his heavenly home. I was twenty-seven then. The loss of a son is so devastating when you are young. I think today that he had come for that short time to enrich our lives; he went when his time was over. The one who creates us destroys too. The potter, who builds so many pots of clay, can always break them at will. Similarly, the divine potter who made us can break the vessels whenever He wishes.

Kumudkanta, whom I called Chhor-da, and Ma called Chhoto-mama, was a choleric man—dark, large, short, bespectacled. His wife, our Chhor-didima, was dark and fat too. She loved food, and she loved feeding others. She laughed as much as she talked. She was as hot-tempered as she was friendly. Husband and wife were 'made for each other' as that Wills campaign used to say.

When I saw them, they had built a house for themselves and had moved out of Hanuman Road. All the rooms in their house had well-designed mosaic floors and large doors and windows. There was a big terrace on the second floor where seasonal flowers grew in pots in great profusion. The lush lawn in front of the house looked ever fresh and green. What I found most striking was the large, beautifully carved bed which was placed in the centre of their bedroom. Many years later, when I read a short story by Narendra Mitra called *Palanka*, I was reminded of that bed. The bed described in the story was made of teak and very fancy. Its four legs were carved in the shape of tiger paws. The head of the bed was finely carved with a floral design on top and bottom and a row of elephants in the centre. Chhor-dada's bed mimicked this design exactly. Four fat pillows and two huge bolsters lay under an embroidered green bedcover, seemingly waiting for the dalliances of the amorous couple, Kumud and his spouse.

After Kumud came Ushabala, my grandmother. She will feature in the second chapter of my story. After Usha came Sisir. If mothers love one child more than others, it creates sibling rivalry. Sundar-ma's excessive affection for her son Sisir made the others very jealous. The chief reason why she had a special weakness for him was that, like her, he loved books greatly. He was always immersed in, no, captivated by, the world of books. From matriculation to master's, he stood first in every exam he sat for. He would close all his books a week before any exam and simply stroll about. If anyone asked, he would say, 'I've finished studying. I'm ready for the exam.' That such a son would shine in the Indian Civil Service examination goes without saying. 'Heaven-born service' it was called—how few Indians qualified for it! In Sisir's case, the stigma of swadeshi leanings went against his being made a magistrate; he got a judgeship instead. The British were suspicious of the loyalty of persons believed to be nurturing patriotic sentiments and were reluctant to arm them with the executive powers of a magistrate. Sisir's last appointment was in the High Court of Calcutta. His wife, the beautiful Rani, had studied in Loreto School and College, then the most elite women's educational institution in Bengal and considered the ultimate in modernity. It wasn't that she didn't want to mix with the rest of the family but her style and attitude did not match theirs. Sisir Sen himself was a very solemn sort of man, taciturn and generally quite unsocial. If you visited him, he wouldn't welcome you with a smile, ask after your welfare or exchange a few pleasantries. How can one like such a person? I didn't, but my father did. 'Don't judge him by his manners. Sisir Sen is a truly honest and upright man,' he would say. Father was proved right. After both Dadamoshai and Sundarma passed away, the house on Hanuman Road was sold, and the brothers gave Sisir the responsibility of dividing the money. Sisir ruled that daughters ought not to be deprived of a share in their parental property. They would get at least half of what the sons received. Such a principle does exist in Islamic law, though in most cases the law was—and still is—bypassed in practice. By Hindu law, before the Hindu Code Bill was passed, daughters had no rights to their father's property, barring a few exceptional instances. Even today, when the law has granted equal gender rights, brothers often persist in scheming to cheat their sisters. Sisir Sen sent his sisters fat cheques, without their asking, or even having any knowledge about it. His sisters were stunned. And, of course, thrilled.

Sisir's youngest sister was Santwana. She looked like her mother. Her parents allowed her to get her master's degree before getting her married. The groom was a doctor in Dhaka,

Shailen Sen by name. Husband and wife were polar opposites in temperament. She was serious and straight-talking; he was a witty, jovial man. After the partition of India, Santwana-didi moved to Calcutta with her only daughter Reba and lived in a rented apartment on the third floor of a house on Cornwallis Street. Dr Sen stayed on in Dhaka where he had a large practice. He visited Calcutta occasionally. He was very attached to his money and this attachment ultimately cost him his life. In 1971, during the terrible communal riots in Dhaka, a Muslim family had given him shelter. They had warned him not to step out of the house. After a few days, Dr Sen decided that since his own house was not too far away, he could run back and retrieve his money. He didn't tell anyone of his plans and simply left. He never came back.

After Santwana was Santosh, Ma's Sejo-mama. I called him Sej-da. I have such tender feelings about him even to this day. He and Ma were great friends. Perhaps that was why he was so fond of me. Sej-da was a famous surgeon and his establishment, Sen's Nursing Home in Delhi, was very well known in those days. Sej-da went to Vienna to learn the latest technique in prostate surgery and was the first to introduce it in Delhi. Jawaharlal Nehru, Jinnah, probably Maulana Azad too, were among his patients. He told me once, 'You are a great fan of Jawahar's. Well, he won't be with us too long. Six months at most.'

'Why? What is he suffering from?' I asked him with great concern.

'I cannot divulge that as a professional,' Sej-da answered. 'Even the little that I told you is against medical ethics. We are not supposed to discuss such things. I don't know why I told you; I'm surprised at myself.' Well, Nehru did die within six months. I wonder whether Sej-da had also known about the approximate time of Jinnah's death. He never told me and I never thought of asking him. Santosh Sen was passionate about his work. As a surgeon, he was as dexterous as he was dedicated. Whether he was as detached as his mother regarding the money that overflowed as a result, I really can't say. He earned plenty, spent plenty and he believed in this simple philosophy. However, Sej-da's deepest attachment was to two people: one seen and the other unseen. His first obsession, the one who could be seen, was his wife Sita. The other obsession was none other than Rabindranath Tagore. The poet was with Sej-da when he first opened his eyes in the morning, while he bathed, while he dressed, while he ate, and while he moved around. He knew many poems by heart. All of *Purabi*, *Kshanika*, *Sonar Tari* and *Gitanjali*. He knew dozens of Tagore's songs from *Geetali* and *Geetobitan*. And while I can't exactly praise Sej-da's musical skill, his memory was commendable. He spouted poetry night and day like one possessed. If I happened to be beside him, he'd stop a little and say, 'Now you say the rest.' If I got stuck, he'd be very upset. 'You forget Rabindranath, Bharati? How can anyone?'

Though I was embarrassed, I asked him a counter-question, 'Sej-da, do you recite Rabindranath even as you operate?'

He said, 'No. When you operate, you have to forget everything else in the world. Even Rabindranath. It's just me and my patient then. A little later, even I disappear. Then it's just the patient and his life. Just one entity.'

I would start laughing. 'So you forget Rabindranath too, sometimes. So why are you bothered when I forget?'

'If you forget Rabindranath, from where will the spring of life flow?' he would respond, looking happy and inspired. I was the only one with whom he could share his love for the poet. There were many Bengalis who lived in Delhi at the time but I doubt if there was anyone else as mad about Tagore as Sej-da. Those who are at the peak of their careers hardly have time for poetry. Sej-da's Punjabi wife Sita Dharamvir and his Hindi–English-speaking children were unappreciative. It was their misfortune, and Sej-da's too.

Sita was the love of Sej-da's life. And that love lasted, untarnished, to the end. I know there was a second woman who was close to him, too close, but Sita and Santosh remained forever true to each other. When he first told his parents about Sita, a storm raged in Hanuman Road. All the conservatism that Sundar-ma and Dada had repressed for many years found a chance to stand up in protest. First of all, Sita's father was Punjabi; worse still, her mother was European. Such a liaison in a Bengali household was unacceptable! However, they had to accept it. Mainly because Subhas Chandra Bose himself arrived in person to play matchmaker. Not only Sundar-ma, he had to persuade the Dharamvirs too. He was very fond of Sita and he was quite impressed by Santosh. He told the Dharamvirs, 'I have met Santosh. He is extremely bright.' He told the Sens, 'Sita's father Dr Dharamvir is a very close friend of mine and I know Sita very well. She's a wonderful girl. I request you to bless her and accept her.' That settled it. Sundar-ma agreed without further hesitation. She built a little dais on the spot where Subhas Bose had sat and the wedding ceremony began from that spot. In due time, Santosh entered 48 Hanuman Road with Sita Dharamvir as his bride.

The couple lived in that house for quite some time. They were assigned two rooms on the ground floor; a separate apartment. They ate with the family, however. Sita was a vegetarian and I can well imagine what Dr Dharamvir's beloved daughter must have felt about the food—a watery curry of round gourd, dal and roti! She still managed to adjust—or at least she tried. Were there no clashes between mother-in-law and daughter-in-law? Of course there were. They were two strong personalities with very different ideas and a culture clash was inevitable. I remember one day, Sita's newborn baby girl Ela was crying at the top of her voice. Sundar-ma, who happened to be around, ran and picked her grandchild up in her arms. Sita arrived at equal speed, took the baby away and put her back on the bed without uttering a single word. Ela kept on squealing. Sita simply ignored her and walked out. Sundar-ma was extremely hurt. Was this any way to behave? Did she have no right to pick up her own grandchild who was crying so hard? Sita should have explained to her: a baby should not be picked up whenever it cries, unless, of course, if it is feeding time or if the nappy is wet. She could have said that, in her opinion, crying just to get into someone's lap was not to be encouraged because that would be spoiling the baby. I'm sure Sundar-ma would have understood if Sita had cared to explain. Sundar-ma misunderstood and blamed it on her Punjabi background. 'No Bengali daughter-in-law would ever do that,' she said. That was not quite fair to Sita. What she did was what she believed, rightly or wrongly. It had nothing to do with her being Punjabi.

The truth is that while Sundar-ma had accepted Sita, she didn't really love her. And neither did I. Not at first. After Sej-da and Sita, whom I called Sej-di, moved out of Hanuman Road and went to live in a huge rented bungalow on Hailey Road, I stayed with them for some time for my studies. The first day we sat down to lunch, it was altogether in the European style. Not a bit at all like at Hanuman Road. Sej-da, Sej-di and their two daughters Ela and Ketaki were seated at the table which was covered with an English lace tablecloth. I went and sat next to Sej-da, feeling very uneasy. The bearer brought in the food. Our places had already been laid with cutlery and fine bone china plates with English floral designs. A matching serving plate contained large pieces of fried fish. A serving bowl of similar design held boiled peas and another bowl was filled with boiled carrots. The third bowl had strips of fried potatoes, which they called finger chips. Salad was served in a large cabbage-shaped plate. Oh my, where was the rice? And the dal? I looked around the table tentatively. Sej-da said, 'There's bread and butter, help yourself.' He looked at my face and said, 'You can't eat without rice, is that it?' He asked the bearer to serve rice and told his daughters to take some too; to keep me company, I suppose. They dutifully took a spoonful each. Now I was in real trouble. How could a rice-guzzling girl from East Bengal survive on just one spoonful? But if the others were taking a spoonful each, how could I take ten? When I came back home after a week, I related to my cousins all my travails at the table of our rich great uncle with a great deal of flourish and fun. I hadn't known Sej-di then.

Later, when I got to know her well, I realized that this reserved lady, with a few sentences, could amaze you with her powerful personality. A renowned gynaecologist, she spent all day at the nursing home, came back and took up her knitting, sewing and household supervision. She was also very dedicated to her husband. One evening Sej-di and I were immersed in Beethoven when Sej-da walked in and said to her, 'It's late, come to bed.'

'We're listening to the Ninth Symphony, Sej-da,' I said in a tone of mild protest.

Sej-da laughed and replied, 'I think she will enjoy our symphony better.' What could I say to that couple, both of whom were fifty-plus?

Just observing Sej-di was instructive; and listening to her too. One afternoon we had just finished lunch when Ela came running and asked her mother, 'Ma, there's going to be a strike at school. They've asked me to attend a meeting. Should I go? What do you think?'

'You think it over and decide for yourself,' Sej-di replied. Ela left the room.

'Why didn't you give her your opinion?' I asked.

'Ela's growing up. She ought to learn to take her own decisions,' Sej-di said.

I was surprised. 'Suppose she makes mistake?'

'People learn from their mistakes,' she replied coolly. 'If it were something serious, I would have given advice. But if she can't make up her mind about little, everyday matters, how will she learn to decide on larger issues?' My reticent Sej-di taught me an important lesson that day: parents ought to help develop their children's decision-making ability and not make decisions for them.

Such was Dr Dharamvir's daughter Sita in the 1950s. We didn't have her with us for too long; she left us suddenly one day without a word of warning. Sej-da and Sej-di were chatting together one evening before dinner. It was time for her to take some medicine. She was about to put a tablet into her mouth when it dropped from her hands. She bent down to pick it up and didn't get up again. Sej-da didn't live for too long after that. As Saratchandra Chattopadhyay neatly expresses in his novel *Srikanta*, 'If the fire dies out, can an engine run on water alone?'

Sundar-ma's son after Santosh was Ajit. He went to bathe in the river Jamuna one day when he was twenty-one years old and didn't come back. They found his slippers near the water. The mystery was never solved. Sundar-ma remained mute for days on end. When she finally opened her mouth, she kept saying, 'I lost my son because I had sinned.' A few days earlier, a teenage girl who lived nearby had come crying to her for help. She was pregnant by her own father. The helpless Bengali girl! She had no one to confide in and didn't have the courage. If the child were born, she would have to take the blame on herself in silence. Who would believe her if she did speak the truth? And even if they did, what was she to do? How would she bring up a bastard child of her own father? She was in extreme distress, so Sundar-ma stretched out a helping hand. The girl was saved from open shame but an unborn child was destroyed. Sundar-ma felt she was guilty of infanticide, so her own son was snatched away as punishment. Her rational mind, her sharp intelligence, all submerged in the quicksand of blind superstition. How amazing is the human mind. More amazing, society's changing mores. In Sundar-ma's time, abortion was considered a sin. It is now legally sanctioned in the interests of family planning. The women's movement considers it to be a woman's right.

Though she lost Ajit, her youngest son Lalli—Ma's Lal-mama, my Lal-da—remained close to his mother till her death. He was a large-hearted, loving, uncomplicated soul. His wife Nivedita was Sundar-ma's favourite daughter-in-law. She was very lovely and Lal-da was enamoured of her. But Nivedita was not only the goddess of his heart, she was also a heaven-sent blessing for Sundar-ma's household. She came from a large joint family based in Calcutta and she blended in with her new family almost instantly. Lal-didi's joyous laughter and chatter infused new life into the dismal atmosphere of Hanuman Road. Sundar-ma finally found someone with whom she could share the joys and sorrows of her twilight years. Lal-didi is no longer with us. Lal-da died four years ago. He was the last representative of Sundar-ma's immediate family.

Or was he? Is there such a thing as 'the last'? Life goes on. From one seed a great tree is born and from one great tree is born another.

THE LARGER FAMILY

Sundar-ma's family was truly enormous. Computing the number of people who visited 48 Hanuman Road and the number who came and stayed there would take great mathematical skill. One of those people who were not related in any way, but whom I later met and grew close to, was Usha Bhattacharya. Usha-di had joined Delhi's Miranda House as a lecturer in philosophy at a very young age. She had been a star student of Dhaka University. How could it be that a young, unmarried Bengali girl stayed in a hostel? Sundar-ma sent a message to the teachers' hostel at Miranda House requesting Usha-di to stay with them in Hanuman Road. Usha-di did not fully accede to the request but she visited so frequently that she became almost part of the family. I heard many stories about that house from Usha-di when we were colleagues in Bethune College. Usha-di would say, 'I can still feel the warmth and sincerity of the people in that house.' Usha-di herself is a happy, jovial and sociable person. After a long career as a college professor, she is now retired. She has to use a walking stick these days but her heart is still young. Very few octogenarians can keep their hearts forever green. Usha-di does.

Unlike Usha-di, I did not see the Hanuman Road house in its heyday. I saw it in its last years. Many members of the family still lived there. Among those I knew quite well were Bibhuti and Amarkanta—my Sundar-dada and Ranga-dada—and their families. They were Gyanada Sen's nephews who had lost their parents at an early age. Sundar-ma and Dadamoshai brought them up like their own sons. Of course, this was not exceptional; on the contrary it was only expected.

Sundar-dada was married to Suprabha-didi. I remember their wedding very well. We even went to Delhi for the occasion. Sundar-dada was very pleased with his new bride. And why not? Orphaned as a young boy, he had at last found someone he could call his very own. She was a dusky young woman of medium build, in a broad-bordered sari, a long, thick gold necklace, a big vermilion dot on her forehead and with a soft, shy smile on her lips. I liked her very much. But Sundar-dada did not like the way I hung around her all the time. Like the proverbial bone in a kebab, I was a real pain. Sundar-dada would come on the quiet for a few stolen moments with his new bride, a quick word or two, or a light caress—and there I would be! In a joint family a husband and wife could only meet late at night when both were tired after a long working day. Once in a while they found a sudden opportunity to meet during the day. Who wants a silly little girl to spoil the moment? One day Sundar-dada had to tell me off straight, 'Leave this room right now. What work do you have here anyway?' I was going away with a sorry face when Sundar-didi drew me into her arms and said, 'Aha, she has no work in this room but she does have with me. Staying close to me is most important for her. Isn't that so, Bharati?' In one moment she threw off my feeling of rejection with those sweet words which I still remember so well. Sundar-didi is gone now. People leave us but their words remain.

Sundar-dada had a pretty ordinary job in a mercantile firm. Compared to all those big shots in the Sen family, he was the least successful. But he was such a lovely person. When Sundar-didi developed white leucoderma patches all over her body, she became very depressed. She used to feel ashamed as if it had happened through some fault of hers. But Sundar-dada couldn't care less. He surrounded her with youthful laughter and love. When their circumstances improved, they moved out of Hanuman Road with their three children and went to live in a small house of their own. Sundar-didi's own household was filled with love and joy. Alas, all pleasures must come to an end. Sundar-dada used to return home every evening on a scooter. Sundar-didi would wait for him standing with her face against the bars of a window. One evening Sundar-dada didn't come back. A speeding car knocked his two-wheeler down. Sundar-dada fell under it and died on the spot. Sundar-didi could never reconcile herself to this sudden tragedy. She still waited for him every evening with her face against the window bars. Waited till the end of her days. Their two sons now work in Delhi. Their daughter Sonali teaches at a school at Salt Lake, Kolkata. She is a bright and charming girl, just like her mother.

Sundar-dada's elder brother Amarkanta stayed on in Hanuman Road for many years. We called him Ranga-dada. He was a senior government officer, very genial and benevolent. His wife Sushila was a beautiful and accomplished lady. She sang very well, cooked very well, and most of all, she could dress very well. In fact, she was extremely particular about her beauty routine and gave all kinds of beauty tips to other relatives in her age group. One such tip, given to my mother, a shy young woman, was to discourage husbands from handling breasts if she wished them to remain shapely. Of course she kept her husband completely mesmerized. But the magic was short-lived. Sushila had an extramarital affair and the couple went through a bitter divorce. At the end of it Ranga-dada breathed a deep sigh of regret and their only son was stuck with the fruit of a poison tree.

Everybody in the family liked Ranga-dada. Every home he visited was instantly in happy tumult. Everybody commented with one voice, 'Such a wonderful person and such a whore of a wife! Amarkanta is one unlucky guy.' I thought so too at the time. But I wonder now whether it was his fate that was to blame or his lack of a personality. Was he a suitable husband for a beautiful, talented and ambitious woman like Sushila? Why do women become wayward? We are quick to find fault with a woman, quick to defame her for her 'loose character'. Perhaps it was Amarkanta who was deficient. Was it all Sushila's fault alone? Did she have no valid reason to walk out, setting aside all the praise and admiration she received, the family wealth and her husband's doting deference? Was she alone responsible for the breakdown in their relationship?

One can't really disapprove of divorce on principle. If a husband is a brute or a womanizer, or a wife depraved or a two-timer, and the couple is locked in a loveless marriage with no physical or mental correspondence, what purpose is served by staying together merely to pay lip service to some holy mantras which they hardly understood in the first place? Weddings in middle-class families are conducted with a great deal of fanfare and plenty of expense. And then, in barely a few months, I often hear that the marriage has broken down. In most cases it is due to a lack of tolerance. Quite often the bone of contention relates to property, ambition, cultural differences and other such issues. Moreover, the women of today are unwilling to conform demurely to their in-laws' wishes. The in-laws on their part refuse to show due respect to a well-educated bride. How can such marriages ever survive? After all, marriages are not really made in heaven; it is a social institution devised by human agency. But the question that still remains is: what happens to the children of such marriages? It is true that when parents begin to disagree, it is better that they live apart and spare children the trauma of ugly domestic scenes. Nevertheless, when I think of Amar and Sushila's son, I am filled with all kinds of doubt. The ugly battle for custody, even kidnapping the boy and spoiling him silly to gain his affection; I have seen such things happen in our wider family. May such disasters never befall any other innocent child. No child comes to earth of his own desire; he has no choice in the matter. Those who are responsible for giving birth to him, what right have they to curse his life? Amarkanta's son is lost to us forever. He lives in a twilight world of semi-consciousness most of the time.

The story of Mona-dada, Sumitra-didi and their children is very different. Mona-dada was another of Gyanadakanta Sen's nephews. I remember him quite well. He was a roly-poly, jovial sort of man. Sumitra-didi too was full of life; always eager for outings and fun and chit-chat. Mona-dada has passed away but Sumitra-didi is still alive. And so are their two daughters and one son. The older daughter Saswati is an exceptional woman. She won a dance scholarship while studying for her graduate degree. Many family elders frowned on this. 'A scholarship for dancing? Of what earthly use can dancing be put to?' But Sumitra-didi and Saswati ignored such old-fashioned notions. And why not? When it comes to learning, there are no caste barriers between one set of subjects and another or between formal school, college or university education, and oral, cultural or physical education. Physics or swimming, there is no basic difference between the two in terms of education. If the student is completely dedicated, her or his efforts are truly blessed. Saswati opted for dance was her chosen field of study and Birju Maharaj as her guru. When this legendary exponent of the Kathak style puts on his ankle bells and goes on stage, what a magic spell he weaves on our eyes, hearts, minds; on all our faculties! A devoted disciple of Birju Maharaj for many years, Saswati is now an exponent and teacher herself. Guruma Saswati Sen.

Satyajit Ray selected Saswati as the traditional court danseuse in the Mughal emperor's court scene in his film *Shatranj ke Khiladi*. Dancing is now Saswati's profession and her very life. It left her no time to spare for marriage. Perhaps she felt no need for it. Saswati's mother lives with her in Delhi. She looks after her aged parent, provides companionship, and goes on dance tours all over the world. Earlier, sons would take care of their aged parents. Today, many daughters have taken over this responsibility. Their tender loving care fills the old people's hearts with much joy.

In the early twentieth century, author Saratkumari Chaudhurani, who was known as 'Lahorini' because she came to Calcutta from Lahore where she had spent her early years, asked 'Why are women so neglected?' A hundred years later women are still undervalued when compared with men. Nevertheless, 'Lahorini' would have approved the likes of Saswati Sen who break barriers and establish themselves on the world stage and take responsibility for their parents in their old age.

BEYOND THE FAMILY

Sundar-ma might have been detached about domestic matters, but not so about the world outside. The times in which she lived were bound to have an impact on her extra-sensitive mind. The independence movement was then in full swing. Gandhiji had appeared in the arena. Thousands of women responded to his call for non-cooperation. It was probably the most refulgent chapter in the history of Indian women. Women, who had for so long been confined to homes and forbidden to even exchange a few polite words with men outside the immediate family, leave alone associating with them, broke their age-old shackles at a moment's notice and came out on the streets to walk in procession side by side with men. The first steps were taken during the swadeshi movement against the partition of Bengal in 1905. Participation in that politico-economic struggle against the British was made easy for women because it was conveniently couched in religious symbolism. Religion has always been women's special domain. The protest movement against colonial rule was called the worship of Mother India. Some of the most respected figures of the literary and artistic worlds, Bankimchandra Chattopadhyay, Abanindranath Tagore and Rabindranath himself, helped in deifying the motherland.

> Your left hand holds a falchion
> With your right you remove our fears,
> A loving smile in your two eyes,
> While your third eye is inflamed.
> Dear Mother, what a vision you present!

Sundar-ma was in Bengal during those stirring times. However, she was merely a housewife The theme of freedom in the inspiring folk drama of the itinerant poet Mukundadas was a popular attraction in the villages and small towns of Bengal. His songs were on everyone's lips, educated and uneducated alike. Of course their message reached the village Kalia in Jessore. Although it was out of the question for Shailabala, the veiled young woman, to be allowed out to witness those open-air operettas, she did hear the songs and was deeply touched. Not just Shailabala, but thousands of women like her. The songs she could not sing as a young daughter-in-law in Jessore, she gave voice to as a middle-aged homemaker in Delhi. Her untrained voice was out of tune and out of rhythm, yet she sang to her heart's content.

Arise, ye dear women of Bengal
Break your glass bangles one and all.

Countless women must have responded to this rousing call by Mukundadas and broken their bangles on the spot.

When the struggle acquired a new momentum under Gandhi's leadership, Sundar-ma was in Delhi by then. She didn't join the Salt March like Sarojini Naidu, nor did she enter active politics like Aruna Asaf Ali or Sucheta Kripalani. But she attended Gandhi's political rallies; along with thousands of other ordinary women, she took off her gold bangles and necklaces and contributed to the Congress fund. In fact, Dadamoshai was reluctant to put any money into her hands for fear that it would immediately disappear as donations to the Congress Party. Sundar-ma would hand-spin cotton thread on her charkha all afternoon, exactly like the Congresswomen. She even wove cloth and made baby clothes and wrappers, stuffed these items into bags and went out with her daughter-in-law Nivedita to peddle them on the streets! Whatever she earned went into the Congress fund. Going through so much trouble for such a meagre amount of money might not have made much sense, but it was her way of serving the national cause. Sundar-ma would recite a poem by Hemachandra Bandhopadhyay as she walked through the streets.

> Blow your horn, sing out loud,
> All the world is free and proud,
> Should India sleep, and be left out?

Hardly anyone remembers Hemachandra Bandhopadhyay nowadays. His poetry is not included in school textbooks and most young students have not heard of him. But at one time his patriotic poems were a source of inspiration for thousands of Shailabalas throughout Bengal.

The Indian women's movement is closely linked with the nationalist movement. Women joined the struggle for independence and at the same time started forming women's groups. There were organizations for women in the nineteenth century too such as the Bamabodhini Sabha, the Uttarpara Hitakari Sabha, the Bikrampur Sammilani and so on. They were all run by men inspired by social reformers of the time but from the early 1920s, women gradually took the initiative themselves. First, Sarala Devi Chaudhurani (b.1872) started the Bharat Stree Mahamandal in Lahore in 1910. In Calcutta, Abala Bose (b.1864) founded her Nari Shiksha Samiti in 1919. In 1925, the All India Women's Conference (AIWC) came into being. In different parts of India, including mofussil towns like Dhaka, Chittagong and Bankura, small women's units started coming up. Their objective was education and skill training for income generation. Women started networking through these little cells, discussed their domestic issues and spread the nationalist ideals. Unlike the Dipali Sangha of Dhaka, or the Mahila Atma Raksha Samiti of Calcutta, these smaller units took no direct part in the nationalist agenda.

Sundar-ma formed the New Delhi Mahila Samiti with women and girls in her locality. The organization was non-political. Members were encouraged to study books and read newspapers and magazines. They discussed current affairs, women's status in society and the concept of patriotism. The poorer women were given some training whereby they could earn some extra income. The idea was simple. Instead of wasting leisure hours in sleep or idle gossip, it would be better to get together and do something useful. They practised handicrafts, made bags, baskets, sweaters and clothes.

Sundar-ma made rag dolls. Pretty basic stuff. The dolls had no noses, their eyes were closed, they were almost bald. Certainly no one today would touch these cloth creations. But that was another time inspired by nationalist ideals; these dolls were a great hit in the market. Sundar-ma also introduced the idea of an annual fete called the Ananda Mela. Women from different regions made a sweet called Ananda Naru with their individual recipes. Others cooked snacks such as samosas, sandesh, rossogolla and badam barfi. A handicraft exhibition was a must of course. The proceeds were distributed among the poorer women. This Ananda Mela is now a tradition kept up in the Delhi Kalibari, the temple of Kali.

We find many exceptionally talented women emerging in those years. They discovered new paths and moved forward eagerly. Those who had learned to read started trying their hand at writing. Apart from reputed women like Swarnakumari Devi, Gyanadanandini Devi, or Kamini Ray, newly educated women—some had studied at home, others in schools and colleges—expressed their inner thoughts quite feelingly. Rasasundari Devi, Kailasabasini Devi, Ambujasundari Das Gupta, along with many other unknown housewives wrote quite well. Some of them published their work in women's magazines. Some others must have written too, but did not publish anything. Their work is invaluable material for social history.

Sundar-ma also wrote. Pages and pages of her diaries are filled with the joys and sorrows of her daily life; about her home, society and political activities around her. Those precious diaries were thrown away as useless rubbish when the house on Hanuman Road was sold. Only two of them somehow survived in a faded, dim and colourless state. I read them today and wonder. Where did she pick up such rich intellectual powers? She had learned Sanskrit by her own efforts sitting at home. She translated the Bhagavad Gita in Bengali verse. She translated sections of the *Kathopanishad* and *Kenopanishad*, also in verse. They were printed so they are not lost. Two volumes of her own poetry were also printed—*Anukana* and *Renukana*. Very simple, very moving, Sundar-ma's writing was of a high standard. The women who took up their pens at home wrote because they were inspired from within. They wrote with passion; from an urge to express their authentic feelings with a natural balance between thought and language. Let me give you one small example of Sundar-ma's pen—a few lines obviously addressed to god:

> I feel proud to have repeated your name,
> Forgetting you're nameless all the same.

Was Sundar-ma a religious person? In my opinion she was inclined towards the Brahmo faith. This is where she differed from Dadamoshai. He was a disciple of Anandamoyee Ma. Anandamoyee, in her early life an ordinary housewife in Dhaka, became a sanyasin later and was known as Anandamoyee. She was truly beautiful and had a sweet voice. She didn't speak much but was always surrounded by her disciples who did most of the talking. Many eminent men, from judges of the high court to high-ranking officials, as well as numerous ordinary middle-class people seemed to be mesmerized by her. Anandamoyee's vast family of devotees spread from Vrindavan and Varanasi right down to Calcutta. In Delhi, the principal disciple who established her fame was Gyanadakanta Sen. He built a small ashram for her in one corner of his garden: two rooms, one bedroom, one meeting room, with an attached veranda. These quarters were opened only when she came to the city. Hundreds of people trooped in to see her. They filled the meeting room and veranda, and spilled over to the garden. They laid out durries and sat on the ground. They sang songs inside, mostly religious songs in praise of Lord Krishna and Radha. Anandamoyee Ma sat on a raised platform and smiled benignly. The last song would be in praise of the Mother—'Jai Ma, Jai Ma, Jai Jai Ma.'

Dadamoshai had almost blind faith in Anandamoyee Ma. He claimed that she was Goddess Durga incarnate. But Sundar-ma said, 'A human being cannot be a goddess. Anandamoyee may be a superior devotee of Durga but goddess she is not.' Sundar-ma wrote in one of her diaries:

I don't like the great fuss they make over Anandamoyee's birthday. I once asked her straight, 'Why such excessive celebrations of a human being's birthday? How do you allow it?' Ma smiled, and gave no answer. That night I saw Anandamoyee in my dreams. She came to my room and told me, 'You must persist with reverence.' Anandamoyee does appear sometimes in one's dreams. She gives answers to many unuttered questions. I have seen it happen many times. I still say, she is divinely blessed. But she is not god.

In my opinion, god did not bless Sundar-ma. Nor did he ever do her any justice. She got no opportunity to cultivate her intellect, being married off as a child. She hardly had any communion of hearts with her businesslike husband. Her successful sons went off and set up their own establishments. The death of three sons—one as a child, one as a young man and the third while on top of his career—and the disappearance, for all practical purposes, of the eldest son in the Pondicherry ashram must have grieved her more than she ever expressed. Gyanadakanta was bedridden for many years towards the end of his life; she had to take care of him. She had just two friends to keep her company: her books and her charkha. She held them close to the last.

Even her last journey was not happy. One morning she was discovered lying senseless at the bottom of the spiral staircase leading to the garden. They thought she must have missed her way to the bathroom, wandered out by mistake and taken a fall. She remained unconscious for three days. Then she went off on her final journey; as alone as ever. She was seventy-five years old. She had written on one page of her tattered old diary:

> I am but a worthless daughter of my motherland. She has so many weaknesses, so many sorrows, so much pain . . . I could do nothing for her . . . People want to be released from the cycle of rebirth. I want to be born again so that I can come back and spend all my time in her service.

Alas, are the deepest longings of human beings ever fulfilled?

DIDI-MA

DIDI-MA'S CHILDHOOD
AND MARRIAGE

Didi-ma, my grandmother Ushabala, was Sundar-ma's eldest daughter. The third child, she was born in 1900, an epochal juncture in history—the twentieth century was beginning and Gyanadakanta's practice in Delhi was yet to take off. He lived in Kalia village with his elder brother Mohitkanta. At that time he was just a fledgling doctor in an average home, eating ordinary food, leading an ordinary life. Ushabala was to later rue her luck. By the time her father became rich and famous, she was no longer young. Her brothers went to good schools and colleges and built great careers. She neither went to school nor had any connection with the outside world. A job, of course, was out of the question, even though she was no less gifted than her siblings. Even her younger sister—who was much younger than her—was allowed to take a master's degree and bask in their father's opulence. Ushabala was just given a basic education at home and married off when still a child.

As a little girl, she spent her days within the walled compound of her uncle's brick house in the village. He was an engineer with the railways—it was a good job. Didi-ma's two elder brothers, Nalinikanta and Kumudkanta, would sit in an outer room, their heads immersed in piles of books. In an ankle-length dress, her curly, jet black hair tied in two thick braids, she would creep up beside them and sit in one corner of their settee, an open book held firmly in her two small fists. Her mother and brothers approved but her father Gyanadakanta did not. Whenever he saw his little girl studying, he would frown. 'What use is it for girls to study so much? Go inside and help your mother. She works single-handed.' Gyanadakanta was unaware that Ushabala had been affected by her mother's passion for books. Having failed to cure his wife of her addiction, he perhaps didn't want his daughter to fall into the same trap. Usha would walk off sadly and join her busy mother in the kitchen. Mohit Sen's wife had passed away and Shailabala was in sole charge of running the house. As her mother's little helper, Ushabala became quite adept at housework at an early age. And while she didn't dislike it, her ears were always open for her father's footsteps. As soon as she heard him leaving the house, she would run back to the study room where her brothers would be poring over their books. 'Please teach me how to write properly!' she would beg them. Or, 'Please buy me Rabindranath Tagore's *Shishu*. I want to learn all the poems by heart!' And indeed she did. Not only *Shishu*, she learnt to recite from *Shishu Bholanath*, *Naibedya* and *Kheya*.

When Gyanadakanta left for Simla and Delhi to improve his career prospects, Usha left with the family. But it was fated that she should be linked to Jessore forever. A certain lady called Swarnamoyee Das Gupta, from the village Banda not far from their home in Kalia, had taken a great fancy to the sweet and gentle little girl. She sent word to Mohit Sen proposing a match between his niece Usha and her son Jyotish Chandra. Mohit Sen was delighted. It was rare that a proposal should arrive from the groom's side. Jyotish Chandra Das Gupta's father, Jagat Chandra Das Gupta, had been a court doctor for the king of Nepal. His sudden and untimely death had meant an economic downturn for the family; but it wasn't of very great import. Young Jyotish was a student at the Scottish Church College in Calcutta studying for his BA with honours in economics. He was a meritorious student and was sure to sail through college and land a respectable job. Mohitkanta was so thrilled, he promptly accepted the proposal. Gyanada and Shailabala received news that their daughter's marriage had been arranged. She was to be sent back to Kalia at the earliest. Shailabala was distraught. A quaking Gyanadakanta pled via telegram: PLEASE CANCEL WEDDING PLANS. But that was easier said than done. After all, Mohitkanta was the elder brother and head of the family. His word would have to be kept. Ushabala was married off at short notice, just as Shailabala's younger sister Indubala had been a generation earlier.

There were no demands for dowry from either side. The bride was sent off with a pair of bridge-pattern bangles, a thick shark-head-design armlet on her right arm, a muff chain around her neck, large ear studs, and a tiara, all of pure gold. Her damask Benarasi wedding sari was a gorgeous deep purple silk with pure silver-thread floral motifs closely spaced all over. The anchal had a row of large silver flowers. The blouse was frilled, full-sleeved and waist-length with buttons down the front. The groom received gold kurta buttons, a watch, and the standard silk dhoti and chador worn during the wedding ceremony. Ushabala Sen became Ushabala Das Gupta at the age of twelve with nary a notion of what it entailed.

The first thing she learnt was that marriage meant hard work. Her husband was a student. His eldest brother Suresh Chandra was a physician in Nepal, thanks to their father's earlier position there. The second brother Jogesh earned very little as a schoolteacher, also in Nepal. The family got along on the money the eldest son sent home. It was a large household living on a tight budget. The little bride spent her days with her head always covered by her sari, her face completely hidden from view. She would wake up at the crack of dawn and clean the rooms and courtyard. She then had to assist her mother-in-law with the cooking. Then she and her elder sister-in-law would walk a long way through dusty and muddy roads to the village stream, wash the household utensils, bathe and bring back two huge brass pitchers of water. When they sat down on the kitchen floor to eat, the elder one would often grumble, 'Some luck we have! How can one eat with a dash of dal and chillies only? I'm waiting for the day when my husband will take me away with him to Nepal.' Ushabala said nothing. Their mother-in-law would lament, 'Oh, my ill fate! I have never been able to take care of you two as I should.' Even at that young age, Ushabala felt sympathy for her. She knew that the lady was good at heart. Indian mothers-in-law have always had a bad name for ill-treating their daughters-in-law but all of them cannot be called oppressors. While some are known to torture their sons' wives, others love them like their own daughters. Take Keshab Sen's mother for instance. She used to quake in fear of her mother-in-law. Even though they had plenty of servants, the mother-in-law made her young daughters-in-law sweep their large rooms and the maids were forbidden to help them. On the other hand, Rasasundari Devi's mother-in-law would pick her up in her arms when she cried, comfort her with sweet words and feed her with her own hand, 'as if she were [her] own mother'. Ushabala's mother-in-law too would caress her gently and take care of her. Ushabala loved her mother-in-law, she was fond of her sister-in-law, and she adored her husband

Jyotish. Jyotish Chandra was a genuine soul. Simple, truthful, devoid of envy, averse to gossip, easy to please, quick to smile, an ever-happy sort of man. He was rather fond of food, keen on physical fitness and unmindful of material loss or gain. There was some doubt about whether this straightforward person was equal to his wife in intelligence, efficiency, spirit or ambition. But there was no doubt that the two were deeply in love with each other—right from the time they were married. Neither advancing years nor the fatigue and frailty of old age could weaken their ardour. In her middle age Ushabala wrote in her diary, 'Where have we lost the rapture of our love?' Beneath this, Jyotish commented in his beautiful hand: 'Who does not know that there is no turbulence in the ocean depths?'

The first crisis that the couple faced was before Jyotish's master's exam. His brother wrote from Nepal saying that he was unable to spare the money for his exam fees. Jyotish was married now; he should look for a job instead of sitting for his degree. Jyotish decided reluctantly to give up his plan. He would have to find a job. Ushabala brought out her tin trunk, the one with the red flower painted on it. From beneath her trousseau, all carefully folded away, she took out her most precious ornament—the armlet with the shark-head design. She looked her husband straight in the eye and said with spirit, 'Go sell this and pay your fees. You have to do well in your master's just like my brothers did.' The fees were paid, the exam was taken but the results were not quite as good as her brothers'. Jyotish was ranked first but in the second class. He had no desire to sit for the civil or imperial service examinations as his brothers-in law had done. Since he was by nature unambitious, how far could his young wife push him? He took up a job teaching economics at Serampore College for a salary of Rs 120 per month. He took his wife and mother along to Serampore and set up house there. His child bride had by then slipped into adolescence, almost unnoticed by others. Usha had become pregnant.

Sundar-ma came down herself to take her daughter back with her to Delhi. Dadamoshai and Didi-ma's first child, a daughter named Kalyani, was born there. Didi-ma's mother-in-law heaved a deep sigh when she received the news. All she said was, 'My Jyotish fathered a girl?' But, three months later when Didi-ma returned with her baby in her arms, her mother-in-law couldn't take her eyes off the child. She had never seen such a beautiful baby in her life. Kalyani looked, she thought, like the moon that rises even before the light of dawn fades. She took the creamy sandalwood-complexioned Kalyani in her arms and remarked in her own dialect, 'Even a rag looks good when it's freshly laundered.' And then she added, 'I will bring her up myself.'

Didi-ma's mother-in-law did not get her wish. She came down suddenly with kala azar, a vicious tropical malaria. She had been on a poor diet for many years—merely rice and dal accompanied by a dry dish of spiced vegetables and fish bones. It was almost impossible for her to find the strength to fight the disease. Ushabala nursed her as best as she could. She prepared her diet as was prescribed; she gave her medicine morning, noon and night; she repeatedly shifted the patient's position to prevent bedsores and kept an eye on her so she wouldn't fall off the bed. Yet the patient's condition only deteriorated. Finally one day Swarnamoyee called her son to her bedside and said, 'Dear Jyotish, I wish to observe the antarjali jatra rites.'

'What is antarjali jatra, Ma?'

'You're a Hindu, yet you don't know what it means? It means that I want to die in the holy waters of the Ganga.'

My poor Dadamoshai was at his wit's end. He sent word to his brother in Nepal. It took some time for him to arrive. The doctor son examined his mother and shook his head. 'No, it's too late. Her pulse is very weak and she is about to breathe her last. We should follow her dying wish.'

The two brothers carried their mother to the river; Suresh Chandra to her right, Jyotish Chandra to her left. They stepped into the river slowly. When the water reached her navel, Swarnamoyee raised her joined palms in prayer. Suresh Chandra held her quivering hands and Swarnamoyee's head rolled on to his shoulder.

Didi-ma was fourteen years old then.

BERHAMPORE: DIDI-MA'S HOUSEHOLD

Time is a great healer. Dadamoshai gradually got over his grief at his mother's death but her absence made him feel unsettled at Serampore. He looked around for a new job and finally found one in Berhampore in the district of Murshidabad.

Murshidabad was famed as the one-time capital of the powerful Mughal governor Murshid Quli Khan, after whom it was named. In British times Berhampore served as the sub-divisional headquarters. It was not far from the main town of Murshidabad. The bustling town of Berhampore that we see today bears little resemblance to what it was in Dadamoshai's time. It was a typically small mofussil with hardly 30,000 inhabitants. Most of the people lived in the old locality known as Khagra and the area around Gorabazar was virtually empty. There were just a handful of tiny houses built in the traditional style; most of them single-storeyed, only a few two-storeyed. The lifestyle still mirrored that of a village. Values were deeply conservative and women hardly stepped out of their homes. There was no girls' school. The men worked in government offices, in the famous Murshidabad silk factories, at the new printing press or in small shops.

The beings that exerted the most power in town were the mosquitoes. The poet Anandashanker Ray once wrote a little rhyme about the virulent mosquitoes of Krishnagore, another mofussil town close to Berhampore:

Monsieur,
The mosquitoes of Krishnagore have made me an exile.
Do you know why the Japanese flew off, one and all?
The uncles of the Krishnagore mosquitoes live in Imphal.

The mosquitoes of Berhampore were perhaps not uncles but first cousins of their Imphal counterparts; such was the fear their tyranny instilled in the people of the town. The flies too were of no less might. Berhampore is a land of mangoes. In those days, 108 varieties of mango were grown in its vast orchards. Each had a distinctive taste. They had beautiful names like Kohinoor, Molayam Jam, Begum Bahar, Rani Pasand, Chhoto Fazli and Boro Fazli. Much like the hundred names of Lord Krishna. The delicious scents so enamoured the fly brigades that they never retreated.

Nevertheless, Berhampore had its own charm. The river Bhagirathi flowed through the heart of the town. Its banks were not properly walled but they were high enough to keep the water out in the monsoons. There were quite a few ghats with steps leading down to the river. Bathing in the river early in the morning was a regular practice for many. Round-the-year water sports and swimming contests brought tides of youthful energy to the river. In April–May, when the weather was hot, boys would swim back and forth. They picked green chickpeas from the farmers' fields on the opposite side. In autumn, tall rows of the kash flower blossomed on either bank. The beauty of the brimming river would flood one's heart with joy in monsoon and in winter the powerful rush would dwindle to a narrow stream. Yet no matter how cold the weather, people continued to bathe in it. They would go in shivering, take three quick dips and pray in the Shiva temples on top of the ghat. The sound of temple bells echoed through the morning air of Berhampore.

Another special feature of the town was the brigade parade ground or maidan as it was popularly known. There was not a single tree on it, just lush green grass. Tall trees bordered the field—sisu, sirish and jarul, also a couple of krishnachura and an ancient neem. Behind these trees on three sides of the maidan stood the barracks. These barracks were of historic importance. It was from here that the 19th Regiment of the Native Infantry joined the revolt of 1857—the first Indian war of independence. It was only natural that they would; for not far from here stood the mango grove of Plassey where a fateful battle had initiated British dominance a century earlier. After the revolt was crushed, the barracks continued to be occupied by troops loyal to the British for quite some time. Not until the British rulers felt safe and secure again were the barracks given over to a civilian workforce.

Many of the high-ranking officials of the district administration lived here. There were three bungalows on one side: for the district magistrate, the district judge and the civil surgeon. A two-storeyed circuit house was also built beside them. On another side, a post office and sundry other offices were gradually constructed. Residences of some respected citizens and senior government officials stood on the third side. Behind the magistrate's and judge's bungalows flowed the great Bhagirathi. On the opposite side, that is, the fourth side of the parade ground, ran the main and only tarred road in town. In one corner of the highway under an old raintree was a stand for cycle rickshaws, which had been the chief means of transport since the 1930s. Prior to that there were only three ways one could travel—by bullock cart, on horse-drawn carriages, or, as a last resort, on foot.

Not far from the parade ground stood Krishnanath College, another place of historic interest. It was established in 1853. Prominent among its founders were luminaries such as Rani Swarnamoyee Devi, the Nawab of Murshidabad, the royal houses of Kandi and Lalgola, the Nandi family of Cossimbazar, the Ray family of Dighapatia, Pulin Sen of Berhampore, Madanmohan Tarkalankar, a close associate of Ishwarchandra Vidyasagar and Drinkwater Bethune. Among those who had taught there were well-known personalities such as Rashbehari Ghose, Reverend Pulinbehari Dey and Gurudas Bandhopadhyay. Among its illustrious alumni we find the names of the historian Kalikinkar Dutta, Professor Bimanbehari Majumdar, the statesman Nalinaksha Sanyal, the intellectual Somen Nandy. Mahatma Gandhi himself had visited Krishnanath College once in 1925, an event still recalled with great pride. All the meritorious students of the Murshidabad district enrolled in Krishnanath College because the quality of teaching there was good and also because there were two student hostels. At first the barracks were used for classes and hostel accommodation. Later the college moved to a building of its own. It was a building that would enhance the pride of any mofussil town.

Jyotish Das Gupta joined this famous college as a professor of economics. He rented a house in Gorabazar—a tiny place, too small even for two people. It had absolutely no place for his books. A few months later, he heard of a two-storeyed house lying vacant nearby. It was said to be haunted and people were afraid to live in it. It was on the market for a mere twenty-five rupees as rent. Jyotish hastily packed all his belongings and moved into the haunted house with his wife. The ghosts never bothered them in any way—they must have taken a liking to the couple. Once Ushabala's brother Kumudkanta came for a two-day visit. Usha made up a bed for him in one of the empty rooms downstairs. Since they were meeting after a long time, they all kept chatting till it was nearly midnight. The next morning, practically before dawn, the Das Gupta couple heard a loud rapping on their bedroom door. They got up in a hurry and opened the door. Kumudkanta was standing outside. Surprised and a little worried, they asked, 'Any problem, Dada? Are you unwell? Didn't you sleep last night?'

Kumudkanta replied in a pathetic voice, 'How could I? A ghost lives in my room; a ten-year-old girl who circled my bed all night. Towards the end she sat at one corner of the bed and said sadly, "I am in great distress. Please offer prayers at the Kali temple for me. Only then will I be set free."' At Kumudkanta's insistence offerings were duly sent to the Kali temple. Still, he did not risk another night there and promptly ran away. Jyotish slept in that very bed the next night in the hope of meeting the ghost but he was disappointed. Perhaps the ghost was indeed set free! The neighbours later told him the story of a little girl who was so hurt by her parents' unkindness that she poured kerosene on herself and committed suicide. Ever since then she had apparently lived in that house as a ghost.

Usha and Jyotish set up home in this haunted house. The ghost, whether free or bound to this earth, proved propitious for them. Ushabala gave birth to five children in that house and Jyotish Chandra gained a sound reputation as a teacher. He worked out his daily routine in that house, a habit he observed all his life. Jyotish Chandra woke at the break of dawn, sat on a mat on the floor and sang a hymn in a thick flat voice, devoid of tune or rhythm.

I pray to thee ere I proceed with my day's routine,
May mine eyes be ever on thine, in my soul unseen.

Ushabala sang along with him and later, the children too as they grew up. None of them had good voices or any musical sense yet they would sing for half an hour. After his morning ablutions, Jyotish performed some physical exercises. Three days in the week he did freehand exercises; on three other days he went swimming in the river. He walked for half an hour with a towel on his head and a fresh set of clothes bundled under his arm. After his swim, he rang the bell in the Shiva temple and walked back home. Then he was off to the market. Being fond of good food, he shopped with great care. Fish was a must; and the other things like vegetables had to fit a limited budget. Usha would wait for him at the kitchen door. She would empty his shopping bags in the middle of the kitchen floor and ask in her sweet dialect, 'What would you like? A spicy fish, or a thin stew, or shall I cook it with poppy seeds? The bottle gourd stalks are so tender! Shall I make a pepper soup with them?' Young Jyotish would smile

back equally sweetly and say, 'Draupadi has a free hand.'
Perhaps Ushabala's cooking could compete with the mythical
Draupadi's. But unlike Draupadi, Ushabala would not vary
her culinary repertoire, cooking at times like a forest dweller
and at others like a queen. Her cooking was always homely
and middle class.

With the shopping done, Jyotish would sit at the only table
in the house and go through his lecture notes for the day.
A good teacher must keep abreast of his subject. Of course
Jyotish Chandra could not spend too much time on his
notes in the morning. By ten o'clock he would sit down for
his morning meal, all dressed and ready in his home-washed
and well-pleated dhoti and shirt, a chador on shoulder and
thick leather sandals. He had no time to pay attention to his
food then—he would be mentally revising points for the day's
lectures. Usha was upset. The poor man could not even enjoy
his lunch in peace!

When he got back from college, Jyotish changed. With a
towel tied firmly over his underclothes, he would go straight
down to the garden, shovel in hand. He looked more like a
common gardener than a college professor. The garden was
small but Jyotish had planted pineapple, papaya and pomelo
trees. There were also vegetable patches for lady's fingers,
spinach and other green herbs and aubergines. The aubergines
became a real headache. Black-faced langurs pestered the
whole town. The simians plucked and chewed the pomelos
and chucked them all over the garden; and no matter how
hard you tried to chase them off, they wouldn't leave without
stealing the aubergines. They disdainfully ignored Usha and
her daughters but were wary of Jyotish and his young son
Arun who was still in short pants. Langurs must be pretty
sexist creatures.

When evening descended, Jyotish Chandra reverted to his professorial persona. He washed up and sat at the table on which piles of books were neatly arranged. He lit a low-powered lamp to save on electricity bills. At that young age his vision was good so while the light was dim, it didn't strain his eyes. He kept at his books till dinnertime. After dinner, before retiring to bed, husband and wife sat under the weak lamplight and tallied the day's expenses. With the low salary he earned they had to live on a strict budget. Conscientious teachers in those days would never do extra tutoring to increase their earnings; they would share their knowledge unstintingly with the students in their classrooms. Jyotish had no extra income to fall back on, so they had to keep track of every paisa spent. They reviewed the expenses to check if they had been wasteful. They counted the change to see that nothing had been lost or misplaced. Only when the accounts were fully reconciled could Jyotish and Usha sleep in peace.

Such was Professor Jyotish Das Gupta's daily routine. An exception would be made for one and a half months in the year when the university exam scripts arrived. As soon as the bundles of papers were delivered, the children would stiffen. 'Oh dear, Baba's *khatas* are here.' Jyotish would finish his exercises or swim and disappear into a room for the entire day. No one could see him unless it was really necessary. The doors and windows would be closed, except for one outside window. The children were reluctant to raise their voices or rush around and play ball. 'Baba's correcting papers, don't you know? Suppose he gets distracted and makes a mistake?'

'Yes, suppose he puts down a zero instead of ten? A student's life might be ruined forever.'

'Wonder which student has scored the highest.'

As if the students' names were written on their answer scripts! As if any examiner ever writes a zero instead of ten. But still the Das Gupta children speculated freely and were filled with awe and fear. When the packets wrapped in brown paper finally left the house, they felt a little proud and breathed a big sigh of relief.

For Ushabala, it was quite another thing. The man of the house being locked in a room for a month and a half was a bit inconvenient but his preoccupation with something as serious as examination papers was a matter of pride for her. She was bathed in reflected glory. A vibrant household, an esteemed and loving husband, devoted children, cordial neighbours. Ushabala beamed with happiness. The vermilion dot on her forehead reflected her inner radiance.

Usha was busy all day. There was nothing remarkable about that. No one ever gave thought to the mountain of chores that a middle-class housewife had to undertake. Author Bhudeb Mukhopadhyay in his article on family matters, 'Paribarik Prasango', ordained that 'a housewife's duties are all-inclusive'. Even those who could afford to keep servants were responsible for overall management. But for the thousands of Ushabalas of Bengal who cannot hire help, the entire burden falls on their shoulders alone.

Like any other professor's wife, Ushabala too had to rise at the crack of dawn, sweep and mop the house and wake the children up for their morning studies before preparing their breakfast. There was no concept of 'bed tea'. Usha served fresh hand-made roti with cane molasses and sprouted chickpeas. Sometimes it was puffed rice and fried groundnuts with boiled green peas in season. Bread loaves did not enter the house unless someone was ill and the doctor had prescribed milk and bread as a diet. That was why little Arun once said to his friend next door who was the son of an income tax officer: 'Bab-ba, you are such rich people! You have bread and butter every day?' Breakfast over, it was time to get the children ready for school, with Usha dancing attendance on them all. It was rush hour indeed. One might be asking for a fresh set of clothes, another might want his shoes polished and a third would need his lunchbox filled. Usha liked to keep her husband's clothes neatly folded and ready. Having seen the children off, she would enter the kitchen. Sitting on the floor she would peel the vegetables and deftly slice them with a sharp-edged bonti. Spices were ground to a fine paste on a grinding stone. Now she was ready to start cooking. The daily fare was simple: plain rice, a vegetable dish, a soup of lentil, gram or some other variety of pulses and fish of course. Sometimes she would prepare shuktoni, or a vegetable crisply fried in clarified butter as extras. A little after 10 a.m., when children and husband had left, it was laundry time for Usha. The earlier she finished the better because then the washing line could get the full benefit of the sun. Hang out the clothes, clean up the kitchen, quickly finish eating. Ushabala She went full speed at this time because she needed three hours to herself in the afternoon to read. This was something she had picked up from her mother.

Three hours later she got back to housework—pick up the sun-dried clothes and fold them neatly so that they would not need ironing. After that on to preparing snacks and savouries for her hungry brood. Both children and father would look out eagerly for the new delicacies she made every day. Mohanbhog. Chhola ghugni. Malpoa. Masala muri. Then it was time for Usha to go back to the kitchen and cook dinner. No fish or rice this time; just a savoury vegetable dish with roti. For Jyotish she set aside a large bowl of milk for his meal was incomplete without it. He soaked roti in the milk, added a banana if there was one, plus a chunk of solid molasses if handy. The children had milk too—it helped develop brain cells apparently. A seer of milk cost just two annas, one-eighth of a rupee, quite affordable even on a tight budget.

Ekadasi, or the eleventh day of the lunar fortnight, was the day Usha cooked special food. That day, Jyotish would fast all day without a sip of water. No one knew why he suddenly adopted this particular ritual. Perhaps it was for the meal that followed when he broke his fast. Usha would pick plump aubergines from the garden and cut them into thick slices or split some green pointed gourd lengthwise and fry them in oil. Or she would shred potatoes thinly and fry them as jhuri bhaja. She would cook two kinds of vegetables and make a delicious payesh with fine rice and creamy milk and sprinkle juicy raisins on it. When it was time to serve the food, she squatted in front of Jyotish with a portable stove and gave him little rounds of pan-fried luchi made from refined flour. Luchis that puffed up into little balls with flaky tops were served hot from the pan one after another. Poor man! He hadn't had a bite all day and looked half his usual size. He needed a little pampering surely? Why the children didn't follow their father's example and start observing Ekadasi surprises me!

Because she liked cooking, Usha bought her utensils with great care. Rice had to be cooked in a heavy brass vessel. For vegetables she chose a squarish brass saucepan. For dal there was a circular brass pot with a raised rim and a karahi for fish. Another thick, heavy-bottomed brass karahi was set aside for milk, payesh and kheer. Ladles were all made of brass. Only the tongs and the flat tawa were iron. Usha never cooked in aluminium vessels. She served the food on bell-metal plates; each person had his own plates, bowls and water tumbler.

The utensils were not of the same size or shape so that they could be easily identified. Jyotish Das Gupta enjoyed buying utensils too—a trait he'd inherited from his mother. It is said that Swarnamoyee had such a passion for these things that as soon as she received money from her doctor son in Nepal, she would secretly buy more utensils and hide them under her bed among her boxes and bundles. Her sons ferreted these out from time to time and scolded the old woman who had sold the vessels to their mother and forced her to take them back. Jyotish was fond of buying the famous Khagra utensils once in a while to please himself and his wife. Ushabala was always delighted by these acquisitions. Cooking in a new pot or serving in a new plate gave her great satisfaction. Poor Swarnamoyee, though, was denied these pleasures.

Usha cooked on a coal-fired oven. At the bottom went sun-dried cowpats. Small pieces of coal came next. The top layer consisted of gul which was a mix of coal dust, cow dung and mud fashioned into small balls and dried in the sun. The evening meal, however, was cooked on a portable chuli with twigs and dry leaves gathered from the garden and stacked in one corner of the kitchen. The thick smoke from that oven made Usha's eyes water. She narrowed her eyes into slits and continued fanning the fire. But she didn't mind. Through the smoke she saw a clear vision of good days to come. For Usha dreaming was another name for life. Her dreams were driven by ambition—not for herself since she was a closed chapter. Not for her husband either for she realized that he wouldn't be pushed too far—Jyotish was happy with his lot. It was on her children that she pinned all her hopes. They were the inspiration for her dreams and the measure of her success as a mother. Her brilliant daughter Kalyani would make her mark in academia. Urmila would be a famous doctor like

Kadambini Ganguly or Jamini Sen. Arun would have to be a powerful executive officer and own fancy cars—which she would ride too! Subhadra was good at sports; she would go to the Olympics! And little Ashok would make a fine engineer. These dreams were where husband and wife disagreed. Jyotish would say, 'Why dream such impossible dreams?' Usha would be hurt by his response and withdraw into herself. But she never stopped dreaming.

It only stopped for three hours in the afternoon; she devoted this time to books. She read the complete works of Bhudeb Mukhopadhyay, Bankimchandra Chattopadhyay, Saratchandra Chattopadhyay and the evergreen Rabindranath Tagore. She learnt long poems by heart—by Nabinchandra Sen, Hemachandra Bandhopadhyay, Kazi Nazrul Islam and by Tagore. She recited these poems in a clear voice as she arranged things in her larder, washed clothes and dusted rooms. She also wrote sometimes—a diary, short stories, essays and belles-lettres. It was her very own private world, one not even Jyotish had access to. She stacked the notebooks on the floor in a corner of her bedroom. One day Jyotish sold them all at the price of old papers, thinking they were useless junk cluttering up the room. He needed a little extra money. In Ashapurna Devi's widely read novel, *Subarnalata*, Subarnalata's writings are deliberately destroyed by her contemptuous son. Jyotish destroyed Ushabala's writings quite inadvertently but the result was the same. Usha, like Subarnalata, did not put pen to paper again.

A sudden happy change occurred in Usha's life. Despite their small income, Jyotish managed to build a house in the newly developed Gorabazar. It was actually his engineer friend Tona-babu who built it for him at an unbelievably low price. Tona-babu was a genius of sorts, devoid of greed, self-effacing and innovative. There are so many such geniuses hidden away in Bengal. Tona-babu looked like any average Bengali—dark-complexioned and portly, with a head full of dark curly hair under which teemed dozens of bright ideas. He was full of life, laughed heartily, spoke loudly and loved good conversation and a good argument. And whenever he got a chance to build a house, he was happy as a child with a new toy. Thanks to Tona-babu's generous help, the Das Guptas could have a house of their own. A little brick path led off from the main tarred road in Gorabazar, just broad enough for two cycle rickshaws to be driven side by side. The lane was well known to the residents of Gorabazar because Dr Moti Das Gupta lived at the end of the lane. He was a bad-tempered, foul-mouthed, fine physician remarkably free from avarice. His son Promod Das Gupta later became an influential leftist leader. Halfway down this lane lived Jyotish Das Gupta. Opposite his house was a walled garden where a tribe of langurs had established territorial rights. You could spot these great devotees of Lord Rama at any time of day. Ayodhya was not a patch on it!

A low compound wall, punctuated by a small iron gate, surrounded the Das Gupta home. The gate opened into the garden. To the left were tall coconut trees, custard apple, pineapple, several varieties of citrus and guava trees. To the right were flowering bushes—homely plants that didn't require too much care but bloomed and shed flowers on their own—togor, karabi, jui, hasnahana. Just outside the gate were two magnolia trees, sown lovingly by Tona-babu himself. They didn't grow too big and they yielded just four flowers a year but when the flowers bloomed, everyone in the neighbourhood knew that Queen Magnolia had arrived at the Das Gupta place.

The house itself was two-storeyed. Three steps led up to the green front door through which one entered the sitting room. There were a few wooden armchairs, a medium-sized table, a book cabinet on one side and a plank settee on the other covered with a durrie. On the table was placed a small brass vase with a few leaves and flowers. It was an ordinary room, no flashiness, and just good enough for students and colleagues to drop in for a chat. The table served well for teaching or correcting papers and even a few cups of tea.

Beyond the sitting room was a large veranda from which a staircase led up to the first floor. Below the stairs was a tiny pantry. You entered it carefully with your head bent low. Inside, the room reminded you of a fairy tale. The room was full of containers of every size and shape filled with rice, pulses, salt, turmeric, pickles and preserves, sun-dried pigeon-pea nuggets, condiments, fried snacks of all sorts, nuts and many other things. There were also moulds stacked for sandesh and other sweetmeats, a little karahi for luchi, another for sweet patties, raisins, cashew nuts and pistachio. Which child would not wish to peep into that room? But children were not allowed inside in case they dropped or broke something. You tore yourself away from the pantry and went along the veranda. A little detached, and in one corner, were two attached rooms, the bathroom and the toilet. The two served separate functions, unlike Western-style toilets. Following the veranda, you would first see the dining room which had no table. For meals, one sat cross-legged on a piri. Next to the dining room was the kitchen where Usha had to spend a great deal of her time. To make her as comfortable as possible, Jyotish had ordered a large, airy kitchen with a large window and three doors. The oven was in the centre of the room with a flue pipe above it to let out the smoke. There was a low wooden seat in front of the oven for Usha to sit on and cook. A long narrow platform against one wall held large brass pitchers of water for cooking and narrow-necked clay ones for drinking. On the opposite wall another such platform was for daily cooking utensils, platters and tumblers. Beyond the kitchen, you walked down three steps and came to a washroom with a tubewell. Some distance from it was an old village-style service latrine which you had to climb eight or ten steps to reach.

The rooms upstairs were aligned with those below. But the veranda upstairs had railings around it. Usha and her daughters often sat there in the afternoon to dry their hair. Sometimes, when women acquaintances dropped in, a reed mat would be rolled out on the floor for them to sit on and chat. It became a women's parlour where they exchanged typically feminine gossip. On one side of the veranda above the downstairs sitting room was Usha and Jyotish's bedroom. There were at the centre two simple beds with no carved designs. Against one wall stood two large wardrobes for clothes, jewellery and other expensive things and cash. One of them had a shiny full-length mirror on one door—great for pleating saris and checking the length of the anchal. On top of each wardrobe sat a huge celluloid doll, possibly to guard its contents. The staircase was next to the bedroom. Above the downstairs bathrooms was the box room. There were boxes made of leather and also of tin. Three large steel trunks were filled with fancy utensils, important papers, and all the extra items that were not for daily use and yet could not be thrown away. Above the dining room was the children's room lined with rows of beds in which they slept at night and studied on during the day with their books spread around. All the siblings shared that one room. Of course there were friendly exchanges and quarrels during study hours but as soon as they heard their father's footsteps, they became quietly serious. Next to the children's room, above the kitchen, was a tiny walled terrace. It reminded one of the house on Hanuman Road. When the weather was really hot, mats would be spread on it for people to sleep on. On winter nights the children would sometimes not bother to go to the lavatory downstairs, but relieve themselves on the terrace!

The house had a third floor too, in the style of 48 Hanuman Road. That floor comprised one attic room and a walled terrace. During exams, the attic was the place where you could read aloud and memorize things. Sometimes clothes were hung out to dry on the terrace. After the monsoons all the bedding and blankets, quilts, sheets and pillows were lugged up there for a thorough sunning. Pickles and preserves were sunned there from time to time. Sometimes the children's friends came over to play—mostly hopscotch or some other game of catch with a small ball. As they grew a little older they held drama rehearsals or practised out loud for elocution.

Beside the top flight of stairs, beneath the third floor, was a loft with a locked green door. Extra bedding, pillows, blankets and towels were stored there. When house guests arrived, Jyotish would set up a wooden ladder and go up there. The children stood around staring up in wonder. How did so many things emerge from that tiny space? Surely there was some magician hidden inside. Urmila would recite a well-known rhyme in Bengali, '*Gharer madhye ghar, taar madhye kaj kare Chand Sadagar.*' A room within a room, and inside it works Chand Sadagar.

There was no architectural beauty to the house but still, it was the Das Guptas' very own. It may not have been grand like 48 Hanuman Road but there was plenty of sunshine and fresh air. Usha's professor husband had built it with a lot of effort and the help of a friend to make his darling wife happy. On the day they first entered their new home a grateful Usha wept tears of joy. Her dreams glistened in her brimming eyes.

DIDI-MA'S FAMILY

Ushabala was the mother of five children. The first, Kalyani, was my mother. Her life forms the third section of this story. Second was Urmila—another daughter! Twenty-year-old Usha shed buckets of tears. Daughters were not in demand at all in those days. (Not so much in these days either.) The poet Kamini Ray wrote in 1917, in her book on women's education, *Balika Shikshar Adarsha: Atit o Bartaman*:

> Why is a daughter not welcome? Because there's no need for her in her father's house. She takes things away but gives nothing. A son can look after his parents in their old age; a married daughter usually cannot. She is part of another family and her time and efforts are devoted to caring for that family. Why, then, is she not cherished by the family that uses her services? For a simple reason. One who becomes your lifelong possession under your control does not need any special attention or respect. Who cares to protect her prestige? Parents think it is a great misfortune to have a daughter; the daughter thinks her life is quite futile. No one thinks of how the precious sons would be produced if no daughters are born.

Kamini Ray was right. If you are marked out from birth as 'another's property', is it worthwhile for anyone to devote too much attention and care to you? Moreover, it is a real headache for a middle-class family to get a daughter married off. The girl is humiliatingly put on display over and over again. Then the dowry has to be bargained over. It was bad luck for Usha that her daughter Urmila was dark-complexioned, though she had a pretty face and lovely large dreamy eyes. Usha thought hard and decided that Urmila must be a doctor. The first Bengali woman doctor, Kadambini Ganguly, faced many obstacles but girl students later gained the right of admission to medical college; long before Urmila was born. Urmila fulfilled her mother's dream and was admitted to the medical college in Calcutta. She secured a scholarship and found place in the college hostel. After two years a problem arose. Urmila fell in love with a doctor; but one who was Kayastha by caste! Ushabala put her foot down—they were of the higher caste of Vaidyas. She would not let a Kayastha into her family. Fierce arguments arose between mother and daughter. Urmila said, 'The caste system has been created by man, not by god.' Her mother replied, 'Society is created by man. If man himself breaks the rules he has made, then the whole social structure will break down.'

Urmila grew defiant. 'If I marry him, what will you do?'

Ushabala's reply was cold as steel. 'I will disown you.'

Ushabala forgot all about Rabindranath Tagore, Sri Chaitanya and Kazi Nazrul whose words she had long committed to memory and recited. But memorizing and internalizing are certainly different things. How much of what we voice do we actually accept in our heart of hearts? We observe every day the tragic consequences of caste and class conflicts in our country yet can we break the iron grip of traditional beliefs that vitiate our minds?

My Urmila-mashi loved her mother dearly. She could not bear to hurt her. She continued with her studies and became a doctor. She took up a job at the Marwari Hospital. A single woman on her own, she lacked in neither patients nor suitors. At this time a marriage proposal was sent by Samir Mohan Sen. He had been a popular college senior when Urmila-mashi first met him as a student at Calcutta Medical College. Samir Mohan was a Vaidya from a well-known family, the grandson of the reputed zamindar Baikuntha Sen of Berhampore. Urmila's parents consented most happily and the wedding took place at short notice. Samir Sen was a man of rare qualities, both as a human being and as a doctor. He had high ideals and was detached about material gain or loss. He was deft with his surgical implements, believed in humane values and loved philosophy. His wife was of a different nature, and they occasionally argued. She wanted a good house, a large car, saris of the latest fashion, and jewellery. He was indifferent to all the things that money could buy. But they did appreciate each other's good qualities and they worked well together professionally. They left Calcutta and built their own nursing home in Jamnagar, Gujarat. Samir Sen was such a well-loved and highly respected figure in the city that after his death the people of Jamnagar rechristened the street next to his nursing home in his name.

Samir Sen's mother, Urmila-mashi's mother-in-law, was a remarkable woman. She was called Aurobindo—Aru for short. Married into a rich landowner's family of Berhampore, she left Berhampore and settled in Calcutta. Her husband Tarak Mohan Sen was struck by paralysis and remained bedridden for many years. Aru-devi stayed by his bedside, a devoted nurse, ever watchful. Aru-devi's lips always wore a gentle smile. Her sari was ordinary, unironed, her blouse was home-washed, two thin bangles adorned both wrists, she wore a thin necklace and a vermilion dot on her forehead. While Aru-devi seldom left the room, what was remarkable was how well she managed the entire household—a landlord's large joint family with visitors and guests galore. She planned the menu, remembered each one's preferences, settled any problems among the retinue of cooks and servants, decided on gifts for everyone for the autumn Durga festival and allocated the budget for each item of expenditure. She was the final authority on every matter. She had two sons, the elder one was a lawyer and the younger a doctor. Of the two daughters-in-law, the elder was a beautiful, educated woman from a rich family; the second was my Urmila-mashi, a doctor. She had lovely grandchildren. Her two married daughters were frequent visitors. But the person who was most important of all was the ever-smiling, sweet-spoken, ever-devoted wife. Everyone praised this virtuous lady.

As long as her husband was alive Aru-devi never left his side unless it was absolutely essential. After his death her younger son, Samir, persuaded her with a lot of effort to go with him to his workplace in Jamnagar. My Didi-ma Ushabala was visiting her daughter and son-in-law at that time. She was amazed to see the change that had come over Aru-devi. Her low voice became strong and powerful, her silent smile turned to loud laughter, her slow steps gathered speed and her sweet speech became sweeter still. She enjoyed herself wholeheartedly and expressed herself without reserve. My Didi-ma thought, Is this then the joy of being free at last? Setting oneself up as an exemplary woman of virtue in the eyes of society certainly takes a heavy toll on one's true personality.

Aru-devi has passed away. My uncle Samir too has left, felled by a heart attack. Urmila-mashi is an octogenarian now, touching ninety. These days age has a way of making you younger and in this respect Urmila-mashi is truly a wonder. Her capacity for enjoyment, her appetite for life, her vibrant spirit, her ability to draw people close to her and her bright smile could easily be the envy of any eighteen-year-old girl. She has two worthy sons. One of them teaches in a university abroad. The other is a reputed architect in India. They both love their mother, but is it possible, nowadays, to live under the same roof with both wife and mother? Even though old-age homes seem to be the norm now, Urmila-mashi preferred to live with her elder sister, Kalyani, my mother. They were really close friends. After her sister died, Urmila-mashi lives in her own flat, alone. Her sons visit her quite often and make all the necessary arrangements for her comfort. They look after her, even from afar.

Didi-ma's third child was Arun, our Moni-mama. He was her darling, her firstborn son. He was fair, round-faced, with large eyes—most Bengalis would call him handsome. But Arun's face and behaviour seemed a little lacking in what they would call 'personality'. He thrilled his mother by sailing through his studies with great distinction, exactly like her own illustrious brothers, and joined Class I central government service. He became an income tax officer and later, a commissioner.

When Arun was prepared to marry, two criteria were set for the prospective bride. She must be a beauty and she must be a college graduate. There was to be no dowry. Numerous girls were examined one after the other to pick out the loveliest of them all. I went along to review one such exhibit—the very thought of it still makes me want to sink into the ground with shame. What a horrible custom! You have to dress up a girl and produce her for inspection in front of a group of strangers as if she were a commodity—a new version of the slave markets of old. Finally, the choice fell on Iva. She was still an undergraduate student studying for her intermediate arts exam. She was a dusky beauty, though with a minor flaw: a big mole on one side of her nose.

We went in a big group to Didi-ma's place for the wedding. Urmila-mashi's phulsajya, the first night she was to spend with her husband on a flower-strewn bed, fell on the same day as Arun-mama's wedding—in two different houses, of course. She dropped in for a short while to attend her brother's wedding—all dressed up in a flaming red Benarasi silk sari, loads of heavy, old-style, heirloom jewellery (gifted by her in-laws), thick garlands round her neck and dazzling vermilion powder in her parting and on her forehead. My doctor aunt looked happy, shy and strangely unfamiliar to me.

Mami-moni, my new aunt, was the daughter of an affluent lawyer of Rangpur. They came to Calcutta to set up a lavish wedding. The *boubhat*, the reception hosted by the groom's parents, would be held in Berhampore where my Didi-ma and Dadamoshai lived. The whole family climbed into an 'inter-class' compartment of the Lalgola Express train to go to Berhampore. Mami-moni was devastated. Leaving her family was sad enough, and now the agony of travelling by 'inter-class' was just too much. Mami-moni wept all the way. The way she used to cry was quite special. Her face remained still as a mask—not a quiver on her lips, not a crinkle on her nose. Only her large, long-lashed eyes shed a steady drip of tears. The teardrops had a shrewd sense of direction. They fell right down the centre of her two cheeks, never to one side. She looked like a film star shedding glycerine tears. The effect it had on Moni-mama was devastating. How could he help but give his whole heart to this damsel in distress?

When we got off at Berhampore station, we went straight into the waiting room. Subhadra, my Moni-mashi, Arun's younger sister, took charge of Mami-moni's make-up. Moni-mashi loved dressing people up, she was good at it too. But, firmly believing that the more powder you wore the fairer you looked, she dabbed on too much.

By the time we reached home, the women of the neighbourhood had already arrived. Chhabi Sen, the income tax officer's wife from next door, was large and bumptious, in keeping with her position as a big officer's helpmate. She had been given charge of the welcoming ceremony. As soon as the bride descended from the phaeton, a red sari was spread out in her path like a red carpet. Didi-ma came forward and led the bride in by the hand. Moni-mama followed with a basket of paddy which he cut with a small nutcracker as he walked. When they came to the veranda, Mami-moni was made to stand on a black, high-rimmed stone platter filled with milk and red alta. Moni-mama stood on a grinding stone. Didi-ma blessed and performed the ritual welcome. This ceremony is of special significance in Bengali homes. The mother-in-law is the mistress of the house and only if she is welcoming will the new bride have the right to enter her home.

The boubhat reception was scheduled for the next day. According to the Berhampore custom of those days, phaetons were sent out for all the guests. They were coming to honour the householder and had to be accorded due respect. They came, they dined, they saw the bride's face and blessed her with a token sum of two rupees or a tiny silver container for vermilion powder. Mami-moni received twenty-four such containers and a total of Rs 144. She took me aside and asked me in confidence, 'Tell me, Bharati, is my face worth no more than two rupees?'

Mami-moni was charming—the centre of all male and female attention at any gathering. She loved saris and ornaments, parties and get-togethers, picnics and cinema, shopping and fashion, good food and entertainment. She loved to enjoy herself and give joy to others. Above all, she loved her home and her children. She was the perfect housewife and a fond mother. When her son Sabyasachi stayed up all night and prepared for his exams, Mami-moni would keep a watchful eye on him so that he didn't fall asleep. If her daughter Debalina developed the slightest fever, Mami-moni would be there with the magical cold compress for her forehead and a fan. When Moni-mama was stricken with Parkinson's disease, she nursed him so well that old-timers compared her to the mythical Sati of the Purana tales.

After Moni-mama's retirement they came to live in Calcutta. All at once Mami-moni developed a disease that required her to go to her son in Delhi for proper treatment. Before she left, she brought a trunk full of her favourite saris to Moni-mashi. 'Why should I keep them in a locked house? It is better that you keep them, sister. I'll wear them again when I get back.' This puts me in mind of that Tolstoy story where a messenger of god sees a woman buying heaps of beautiful things even as death stands behind her. In the Mahabharata too, Yudhisthir tells Dharmaraj, who appears to him in the shape of a heron, about how oblivious man is of his own death. Mami-moni had wished so much to live. But no amount of wishing could prevent the breath of life from forsaking her at an untimely moment. Moni-mama, too, in his half-conscious, half-unconscious state, somehow realized that Ivu, the apple of his eye, would never return to him. He did not survive for very long after that.

Didi-ma's fourth child was Subhadra, my Moni-mashi. Everyone sighed sadly when she was born. 'Another daughter for Usha,' they said. Moreover, this girl was neither as pretty as Kalyani, nor as attractive as Urmila. She was dark and ordinary-looking. All her life Moni-mashi felt unwanted and kept herself in the background as far as possible. The description that author M.M. Urquhart gave in the early 1920s, in her book *Women of Bengal*, of the passivity of Bengali women and of how they silently suffered all kinds of oppression and injustice would fit the child Subhadra exactly. She had little opportunity to play with other children outside her home. Her mother had been weakened by repeated surgery. Who but Subhadra could remain at her side and do her bidding? By the time Didi-ma regained her strength, Subhadra was already eleven years old. Everybody then woke up to the fact that Subhadra had not been admitted to any school at all. Dadamoshai hurriedly calculated her age and got her admitted to Class V. In those days children and their parents did not have to compete for school admissions—the girls' schools were happy to admit the few students they got. But learning does not happen automatically with age. Poor Subhadra was as helpless in class as a novice swimmer in the Atlantic Ocean. In the Bengali language class, the teacher would say, 'Write an essay.' For Subhadra, it was like a sentence of death. How does one write an 'essay'? What is meant by 'translation'? The English teacher was very particular about correct pronunciation and she made each student read out aloud. Subhadra would stand up when her turn came. Her lips moved but no sound came. The maths teacher would write out a problem 'Simplify—', and then put a large zero on the blank page she received. All the teachers were convinced that this girl was unintelligent; she would never pass.

Their prediction proved correct. Subhadra failed her exams. Dadamoshai was stunned—he didn't speak to her for seven days. For seven days Subhadra's little heart shook all night with unshed tears. Of course everyone knew that Subhadra was an inferior creature. Subhadra thought so herself. Urmila said, 'Subhadra is the darkest, the shortest and the stupidest of us all.' Her parents shook their heads sadly and said, 'She's as stupid as Kutu, our second sister-in-law's mentally handicapped son.' The first to sing a different tune was her eldest sister. The newly married Kalyani had come to spend a month at her parents' home. Living in Delhi had made her lose touch with her own siblings. Nevertheless, coming back to the parental home again felt good. Everything about Berhampore delighted her. The sky had a special charm; the air was sweet as honey, her little sister Subhadra, who was twelve years younger than her, was adorable. Kalyani folded Subhadra into her arms. She showered her with kisses. Subhadra broke down in tears. 'Why do you love me so much, Didi? I'm just like Kutu.'

Kalyani looked her in the face for a brief moment and said, 'Why should you be like Kutu? You aren't!'

'Yes, I am stupid. I don't know anything and can't do anything right.'

Kalyani's voice thickened. 'You'll do everything and know everything. I will teach you. Listen to me carefully, you are *not* stupid.'

To this day, even when she's past eighty, Subhadra recalls those words with tears in her eyes. The first reassuring words she heard. How could she ever forget?

Kalyani kept her word. She tutored Subhadra assiduously for a month every year when she came back to Berhampore.

Gradually Subhadra achieved enough ability to pass with average marks. But she yearned to come first. And she did, not in class, but in a race organized at school. Subhadra was so delighted that she decided she would excel at sports and make her parents happy. She joined Habi-babu's gymnasium. She woke up at four every morning to practise running and to exercise. Dadamoshai breathed a sigh and remarked, 'If she worked as hard at her books as she does on the field, Subhadra could be another Urmila.' Subhadra's efforts were rewarded. In the All Berhampore Sports Competition organized by Habi-babu's gymnasium, Subhadra was declared a champion. Dadamoshai was among the spectators. He came back and said, 'Truth to say, Debjani performed better than you. Habi is fond of you, so he favoured you and made you the champion.' Perhaps Dadamoshai saw it that way and spoke his mind. But is it necessary for us speak our mind on every occasion? It could be that Dadamoshai wished to encourage his daughter to compete even harder. Parents always act in the best interests of their progeny but in the efforts we make and in the strategies we adopt, we fail again and again. Subhadra did not sleep that night.

However, she didn't totally drop out from field sports and even competed at the state level in the Bengal Olympics for the javelin-throwing event, though she didn't come first. She was a fine cyclist too. Sportspersons are usually well liked by others. Subhadra was a popular girl in the locality as well as in school and college. But it was not the kind of attention she longed for as a growing adolescent. The boys she had grown up with, why, even her own brother Arun, would stare at her childhood friend Gouri as if they had never seen a young woman before. They threw flowers at her feet as if she were a goddess to be worshipped. Why did no one look at Subhadra like that? Why did they never throw flowers at her? Of course, Gouri was special. She was good-looking and carried an aura of aristocratic refinement which is rare. Every young man in the neighbourhood was charmed by her. However, Gouri was enamoured of only one person: Partha-da. Gouri's family was middle class, Partha's family was rich. Gouri had free access to his house. Gouri had decided secretly that Partha-da was her husband and she gradually moulded her behaviour to suit his preferences. When her friends asked, 'Why did you give up your dresses and take to wearing a sari so soon?', Gouri replied simply, 'Because Partha-da likes it.' Gouri and Partha grew up together but then Partha moved to Calcutta for higher studies and then there was no sign of him. Days turned to months, months to years and so ten summers passed. A stream of marriage proposals came for Gouri but she turned them all down. 'I already have a husband,' she said.

As luck would have it, Subhadra bumped into Partha's sister one day on a street in Calcutta. The two childhood friends were delighted to meet each other after so many years. They had so much to talk about. At one point, Subhadra asked, 'Has Partha-da married?'

'Don't talk about it. He hasn't. Where's the time? He's too busy with work!'

'You remember Gouri?'

'Gouri who lived near our place? Of course I remember her! Where's she now?'

'In Berhampore. She hasn't married. Still waiting for Partha-da.'

'You don't say! That's amazing! Still dreaming of Partha?'

'She is,' said Subhadra.

When Partha got the news, he was so surprised and thrilled that he rushed to Berhampore and swept Gouri off to the wedding pavilion. It was as if the mythical Uma's penance for husband Lord Shiva was rewarded at last. Subhadra's wedding present for her dear friend was a pair of silver ankle bells with a little line from a popular dancing song—*Sohag chand bodoni, dhoni, nacho toh dekhi*—Dance, pretty maiden, dance in joy. Who can say that Saratchandra Chattopadhyay's popular novel *Parineeta* is just a sentimental, unreal, romantic tale? It only mirrors the real life story of Gouri and Partha!

Meanwhile, Subhadra's wheel of fortune was also turning. She passed her BA and then her Bachelor of Teacher's Training exam. She was teaching at a school and earning success and goodwill, just like her older siblings. Marriage proposals started pouring in—perhaps because of all the praise she received from the residents of Berhampore. Subhadra was adamant—anyone who even mentioned dowry or any other form of exchange was disqualified. In the end, she won. Her marriage was arranged with Ajit Sen, a Class I government engineer, with no dowry or any other claims.

Ajit Sen was an honest and amiable man; gentle, sensitive, conscientious. He loved having people over for meals and he especially loved relating stories of his own childhood. How he jumped on to the school bus, all spic and span in white drill half pants, white twill half-slewed shirt, white socks, those white canvas shoes called keds, with a tiffin box under his arm. How he found the daily lunch, rice and fish curry, boring and how he used to run as soon as he heard the street vendor cry, '*Noni makhan, naram makhan . . . chaa-ai!*' How delicious it was—that creamy butter spread on slices of bread with a sprinkle of sugar on top! Far superior to any sweetmeats he'd ever had. He always said that boys dressed very simply in his time. When he was in Class X, his father Samarketu Sen, a doctor with the Railways, had bought clothes for him for the whole year. Two *addi panjabis*, two khaki half pants, one white half pant, two white twill shirts and one cotton printed full-sleeved shirt. An entry in Samarketu's diary dated 22 June 1941 reads thus:

Ajit's Clothes:
(1) Two khaki & one white half shirt.........Rs 2-4 annas
(2) One printed shirt ....Re 0-8 annas
(3) Two white twill shirts @ 6 ....Rs 0-12 annas
(4) Two addi panjabis @ 10 annas..............Rs 1-4 annas
(5) Buttons ....Re 0-5 annas
(6) One bedcover ....Rs 2-0 annas
(7) One bedsheet...Rs 1-11 annas
(8) Two sets dhotis.......................................Rs 6-3 annas

That was all the civil surgeon had to spend on his elder son's clothes while he was in school. For the annual festival, of course, there were two extra sets of clothes for the first and last days: Sasthi and Bijoya. The weaver would come to the house long before the puja with bundles of saris and cloth for the women of the house. Ajit's mother and aunts selected broad-bordered saris for themselves. For the children they bought printed cotton shirt lengths at two annas a yard and khaki cloth for half pants to be sewn by the tailor.

Theirs was a joint family in both organization and spirit. The family home called 'Senabash' was situated in Ghoom near Darjeeling. Once a year during the pujas, the whole family would gather there. During the bone-chilling Himalayan winters at Ghoom, members who lived at Senabash would come down to the plains where Ajit Sen's father Samarketu held a transferable job. My Meshomoshai's third uncle, his Sejo-kaka, would keep the whole house in a state of excitement while his mother Hemlata Devi would deep fry tender green pointed gourds with expert care. She laid them side by side in hot oil and turned them over once at just the right time for a crisp golden brown skin and a soft, well-cooked core. Just the way it should be to accompany luchis. Frying the luchi came next. Hemlata heated pure ghee in a karhai. Sejo-kaka rolled out the white flour mix into little rounds and tossed the pieces one at a time, perfect potshots into the hot oil without the tiniest splash. After this fun-filled cooking session, they all trooped in to the sitting room for a real treat—Sejo-kaka's amazing magic tricks with cards. Ajit Sen need only close his eyes to recall those sweet memories of unalloyed fun.

The spirit of togetherness lasted in the Sen family for many years. After Samarketu passed away, his fourth brother took over. Thanks to his wonderful personality and decision-making abilities, this bachelor uncle became the very soul of the Sen family. As long as he was alive, his nephews and nieces and their spouses revered him like their own father.

It wasn't difficult for Subhadra-mashi to blend in with such a family. Her mother-in-law Hemlata used to say, 'My eldest daughter-in-law may be dark of skin, but shines bright with goodness.' Subhadra's husband's younger brothers and sisters respected her. Setting high standards for children was in her blood. Her two sons, whom she brought up with infinite care, turned out to be fine young men. One joined the Indian Administrative Services (IAS) the other became a bank official. They have lovely wives with whom they have set up their own happy homes. Subhadra can take much of the credit for her sons' successful careers.

Subhadra's first child, however, was her daughter Nandini. Perhaps mimicking the neglect she herself received from the time she was born, Subhadra treated her baby girl with indifference. Why is it almost invariably so? Why does a persecuted daughter-in-law treat her own son's wife badly when she assumes the role of a mother-in-law? Why does a woman who has suffered the curse of discrimination as a girl-child give preference to her sons over her daughters? In psychological terms, it is the 'intimate enemy' that Ashis Nandy talks of in his book of the same name. We internalize the enmity we face from the outside world and in similar circumstances, we are transformed into the very image of the enemy.

This is not to say that Subhadra neglected Nandini. She encouraged her to become a doctor, after which she arranged her marriage. In her opinion a husband was an absolute necessity for a woman. She often repeated her favourite saying: 'A bad husband is better than a good brother.' She could not conceive of the fact that the effect of a brutish husband on his wife can only be poisonous. She held on to the belief prescribed by the ancient Indian scriptures—a husband is a woman's chief recourse. This is true of many older women in middle-class homes. When will Bengali women's luck change? Not their husband's luck but their own? Whether the husband that her mother has chosen for Nandini will indeed turn out to be better than her own fine brothers, only the future can tell. What is undeniable is that Nandini is a proficient and caring doctor with the rare virtue of selflessness. On the one hand, she is a dedicated professional and on the other, she keeps a careful eye open for her parents' well-being. These days many parents of self-reliant, working daughters depend on them for attention and care, often more than they do on their sons. Nandini is a living example of this change. One hopes that such examples will go a long way in changing our attitudes so that the birth of a daughter will not make parents weep but rather blow joyous conch shells—as they do when a son is born—to announce their good luck.

Now on to Ushabala's youngest child: her son Ashok, our mamu, maternal uncle. Like I mentioned earlier, as children we were very fond of each other; we still are. We talk for hours on end about our happy childhood days in Berhampore as well as about the problems and interests in our lives today. He is an engineer—simple, uncomplicated, straight-talking—as artless as a child when it comes to verbal skills or politicking. He loves reciting poems, loves food and playing cards and he loves his wife Chitrita. She is good-looking, sings beautifully, talks charmingly and displays grace in everything she does. She has won the hearts of the whole family. Her only child Dolan is bright and vivacious and has two children of her own. They live on the upper floor of Mamu's house—a boon for all of them. Chitrita adores her grandchildren—her life revolves round them. It is a happy arrangement for all.

THE LARGER FAMILY

Didi-ma was well spoken, a caring person who knew how to make people feel welcome. A steady stream of relatives visited her home. Her elder brother-in-law's children Ranu, Chinu, Anu, Jamuna, Chhoto and Kutu came over to their aunt's place whenever they were on holiday. Dadamoshai climbed up to the loft to bring out extra mattresses, pillows and sheets. Didi-ma set up one big bedding arrangement on the floor for all the children. She swept the sheets with a broomstick and tucked them around the mattress to ensure they were stretched smooth and tight. She placed a cool pitcher of water and two bell-metal tumblers in one corner—stainless steel had not come into vogue then. For food there was fish curry in a huge brass karhai for everyone and a huge brass pot of fried moong dal and a dish of mixed vegetables. It wasn't grand, but enough. She did fry luchi for the visitors once in a while, and served it with fine rice payesh topped with raisins and a drizzle of finely cut nuts. This was a great favourite of the Das Guptas.

Their niece Chinu was the one who visited most often and stayed the longest. She would sit in Didi-ma's prayer room and sing Shyamasangeet in a loud, open-throated style. I remember one song sung in envy of the red hibiscus that finds a place at Goddess Kali's feet—*Bol re jaba bol, kemane maar charan peli tui tamashi jaba*. Chinu-mashi's elder sister Ranu-mashi used to come for four days during the puja—much like Goddess Uma who is believed to visit her parents' home in autumn. It is actually Uma's (Durga's) supposed homecoming that the four-day Bengali puja celebrates. Ranu-mashi couldn't come more often because her engineer husband was perpetually on tour—it was a job that paid well. They settled in Kalyani after he retired. But, with increasing age, many health problems beset the couple. Old age is hard for everyone and if you live long, you cannot escape decrepitude. It is a losing battle—you lose your youthful vigour and the regular income of a salaried job. Ultimately, the old couple had to sell off their home in Kalyani and live in Calcutta with their son's family. Ranu-mashi had acute diabetes and she wanted to eat all the time. She would stare longingly out of the window at the street vendor carrying a box of puffed rice on his head, or at the man with a pushcart hawking masala muri, or listen eagerly to the voice of the banana seller. And while she yearned for these snacks, she felt diffident about asking her son for money.

Her husband, on the other hand, wouldn't give her a single rupee, no matter how hard she begged. He would say, 'Here we are, two sick old people living off our son. He has so many expenses to bear. We ought to help him out but we don't have the means. I do not have money to waste.' A heartbroken Ranu-mashi wrote to her aunt Ushabala once: 'I don't have even two rupees of my own to buy anything or give a small present.' Her grandchildren too didn't take too well to her. And one can't blame them at all. Their idea—the usual with most Indian children—of a grandmother was someone who would tell them stories, make coconut sweets and all kinds of savouries, someone who would spoil them utterly when they had to escape their parents' strict discipline. How could they love a sick and old grandmother who suddenly descended on them? Unfortunately, one day a lighted joss stick fell on Ranu-mashi's nylon sari and she burnt to death. Everyone said it was an accident.

There was another frequent visitor to Berhampore: Didi-ma's widowed sister-in-law Kamala. Kamala is another name for Lakshmi, the goddess of wealth and good fortune, but for no apparent reason, Kamala-didima had never been in the goddess's good books. She was widowed at an early age with three small children to look after. Her eldest son Kuchu just managed to pass his school-leaving exam and find a low-paid job. He could barely make ends meet. Kamala-didima got Kuchu-mama married. Hardly a month later, his wife ran off with her former lover. Kamala-didima's daughter Chhabi was an unusual beauty. Borrowing the words of Rabindranath, one might say, Goddess Lakshmi 'did not shower fortune on her namesake Kamala', but she blessed Kamala's daughter with her own looks. Beauty is much valued in the Indian marriage market. The beautiful Chhabi was wedded to the

England-returned barrister Prabhat Sen. His father's mansion was grand and Kamala-didima was overjoyed by her daughter's unexpected good fortune. A few months after Chhabi was married, the mansion was sold to settle a huge debt and Prabhat-babu's father died of a broken heart. At his job, Prabhat Sen remained briefless and soon Chhabi-mashi's family could not afford two proper meals a day. My mother found her a job in a canteen run by a branch of the All India Women's Conference. The salary was Rs 30 per month plus two free meals a day. Chhabi-mashi would pack up her own share of the food and take it home—she had a son and a husband to feed. She was so grateful for the job she almost fell at my mother's feet. 'You've helped me so much, Kalyani-didi. At least we can eat once a day.' Chhabi-mashi gave birth to yet another daughter. The girl was half dead at birth but she somehow survived. It may sound heartless, but she would have been better off dead. A sickly, mentally handicapped girl, she ate up all her mother's share of food. And that, in a home where everyone was hungry all the time. I once saw Chhabi-mashi at my mother's place push her daughter off with her left hand while she ate the fish and rice served with care by my mother. 'You eat up all my food. Today it's my turn.' It was a picture straight from the disastrous famine of 1870 in Bengal. Anaemic and starved Chhabi-mashi fell down unconscious one day and died without any medical care. However, events after this proved that real life is sometimes stranger than fiction. Some months after Chhabi-mashi's death, Goddess Lakshmi changed her mind and decided to settle in Prabhat-babu's home. He started making money; he earned a good reputation as a barrister; his unlucky, deformed daughter died and his son established himself well. Only, Chhabi-mashi remained a picture in a frame.

Chhabi-mashi's brother Ram, Kamala-didima's youngest child, was our Ram-mama. Looks-wise, he was the exact opposite of his sister. But if the quality of one's heart can be considered a measure of beauty, then Ram-mama was a wonderfully handsome man. The great poet Kalidasa's *Raghuvansha* contains a description of Raja Dilip as a strapping figure of manhood, 'broad-shouldered as a bull, tall as a sal tree'. Ram-mama was even more handsome than that. What if he was pitch dark, and painfully thin and frail? Is beauty merely skin deep? Ram-mama had only to hear of anyone in trouble and he would rush in to help, no matter what. One day Dadamoshai said, 'Oh! I bought some bananas today and left them in the shop.'

Ram instantly responded. 'Please tell me which shop it was. I'll go and fetch them.' The bananas arrived. Ram-mama was happy to be of service.

On another occasion, Ma remarked at dinner that the mosquitoes in Berhampore were really terrible. Even a mosquito net would not stop them. Ram-mama jumped up with his food still half-eaten. Ma said, 'Hold on, brother. You can hang the net later.' But Ram-mama had disappeared by then. After a few minutes he bounded downstairs again, beaming from ear to ear. 'I've tucked the net in good and proper. Be careful when you get in, Kalyani-di. Don't take the mosquitoes to bed with you.'

Another day I made him a special request. 'I've written a long letter to Baba. It will need extra stamps. Will you go to the post office tomorrow and post it for me, please, Ram-mama?'

'Why tomorrow? Give it to me now. I'll run and post it right away.'

'You don't have to run. It's two in the afternoon, really hot outside. Tomorrow will do fine.'

'Not so hot at all. You wrote it today, so why waste a whole day? Isn't your father waiting anxiously for your letter?'

He practically snatched the envelope from my hand and ran off.

One afternoon Mamu said, 'I won't go out to play today, I've got such a headache.'

'What! Whoever skips games for just a headache? I'll massage your head. The headache won't know where to run.'

And the headache really did vanish with Ram-mama's skilful massage.

Such was Ram-mama. He went to college in Balurghat and passed his intermediate arts exam—something his elder brother Kuchu couldn't manage. Now he wanted to study for his BA. He was sure to get a good job if he graduated. However, Kuchu-mama couldn't afford to feed him and put him through college too. So Kamala-didima appealed earnestly to my mother. 'Kalyani, you have a very large house, I'm told. Will you request your generous and kind husband on my behalf, please? No, no, you don't have to feed Ram. We have a relative who lives in nearby Bhowanipore. Ram can run there twice a day for his meals. Spare him just a little space in one corner of any veranda; I'll send him a mat and bedroll to sleep on.' My mother has always been a woman of few words. She tilted her head to one side and agreed to put forward the proposal to her husband. When she got back to Calcutta and told my father, he was livid. How could she even think of such a thing? Her own cousin, wanting to stay in our home and study, and he was to run from Ballygunge to Bhowanipore twice a day for his meals? 'The two of us, our three daughters and my sister, there are meals for six of us and we can't accommodate one more?' Ma wrote to Komala-didima right away. Ram-mama would have bed and board at our place and there was no need to send any bedding, we had enough at home. Books too would be bought by us. All she had to do was send Ram over with his clothes.

We—my sister Tapati and I—were happy beyond words. Ram-mama would live with us, how exciting! We wouldn't have to put up our own mosquito nets, Ram-mama would help. If we had a headache, Ram-mama's deft hands would massage our heads. If we didn't want to go to the post office, Ram-mama would oblige. If we ever felt low, Ram-mama's delightful stock of stories would cheer us up. We waited eagerly for Ram-mama to come.

On the day he was to arrive—he was expected around 10 a.m.—we kept a lookout for him from the morning. Ten o'clock struck. The hands of the clock moved on to eleven, twelve, one, two. The rice on his plate got cold but there was no sign of Ram-mama. We finished eating with sad hearts. We never imagined he would let us down in this way. Baba came home from office in the evening and remarked, 'Boys these days are so irresponsible. If he was not coming, he should have let us know.'

Ten days later Dadamoshai arrived suddenly and immediately set up a din. 'Isn't Ram back from college yet? When does he get back normally, the rascal? Kamala is very upset with him. He didn't bother to write of his safe arrival. Kamala wrote to me saying, "I'm feeling very anxious, Chhor-dada. Please go and see for yourself how Ram is doing at our son-in-law's house."'

We were stunned. Ma spoke softly and hesitantly. 'Ram didn't come here, Baba.' The question that immediately sprang to our minds was, then where did he go? Did he go to his relatives in Bhowanipore? No, he didn't. Was he upset with his mother for some reason? Had some vile gang in Calcutta kidnapped and killed our naïve boy from Balurghat? After three days of running around, Dadamoshai brought news from the police station. He had identified Ram from a photo, a tin trunk and a few clothes they showed him. The third-class compartment of the train to Calcutta was so crowded that Ram-mama had been forced to stand on the footboard and hang on desperately to the door handle. He hit one of the heartless concrete pillars that stand along the rail tracks and fell to instant death.

My workaholic father, who seldom missed office, and who had never set eyes on either Ram-mama or Kamala-didima, stayed home for two whole days mourning and saying sadly, 'May even my worst enemy not meet such a fate, O lord!'

Kamala-didima's lamentations did not reach our ears. We heard she did not shed a single tear. She said to Didi-ma a few days later, 'Look at me, Chhoto-boudi. I eat, I sleep, I wake up every morning. Isn't it amazing?'

Kamala-didima is no longer with us. Death has relieved her of her pain.

LAST ACT

Dadamoshai and Didi-ma had a good life in Berhampore. Dadamoshai's students held him in reverence. Didi-ma was looked up to by the women in her neighbourhood. She could talk well, she kept up her reading habit and had a good knowledge of Bengali literature. She had also learnt some English from her elder son. Following her mother's example, she put together a women's association in Berhampore. The district magistrate's wife was its patron and Didi-ma was president. Berhampore was a conservative town but by then the Gandhi era had begun. Though men still frowned if women were seen outside the house in the morning or evening, it was all right for housewives to spend a couple of hours at the women's association offices in their spare time in the afternoons.

In 1916, when Begum Rokeya Sakhawat Hossain established the Bengal branch of the Anjuman-i-Khawatin-i-Islam—the All India Muslim Ladies' Conference founded in 1914 at Aligarh—in Calcutta, she was able, after a lot of pleading, to persuade just a handful of women to turn up at the first meeting she called. And this was in Calcutta city, not in some district town. After the session one woman came up to Rokeya and remarked, 'You brought me out of the house to attend a sabha. But I didn't see any such thing.' Rokeya had to explain to her very patiently that the discussion held just a while ago was called a sabha. While Didi-ma didn't need to take the pains Begum Rokeya did, she did have to visit every single home for days on end to recruit members. She had to explain why joining a women's group was a good thing. At the association, they read newspapers, spun cotton thread on charkhas and learnt to make handicrafts. The items they produced were sold and the proceeds donated to needy women. And while it doesn't seem like much, it was important for them to be able to get out of the four walls of the home. It was addictive, this sharing of thoughts and discussing with one another. Didi-ma would say, 'This is so liberating. Oh, the joy of stepping into a world outside the home! To be able to open your doors wide!'

There were two other sources of joy for Didi-ma in Berhampore. One was bathing in the river—she was a great swimmer. Sometimes she went with Dadamoshai and at other times with a group of women friends. On the face of it, the swim was a holy dip. In reality it was only an excuse to submerge herself in joy. The other thing that gave her great pleasure was playing bridge. Didi-ma learnt the game after the children grew up and she had more time on her hands. There were not too many women bridge players in those days so Didi-ma held bridge sessions at home. The group consisted of her husband, herself, her elder son and his friend Dilip from next door and sometimes two of her husband's friends. If her bridge enthusiast brother Santosh arrived, or some other guests who were keen on the game did, she would be delighted. The normally quiet evenings in the Berhampore home would be filled with fun and laughter.

All in all it was a good life for them. But in her later life Didi-ma made one big mistake. As soon as Dadamoshai retired, Didi-ma decided to fold up her establishment in Berhampore and live with son Arun and his wife. Dadamoshai didn't like the idea and cautioned her repeatedly. 'You're a proud woman. Living with your son's family might hurt your pride.' Didi-ma ignored his warnings. She had taken such pains to raise her sons well and made so many sacrifices for them. Surely she had every right to share in their good fortune now? She had been a rich man's daughter. She had seen her brothers living in the lap of luxury yet she had never allowed herself the least bit of indulgence. She always thought that one day it would be her turn to live in style and luxury. At public functions in Berhampore the district magistrate and his wife, and the wives of other high-ranking officials, sat in the front row. Didi-ma, a professor's wife, sat somewhere behind. She saw this and thought that one day, when her sons became officers, she would take her rightful seat in the front row. Didi-ma's brothers drove huge cars and travelled back and forth between Delhi and Agra as if it were no distance at all. Didi-ma would dream, 'My Arun will own a big car and I will drive around in it wherever I like as much as I wish.' In her thoughts, her inalienable right to her son's money was clearly established.

Reality shattered her dreams. She saw that, as she told me, 'A husband's money and a son's money are not the same.' She had always imagined that the desire for earthly pleasures, which she had always suppressed but not killed, would one day be fulfilled. But when the time for their fruition arrived, she saw that the gushing stream she had imagined was only a thin trickle. Once in a while her son and his wife invited her to see a film or to visit the famous Red Fort or make a pilgrimage to Mathura. But the warmth and sweetness she had expected was missing. Her son Arun was very fond of her, her daughter-in-law Iva was not unkind, but did Ma have to tag along wherever they went? When Iva-mami had first come to her home as a bride, Didi-ma had said, 'I will see my daughter-in-law in the magic light of an oil lamp. May that magic last forever.' But does it really last?

Kailasabasini Devi in 1863 castigated mothers-in-law who are unkind to their daughters-in-law in her book that brings to light the sad plight of Hindu women, *Hindu Mahilaganer Hinabastha*:

> Mothers-in-law bless their new daughters-in-law with much ceremony: they make them stand on a stone platter filled with milk and vermilion, place a basketload of fresh paddy on their heads, hand them a soft fish and rice paste and

a pitcher of water, and welcome them with music and the blowing of conch shells. But very soon afterwards many of them treat the young women in an oppressive manner.

Kailasabasini's days have long passed. The year 1863 has entered the pages of history. Times have changed. In a magazine award-winning letter that Didi-ma addressed to her granddaughter Bharati (that is, me), she mentions that she has witnessed great social changes:

> In my time, I was always anxious to please my mother-in-law. Nowadays mothers-in-law worry all the time about how to keep their daughters-in-law happy.

Didi-ma never ill-treated her sons' wives—neither Iva the older one, nor Chitrita the younger one. But at the same time, she certainly didn't give much thought to keeping them happy either. She never became fond of them. In fact, I think she rather envied them. It is a difficult thing for mothers to love their sons' wives. Particularly when they are not child brides as in Kailasabasini's time, but proud young women confident of their husbands' love. First of all, there is the inevitable conflict between youth and old age. Then, there is the struggle for power: two women fighting for influence over one man. On the one hand is the woman who has raised him, loved him with all her heart and earned his trust and devotion. On the other is his wife who has gained the right to love him and be loved in return. A battle is inevitable.

I have already said that this is a story of ordinary women. None of them are angels descended from heaven; they aren't like Mother Earth, nor are they mythological characters like Damayanti or Arundhati, reputed for self-sacrifice and wisdom.

My aunts were ordinary young women and so was Didi-ma. The resentment, the petty battles of egos, the self-interest, jealousy and the little squabbles that erupt in the process of everyday living angered them all in equal measure.

Didi-ma's diaries written in her last days are filled with grief, mortification and regrets. She writes on a particular day:

> I sit and think of the present and the past. People are very self-centered these days. All they think of are their own children and their wives. That's it. Earlier they would think of their brothers and sisters and of others too. Once a son gets married, he becomes completely devoted to his in-laws. It wasn't so in the old days.

This expresses her resentment against her son and his wife. On another occasion she blames herself:

> From the time I was very young, I've always hoped and prayed that my sons receive all that is good. I didn't want anything for myself. It turned out to be true. I didn't get anything. My sons are blessed with so much. I think this is the result of my lifelong prayers. This is just what I had wanted. But I am a sinner. Which is why I cannot find any pleasure in their happiness.

Ushabala left her son Arun's home in Delhi with such turmoil in her heart and came to live with her son Ashok in Calcutta. Her brother Santosh wrote to her saying, 'I heard that you have shifted to Calcutta. I think you will be well looked after in your younger son Ashok's house.' But Ushabala was not destined to live happily even with Ashok. Jyotish Chandra died at Ashok's place. He had been feeling a little under the weather for some days. One evening Chitrita had made Jyotish his favourite tea and brought it to him on a tray. But Jyotish Chandra pushed the tray aside and rushed out to the veranda. The tray fell from Chitrita's hands, the cup shattered and the tea splashed on to the red carpet beside the bed. A stunned Chitrita followed her father-in-law to the veranda. She saw him lying on an easy chair, exhaling long breaths. When the last breath left his body, Chitrita realized why he had pushed her aside. He believed, like his mother, that one must not breathe one's last in a closed room, but out in the open air.

After Dadamoshai's death Didi-ma lived for five more years. Her diary holds evidence of her weeping heart:

> Today is the 6th of Baisakh, 19th April. It has been four years since he left me. He said I would live for three years or so after his death. That didn't happen. I am feeling very depressed. My heart is restless . . . I feel as if I have no one to call my own.

Ushabala's days were numbered. One day she breathed her last in Ashok's house without a word to anyone. She too died in the veranda, but not in an armchair like Jyotish Chandra, nor in the presence of Chitrita. One morning she just lay on the cement floor. When Ashok and Chitrita saw her lifeless body lying there, they were at a loss. Then the rest of the household gathered around her. Her daughters came, her nieces and other relatives. She was laid on fresh clean bedding. They dressed her in a fine white sari with a broad zari border, placed white flowers on her and bade her a tearful farewell.

One life came to an end. One life that covered three-quarters of a century. An ordinary life.

MA

CHILDHOOD AND MARRIAGE

This part of my story starts from almost the end. My mother Kalyani is bedridden. She is over eighty-five. There are those who traipse around the world at that age. Politicians vie for ministerial positions, artists produce new works of art, industrialists stay at the helm of their business empires and men of letters write new books. My mother's brain is clear but Parkinson's disease has immobilized her. Her golden complexion has taken on a coppery hue; her thick black curly hair is thin, bald patches show; she has no teeth, her cheeks cave into her mouth, her sunken eyes are dull and her skin is loose and withered. Her legs are twisted and misshapen, just thin bags of bones. She speaks so low that one can hardly hear her. Her words are garbled and it is hard to make out their meaning. She can think but she cannot express herself. Who would say that this is the same Kalyani Sen Gupta of years ago? Is this then the inevitable end of a harmonious life? Could this happen to me too? Will I grow bald, my body crumple, my lips hang, my speech slur and my eyes be expressionless? Who can see into the future?

Instead of the future, what one can see is the past. There were many who were envious of my mother. 'Kalyani is a fortunate woman,' they would say. Even her later-year attendants would say, 'Your mother is really lucky. You people visit her regularly. You give her good food. You keep attendants night and day.

All old people fall ill. How many get so much care?' When I sat at her bedside with her left hand in mine, she would place her shaky right hand on my head and say, 'You're such an angel! Such a good girl! Bless you, bless you.'

No, Ma, I am not your good girl. Not an angel at all. I don't deserve your blessings. If you knew the thoughts that came to my mind as I held your hand, you would be shocked. People, if they knew, would be appalled. As I stroked your face, your neck, your arms, I did not pray for you to keep well; not in the same way that you did for me. I never wished for you, or for myself, a spent life; one in which sheets have to be changed repeatedly, in which one's speech is so slurred that it can be barely understood, where there is the constant danger that limbs will break if one tries to climb out of bed on one's own, where food has to be spooned into a thin, helpless mouth. Your 'angel' prayed, without anyone's knowledge or approval, for your speedy release from this life. May the present be erased. May your past live on.

Ma was born on 1 April 1915 in Delhi. A few weeks before she was due, Sundar-ma had taken Didi-ma to Delhi—the custom in middle-class homes in those days. There weren't so many nursing homes then. Some babies were born in hospitals; most were born at home. Midwives were given no medical training but they usually had no problem in helping babies emerge from their mothers' wombs. The first child was generally born at its mother's natal home, because an expectant daughter was taken care of by her own mother before and after delivery. Three or four months later the new mother with her baby in arms would return to her husband's place, leaving her own family in tears for the second time. Three months after Ma was born, Didi-ma took her to Serampore, where Dadamoshai eagerly waited for them.

Ma grew up pampered and happy. When Dadamoshai shifted to the 'haunted house' in Berhampore, she happily played there, the ghost notwithstanding. I don't think she would have taken fright even if she did see the ghost of the little girl. She was very brave right from childhood. Between playtimes, she sat down to lessons. Her parents were thrilled to discover how bright their little girl was. But suddenly, at the age of eleven, an attack of typhoid made her forget everything. She even forgot how to speak! However, she did gradually regain her speech and, with a lot of patient tutoring from her parents, got back her memory. They decided then that Berhampore was no place for her—there was no school there, no proper playgrounds. All she could do was run around in that haunted house from morning to night; so they packed her off to Delhi. At the same age that Didi-ma had left home as a child bride, her daughter left home to pursue her studies. What she had to forgo was the company of her three siblings; the joy of playing with them, quarrelling with them and sharing little secrets.

In Delhi, Gyanadakanta's family was at the peak of its good fortune, rolling in money, fame and social prestige. The house on Hanuman Road was abuzz with the activities of six precious sons—their studies, their animated discussions, their swimming and badminton and driving motor cars. They were Kalyani's six uncles—Didi-ma's brothers. She was their one and only darling niece. The fourth brother Santosh, her Sejo-mama, was most impressed by her fine qualities. Ranga-mama Amarkanta thought she was a real beauty. The youngest, whom everyone called Lalli, was her bosom friend. Aunt Santwana kept a loving eye on her at all times. Her grandmother, our Sundar-ma, despite her general reticence, would show some fondness. Kalyani was happy there. She was good at her studies—first in school, first in college. And she was good at physical activities—she could climb trees, ride a bicycle and drive a car, all equally deftly. She had nothing to do with household work. Sundar-ma did try at times to persuade her. 'It's not right for a girl to spend so much time outside.' If she did stay at home some day, she would be immersed in a novel for hours on end and not put it down until she had finished the book. She spoke fluent Hindi as well as English. She read English novels and corresponded with authors. She came first among girls in her matriculation examination under Delhi University and was awarded a gold medal. She wanted to study medicine but Sundar-ma wouldn't let her. 'She's such a pretty girl. Suppose she gets into trouble in medical school?' Kalyani was not obstinate enough to disobey her grandmother. She joined Indraprastha College instead to study mathematics and economics. Soon after, an urgent message from Jyotish Das Gupta arrived. She was to return to Berhampore since her marriage had been arranged. Byomkesh Sen Gupta, the prospective groom, was a fine young man, good-looking and an officer in the coveted Bengal Civil Service. His family was rich in culture if not in wealth. Kalyani obeyed her father and married Byomkesh. Sundar-ma bore the expenses for the wedding. She gave the bride a ruby set: a necklace, peacock-design earrings, a ruby-and-pearl-stringed dostana for her hands, a gold muff chain, and twelve gold bangles. The wedding sari was a golden yellow Benarasi silk with multicoloured zari-work flowers all over. To the groom she gave gold kurta buttons, a watch, and a silk dhoti-chador for the ceremony. There were no metal utensils; the groom's family had not asked for these 'gifts', so none were given. However, they did demand a dowry of one thousand rupees to cover expenses for the reception they were to host! Dadamoshai hadn't told Didi-ma about this earlier. When he did tell her, she became really angry. This was perhaps the first serious quarrel they had. Dadamoshai said, 'Only recently has their son started to earn. They really can't afford wedding expenses now. I didn't want to give up such a wonderful match for a paltry thousand rupees.' Didi-ma snapped. 'It's not the money but the principle. I will not give dowry. Cancel the wedding.' She was pacified somehow. I'm dead against dowry myself but I thank god that Didi-ma finally relented. If the wedding had been indeed cancelled, where could I have found such a wonderful father? On their wedding night, Baba told Ma, his head hanging low, 'I accepted dowry to marry you, Kalyani. I feel so ashamed. I don't have the money today and so could not argue against my family. But I promise I will save and give the money back to your father.' He kept his word and returned the money to Dadamoshai. Dadamoshai bought Ma a steel wardrobe with that money. It's part of my furniture now.

Jyotish Das Gupta hailed from Jessore and Byomkesh Sen Gupta from Dhaka. The Sen Guptas' ancestral home was in a village called Bera in the Tegorhia district which lies across the Buriganga river that runs through Dhaka. They owned some land in the village that they rented out to three or four tenant farmers and were not very well off. The paddy grown was just sufficient to feed the family for a whole year. There was fish in the pond attached to their home but there was no income by way of hard cash. My Thakur-da (grandfather on the father's side), Jagatchandra Sen Gupta, who was born in 1847, was a lowly court clerk receiving a pension of seventy-five rupees a month when my father was but a young boy. The house they lived in was made of clay. There were only three or four pucca houses in the village; the rest were all made of mud and had thatched roofs. Such houses get blown away in a storm and melt down in the rain; the straw rots and starts to smell, and so these houses need frequent repairs. Still they provide cool shelter in summer. Bedrolls stacked in a corner of the room can be laid out on the floor for a good night's sleep. Jagat Sen Gupta's cottage was a medium-sized one. The joint family was large. His four sons and six daughters, his deceased elder brother's son Suresh whom he loved even more than his own, Suresh's widowed mother and Jagat Sen's widowed aunt—his mother's sister. After Suresh got married the family came to include his wife—Baba's bouthan—and their three sons and one daughter. Thakur-da and Thakur-ma (paternal grandmother) had to feed and clothe them all. Money was always scarce.

Jagat Sen may have been short of cash but he was enormously respected in the village as an upright and zealous man of god. Every evening he crossed the river by boat and went to Dhaka town to listen to readings from the Bhagavad Gita. The ferryman would not pack up for the night until he returned. Sometimes on a dark and stormy night a would-be passenger would ask, '*Majhi bhai, nouka ki tuila dichho naki?*' (Brother boatman, have you finished for the day?) And the man would reply, '*Na korta. Tuli nai. Gour-babu ohon tok ahen nai. Kheya bondho korum kamney?*' (No sir, I haven't. Gour-babu is not back yet. How can I close down?) It was for Jagat Sen's fair skin that the village folk had given him that name, Gour-babu, the fair gentleman. The village ferry service stayed open for him no matter how late.

But respect and reverence and readings from the Gita cannot help run a home. Sure there was rice and fish for everyone. But what about clothes? What about school fees and textbooks? The boys wore dhotis and went to school bare-bodied as was the norm in any village. Thakur-da was detached from mundane matters. Thakur-ma, Bhabasundari Devi, had ambitions. She wanted to bring her sons up well and she didn't mind accepting money secretly from her brothers to ensure that the boys' studies were not hampered. She sent her three elder sons to college in Rajshahi. They stayed there with an older cousin, Sundar-dada, who was their father's sister's son. In those days people didn't think twice about putting up two or three cousins—whether studying or looking for a job—for several years at a stretch and the cousins remained grateful for such generosity. At least my uncles did. I heard them always speak of their Sundar-dada in glowing terms. Their youngest brother Byomkesh being their mother's pet—her dear 'Khoka'—and greatly attached to her, was not sent away to Rajshahi. He remained in the village.

How could he have left his mother anyway? The year he finished school, was the year his father died. The sixteen-year-old young man saw how a widowed woman spent her days. His mother's cropped hair and her borderless white cotton sari pained him lifelong. Thakur-ma followed all the diet restrictions prescribed for Hindu widows through the ages. She gave up fish, meat and the parboiled rice that was made from the paddy grown on the family's land. Byomkesh didn't adopt the same attire, and his hair was short in any case, but he became vegetarian and followed the same strict diet as his mother—no parboiled rice, no onions or garlic, no fish or meat, or even eggs. He stuck to these rules all his life. Byomkesh stayed on in the village. He crossed the river every day, walked all the way to the college in town, and later to university, and completed his studies. He sat for the Bengal Civil Services (BCS) examination. He was called for an interview in due time. But how would he go? He had nothing suitable to wear, no long trousers and not a single good shirt. So Rakhal, one of his elder brothers—we called him Moni-jethamoshai—came forward to help. He was in Calcutta, working at some low-paid job in the railways. He borrowed money to buy a suit and shirt for Byomkesh. Byomkesh appeared for the interview, came second in the BCS examination and was appointed a deputy magistrate. In those days hardly two or three men from Bengal would qualify for the BCS Only two or three candidates from all of India were selected for the Indian Civil Service (ICS) every year. Byomkesh did not dream of joining the ICS—even trying for the BCS was an act of daring on his part and he did so only on the urging of his professors. Byomkesh Sen Gupta was a handsome man: tall, fair and well built, with a sharp Grecian nose and strong jaw. His face bore the clear stamp of strong character. He had strict principles, was deeply religious, and had an immense love for humanity. He received great respect, both at home and outside.

My mother got married to such a man at the age of eighteen. Eighteen is just the right age for love and romance —as soon as Ma got married, she fell promptly, deeply in love with her husband. Falling in love is not a sin, whether within marriage or outside it. But while people are strongly censorious of extramarital dalliances, they sing hymns to a loving and devoted wife. It seems to me that while loving one's husband is a good thing, erasing one's self completely in order to meld with one's husband's is not such a great idea. And this is what happened to my mother. She conceived shortly after marriage but managed to reach Delhi and sit for her BA finals with me tucked away inside her. The results were excellent. She was ranked first in mathematics and economics among the girls of Delhi University. Ma was overjoyed. Who wouldn't be? A gold medal accompanied her first child!

But after that, there were to be no more studies for Ma. She didn't even think of coming back all the way to Delhi for her master's, or of joining Calcutta University which would have been closer, or at least taking the exam as a private student. I suspect Baba didn't encourage her and I can't praise him for that. But few husbands are inclined to let their newly married wives out of sight for too long or to have them turn their attention to books, even in modern times. For my conservative father and my loving mother, an MA did not enter the picture. And so it was that my mother plunged into the role of a full-time housewife with two baby girls and an ocean of love for her husband. She gave up sports and studies—the two fields that she had excelled in.

Why did you make such a mistake, Ma?

MA AS HOME-MAKER

From the first days of her marriage, Ma was mistress of the household wherever Baba was posted. Or perhaps she wasn't. Thakur-ma accompanied them; she exercised a powerful influence on all her ten children and most certainly on my father. Ma was a simple, easy-going young woman; Thakur-ma was possessed of a sharp intelligence and a tremendous personality. Had Thakur-ma wanted, she could have completely marginalized Ma. But she didn't. In those days, salaries were paid in cash, in sealed envelopes which came directly from the treasury and not via cheques like today. On the first day every month, Baba brought his pay packet home and placed it at his mother's feet. Thakur-ma blessed him and the instant he left, handed the entire packet to Ma. Never did she take a single rupee out of it. If she ever needed money she asked for it from Ma. I never heard mother and grandmother raise their voices though there was never any doubt about who would win hands down in case of an argument. Perhaps both of them were aware of it and so never crossed swords.

In summer Thakur-ma would say, 'Mangoes have come to the market. Is it time to make amsatta now?' The very next day half the mangoes in the market would be brought home along with some twenty cane trays. Thick mango pulp would be spread in layer after layer on each tray. The amsatta would be of several varieties: plain, with milk or kheer. The trays were set out in the sunny veranda and we two sisters were put in charge of scaring the crows away. We stared at the delicacies as greedily as crows and would break off a tiny bit from a corner a few times. But such thieving was obvious from the uneven edge it left. Jujube pickle was easier to pinch. When winter came and brown jujubes flooded the market, Thakur-ma would ask Ma, 'Padmini, would you like to make berry pickles for the children?' (Thakur-ma gave Ma the name Padmini because another of her daughters-in-law was called Kalyani and also because Ma looked rather like a lotus.) The next morning, basketloads of ripe berries would arrive from the market and pickle would be made in high-rimmed platters of black marble and white marble—sweet, hot and sour pickle swimming in oil. Again, towards the end of summer, Thakur-ma might say, 'Won't you make dried lentil balls, Padmini?' At once, a variety of pulses would be laid out before Thakur-ma—moong dal, kalai dal, masur dal. Thakur-ma ground them into paste herself. She made them into small pellets and arranged them on large platters to be dried in the sun. Ma helped her. The sun tanned their backs and necks.

Thakur-ma's bare, bent back, with just a white sari worn in the Bangla style, would itch all over and bend even more. Ma's blouse would drip with sweat. When later it came to cooking those pellets they forgot about all the time and effort they had spent on them. As long as they were fried to a crisp and Baba and we enjoyed them, it was worth their pains.

Two or three days after Ma had been married, Thakur-ma told her that she had four sons but the youngest was her dearest. She would visit the other three from time to time but she would like to live with the youngest. The problem was: who would cook for her? Ma said she would do it. Thakur-ma looked sceptical. 'You will cook? You're a BA-pass girl, do you know how to cook?'

Ma said she could learn from Thakur-ma. And she did learn really well. She woke up early, had a simple breakfast of tea and toast and went off for a bath. Her hair wet, wearing a fresh cotton sari, she entered the vegetarian kitchen. Thakur-ma finished her prayers and joined her there. First, the kitchen had to be swept and mopped and all the utensils wiped with a damp cloth while Thakur-ma cut the vegetables. A portable oven was used with coal below and gul on top for fuel. The two of them prepared the gul themselves in their spare time in the afternoon—little balls of coal dust and cow dung dried in the sun. Initially Ma used to have problems fanning this fuel to light the oven properly. The smoke made her eyes smart but she got used to it later. The utensils were made of brass. Food was cooked in the order it would be served. First came saag, the greens. There were so many kinds available in the small mofussil towns of Bengal—beter saag, lal saag, palong saag, methi saag, helencha saag—helencha was a great favourite of Thakur-ma's dear son, my father. After the saag, the bitter dish, shuktoni or betak, was cooked. Have you ever tasted betak? It is baby cane, slightly bitter but soft and delicious. It is boiled, a few drops of mustard oil are added and the dish is eaten with rice. The next item to be cooked was dal. Masur dal was forbidden for Hindu widows. The currently popular rajma, kidney beans, was not in vogue then. And none of us liked kalai dal because of its texture. Ma cooked sona moong which she fried first or matar dal. She made dal in many delicious flavours—with a little bitter gourd or tangy chalta. Chhola dal with diced coconut and raisins. And to go with the dal there'd be vegetables deep fried in gram-flour batter. Of all these fried vegetables, pumpkin flowers were the favourite. The next item was a vegetable dish. Thakur-ma loved dishes like mochar ghonto, banana flowers cooked with coconut; chhanar dalna, a delicious curry made out of cottage cheese; kumrho charchori, pumpkin with mustard and so on. Aubergines were cooked once in a while but Ma and Thakur-ma considered it to be a useless vegetable with no food value at all; good only for frying or to put in a curry. Or blanched, if you were in a hurry.

This was the daily menu. Not all of these dishes were cooked on the same day, of course. Just four items plus rice. On special days there could be an extra dish, made with banana stem, or moshla charchori, ground spices fried and dipped in ghee. Both tasted wonderful but were time-consuming to prepare and cook. The last item Thakur-ma ate for lunch was milk and rice. A Hindu widow could have one meal a day so at night she had a bowl of milk and a light snack of something uncooked.

All the vegetarian items were sent to the non-vegetarian kitchen. Baba ate the same food as Thakur-ma but we still had a separate non-vegetarian kitchen where fish was cooked for Ma and the children. Baba would be displeased if we missed out on fish. He bought it himself quite often. A village boy from the other side of the river Padma, he, of course, knew all about fish, though he didn't eat any himself.

The hero of the non-vegetarian kitchen was Jogen-bhai. He had been with Baba from the time Baba landed his first job. Teatime snacks, lunchtime fish and dinner were in Jogen-bhai's hands. Thakur-ma's kitchen was not used in the evening. Dinner was pretty simple—meat appeared very rarely and eggs once in a while—mostly dal, vegetables and fish with rice. The modern practice of serving chapati for dinner had not started yet. In the kitchen we hung on to Jogen-bhai's arms like bats but he carried on with his cooking regardless. He called me Boro Kuncha, and Tapati Chhoto Kuncha. Heaven knows where he got those names; perhaps it was his loving heart that invented them. He loved us dearly and though he kept us in line, he wasn't ill-tempered. He could sense our little sadnesses. He never had to ask; he only smiled a little and made a quick snack to cheer us up—jhal murhi, chinabadam tokti or pakora. One day our dear Jogen-bhai suddenly quit and went off to Jalpaiguri, weeping copious tears and making us cry too. The riots that followed Partition devastated his family in Noakhali. His brothers and their families had crossed the border and arrived in Jalpaiguri. They needed help to settle down in this new place so they sent word to Jogen-bhai. Jogen-bhai had to go but he never forgot us. He visited us many times. He cooked our favourite dishes and brought them as gifts and he poured on us his love and blessings.

Getting back to Ma; after she cleaned up Thakur-ma's kitchen, she came to the dining room table to have her lunch with her two daughters by her side. After lunch she tutored us for an hour and then took some rest. Once you get used to napping in the afternoon, it's difficult to give it up—for Ma, a siesta was a lifelong habit. By three o'clock, she was up again. She brought in the dry clothes from the clothesline, folded them neatly and put them in their owners' rooms or in the cupboard. There was something else Ma did in the afternoon—stitching. It was almost like an addiction. Whenever she came across a piece of cloth—old or new—she would promptly stitch it up into something useful. Not only the curtains in the house, pillowcases, quilt covers, dusters, napkins and tablecloths, she even made our dresses, pennies and bloomers. Girls of today would probably turn up their noses at our dresses but we wore them with great pride and happiness until it was time for us to switch to saris. We never saw a tailor at home. When Baba bought a sofa set, Ma made covers for it with great care. She took measurements again and again to make sure they fitted exactly. And they did.

Ma made teatime snacks with Jogen-bhai. Chura bhaja, singara and narkel muri were everyday items. When we were in Patuakhali, a man named Rohini taught Ma how to make sweets such as rossogolla, gulab jamun and sandesh and she made these quite often. She also made superb chhanar payesh, khee-er luchi and elojhelo, malpoa and halwa. Thakur-ma's scepticism notwithstanding, Ma had a knack for cooking. And Jogen-bhai worked with great speed and efficiency. Needless to say, teatime snacks were something we looked forward to eagerly.

As evening descended and the stars lit up one by one, deep darkness settled in the small mofussil town. There was no electricity, just the mild light of hurricane lamps. Ma and Thakur-ma sat on the veranda amidst the chirrup of crickets and waited for Baba to come home—Thakur-ma would eat only after he returned. Ma heated a bowl of milk for her and served it along with puffed rice, and dry jaggery. Baba and Ma sat down to dinner after Thakur-ma had eaten. We sisters sat on chairs placed between those of our parents. Thus the day ended.

Even after Thakur-ma died, Ma's routine did not change. In a few days' time, our widowed aunt, whom we called Sundarpishima, came to live with us. She was given Thakur-ma's room and she stayed there as Thakur-ma had done. Ma cooked for her in the vegetarian kitchen. The work wheel turned in the same old way but was never tiresome. Ma wasn't bored. In fact she always had a smile of satisfaction on her face.

There was also some space for variety in Ma's daily life—something that most other middle-class housewives lacked in those days. My aunts certainly were not so lucky. In the late afternoon, just as the sun went down, Ma would dress up in a fresh and pretty sari, apply Hazeline Snow and Coty powder on her face, wear long danglers in her ears and go out to meet her friends in the neighbourhood. She made new friends wherever Baba was posted. Sometimes the women's chat sessions would be held in a house. Sometimes, when we were in Patuakhali or Kusthia, they would all go for a stroll by the river. In Jhargram and Chittagong, they would stroll along the road beside the forests of mighty sal trees and palash with its gorgeous red, scented flowers. Going out in the evenings was always a habit with Ma.

Then there was badminton. In Patuakhali, Kusthia and Jhargram, Ma had badminton courts prepared within our compound. She had learnt the game in Delhi and she played, if not to Olympic standards, but very well indeed. Two or three of Baba's friends came to play along with their wives. I think Ma preferred playing against the men. In Patuakhali, Ma played every evening with a police officer friend called Pranab Sen. He was still a bachelor then. Baba came back late from the office and Thakur-ma stayed in her room. Ma made us two sisters sit on the steps. She would say, 'Watch the game. Learn how to play.' I understood the real reason she made us sit there only when I grew up. Patuakhali was a small town after all.

Ma had to give up her favourite game suddenly when Baba was posted to Chittagong. The house there was small with no grounds to play on. Ma took to reading novels instead and that became her new passion. Once she stretched out on the bed on her stomach and started reading, nothing would enter her ears. She paid no attention to anything anyone said and that used to put us off completely.

Ma was obstinate about one thing. She had to spend one month at her parents' place. She valued Baba's opinion on all things except this and when it was time for her to go, nothing could keep her back; Thakur-ma's or Pishima's food, or any other problem in the house. Every three or four years, she visited her grandparents in Delhi, otherwise it was Berhampore, and her parents, once a year. She took the two of us with her. We used to observe with wonder how very different a person she became. The way she talked, walked, laughed; she was like a monsoon river in full spate. In Berhampore, she had no childhood friends. She didn't even peep into the kitchen. She chatted with her parents, taught Moni-mashi, and read novel after novel. And in the morning, as soon as it struck nine, she would go off to the river for a swim. She was an excellent swimmer and she didn't need a swimsuit. She simply tucked in her sari and swam right across to the other side of the Ganga (the branch that ran through Berhampore) and back with ease. She swam under water, did a fine backstroke. She could also float on her back without moving a limb. Much

like a dead woman or a yogini. 'Is the river a bed, Ma?' we
would ask her. 'You lie there so peacefully.' Ma laughed out
loud like a little girl. It is difficult to guess what the main
attraction for her was: the river or her mother.

Another attraction for Ma was going on tour with Baba.
Wherever Baba was posted, he made a tour of the entire area
he was meant to administer. During the early years, he went
by bicycle as far as possible. Later, there were other means of
transport. A launch in Patuakhali, a truck in Jhargram, a jeep
in Kurseong, the charming town in the district of Darjeeling
in the Himalayas, a car in Chittagong and in Calcutta.

I remember Patuakhali very well. A subdivisional town in
the Barisal district, it is networked with rivers and streams.
Baba would go out on tour for two or three days at a time.
Ma would pack a huge hamper with rice, vegetables, dal, oil,
salt, sugar, spices. Utensils and a stove would be fitted in too.
A bottle of kerosene oil was carried separately. Baba didn't like
buying things locally because the launch hands who went out
to do the shopping wouldn't accept any money from him. Baba
suspected that they didn't bother to pay the poor shopkeepers.
Ma would often cook khichuri, rice and dal cooked together,
topped with potatoes and cauliflower. Floating on the river on
those 'dream boats' as we ate, the khichuri tasted like some
exotic fare from another world. Not that the dreams were
always pleasant. In 1941, when the terrible cyclone struck, we
were out on the river. The launch heaved and rocked perilously
all night. Death stood knocking at our very door but Baba
and Ma had no intention of allowing him in. They decided
that should the water level in the launch rise dangerously, Baba
would carry me, while Ma carried Tapati, and jump into the
river. I was older and heavier than Tapati and Ma was a far

better swimmer than Baba yet he followed custom and chose the heavier load. Thankfully, they didn't have to execute the plan. The storm subsided at dawn.

On board our launch was a deckhand called Hossain who showed us magic tricks. Five fingers on his hand would turn to six, and then become five again. There are many such clever, talented people hidden away unknown in our villages that we don't really care about. I should have learnt that trick from Hossain.

From the wonderful launch in Patuakhali, we moved to an open truck in Jhargram. Ma travelled in it with Baba, covered in dust from head to toe. Baba would be busy at work while Ma had nothing to do, and there was no place to rest, yet she went. It is strange, though, that Thakur-ma never went along. Didn't she ever wish to? Perhaps not. She had never known such opportunities, so perhaps she did not dream of such things when she was young; or maybe the dreams had withered. It might even be that she wanted to give Baba and Ma the opportunity to enjoy each other's company outside the daily mill of living at home.

The most exciting tours Ma went on were in Kurseong. Baba would go to Mirik, Bogurha, Tindharia, Darjeeling. The jeep would drive through the fragrant pine forests as Ma sang softly to herself. Nights were spent in dak bungalows where the caretaker would cook for them. Ma would float through the rose-scented pathways of Tindharia, the pine forests high up in Bogurha where the undergrowth was thick with leeches, the mountain streams in Mirik, and the hilly lanes and bylanes of Darjeeling, resplendent under the proud gaze of Mount Kanchenjunga. Ma's spirit would reach out and extend itself in the lap of nature. When she came back home, she felt enriched. Like a bird that had felt the caress of the open, sunny skies and was content to return to her peaceful nest in the evening.

MA'S HOUSEHOLD

Ma's household revolved around her husband. 'Women are of two types,' Rabindranath Tagore wrote in his novel, *Dui Bon*, 'They are either mothers or lovers.' Judging by that, Ma would fall into the second category. She had motherly love for her children and she discharged all her duties towards the household. But above all else was her love for Baba. What he would wear, what he would eat, what he would do—these were her major concerns all day. Yet Baba was no gourmet. He was an abstemious vegetarian, and remained unconcerned about his attire. He had a large heart and sympathy and affection for a wide range of people. He loved his wife and children, his mother, his brothers and sisters and their children; he loved the friends of his childhood from his native village of Bera. Poor people from his village, the lower division workers in his office, as well as needy relatives would come to him with all kinds of personal problems. He gave them time, advised them and helped them with money. Ma used to manage all regular monthly expenses. If someone asked for money towards the end of the month, Baba would insist on giving it. This displeased Ma and she protested mildly. 'We're nearing the month's end; where will I get all that money?' Nevertheless, she did somehow manage to find it.

Baba had a transferable job so we had to live apart from the rest of the extended family. But in our heart of hearts we thought ourselves part of the same joint family unit. Of course Baba's idea of joint family wouldn't match the narrow definitions offered by sociologists like Milton Singer or K.M. Kapadia. According to them, three generations of blood relations, patrilineally defined, living under the same roof or sharing the same kitchen constitute a joint family. But by Baba's reckoning, not only his siblings and their spouses and children but his cousins, their children and grandchildren, their daughters-in-law, his brothers' brothers-in-law, his sisters' relatives by marriage, even distant cousins, and importantly, every tenant who had worked the family land in his father's days, were all included in his joint family. Accordingly, people who are considered no more than vague acquaintances these days seemed like close relatives to us. They visited us frequently and stayed with us for days on end. Once when Baba was posted in Kurseong, our family of five members had as many as twenty-six house guests. It amazes me now, but it didn't then. My mother remained as placid as ever—she was not given to expressing her feelings too strongly, whether positive or negative. Sleeping arrangements were set up on the floor; pulses, vegetables, fish curry and rice were prepared for one and all. Who knows how Ma managed to lay out so many mattresses, sheets and pillows. When she needed an extra pillow the first one she pounced on was mine, because I can sleep like a log all night without a pillow. The next pillow she took was Tapati's. She, poor thing, was rather particular about her clean sheet and fat pillow; she couldn't sleep at all without them but she had to put up with the changes. I tried to console her. 'Sleep like I do. What's a pillow got to do with it? Can a pillow sing you to sleep?' Ma would fold up an old curtain, stuff old saris in it, and improvise a pillow. We had stacks of quilts that Ma made by joining three old saris with fine kantha stitches. They were very comfortable to use when the winter was mild. Our winter visitors brought their own blankets, I think. If not, blankets could be hired in Kurseong.

Of the people whom we call 'distant' relatives these days, the one I remember best is Santosh-da. He was thin as a reed, innocuous and ordinary-looking. Timid, one might say. Yet he was the member of an underground revolutionary group and what safer place for a revolutionary to be in than the sub-divisional officer's home? He would visit us in Kusthia in the early 1940s, suddenly turning up, staying a few days and going off again. Our dining room was shifted when he arrived. Instead of the large room near the front door, we ate in a small corner room. Ma said, 'He's come from the village, he's more comfortable in small rooms. Let's all go and keep him company.' Santosh-da never stepped out of the house. Ma said, 'He's a village boy. How can he like the town?' Ma also said, 'He's very shy and doesn't like mixing with anyone. You had better not talk about him with your friends. If they come to see him, he'll feel very embarrassed.'

I would immediately pipe up, 'What's there to say, anyway? He hardly speaks to us, what can he say to our friends? All he does is sit with his hand on his cheek and think all day.'

Ma said quietly, 'He thinks about our country.' But her explanation was one that a child's mind would easily accept: 'He loves your Baba very much. That is why he comes here.'

There's someone else we saw often: Bidhu, an old tenant from back in Bera. Bidhu's feet were dusty and his singlet barely clean. He wore a dirty dhoti, hitched up to his knees. Yet Baba would take Bidhu by the hand and lead him to the sitting room sofa or to the easy chair in the veranda. Bidhu invariably brought two coconuts for us. We sipped the coconut water and polished off the thick white kernel with great relish. If possible, we would have eaten all of the coconut—coir and shell! The coir was used later to light mosquito repellent incense. The outer shells were stored in the kitchen for rough use. Bidhu used to come in the late 1940s and early 1950s. Baba would talk with him so intimately, it irritated us. Yet we didn't dare protest—we understood that this man was someone very close to Baba.

Another of Baba's bosom friends, whose arrival brought smiles to his face, was Makhan-jethamoshai. A school friend of Baba's, Makhan-jethamoshai was a fat man with a stubbly beard and paan-stained teeth. His son Jangu, whose proper name was Mriganka, also came with him. Ma would cover her head in Jethamoshai's presence as a mark of respect. He never spoke to her. They thus maintained the old rules of conduct between a senior brother-in-law and younger sister-in-law. He was headmaster of the village school and normally a sober and dignified man. But the minute Baba came back from office, how he laughed and talked. The two friends joked and reminisced for hours on end in their Dhaka dialect. Some of the conversation we understood, some not. But one thing was very clear to us—their love had been cemented in their childhood and was precious and rare. The boy Jangu was a great talker too. Makhan-jetha is gone; where Jangu is today, I don't know.

With all his house guests Baba was as sweet as honey. There was one exception, though. Nalinikanta Sen was a brother-in-law of Moni-jethamoshai's first wife. He took up a job in Kurseong and came to live with us. Month after month passed yet there were no signs of him moving out. And it wouldn't have ever been necessary for him to leave had he not made one big mistake. After Thakur-ma died, a photograph of hers hung in one room. Baba lit incense sticks before the picture every day. One day Baba saw Nalinikanta walk through that room in his shoes and said, 'My mother's room is like a prayer room for me. Please don't enter it with your shoes on, Dada.' The gentleman must have misjudged my sweet-tempered father. He had tasted the honey but never felt the sting of the bee. The shorter way to Nalini Sen's bedroom was straight through Thakur-ma's room while the other way, through the outer veranda, was longer. The next day he was walking through Thakur-ma's room again with his shoes on when Baba noticed him. Baba simply said to him, 'Please look for another place. Our house does not suit you.'

Unrelated relations like Nalini-dada notwithstanding, our house always hummed with much closer relatives. We loved them all dearly. Baba had three older brothers and one older cousin: his father's elder brother's son, our Boro-jethamoshai. Baba loved this cousin, their seniormost dada, the most. Boro-jethamoshai's first wife, Baba's Bouthan, Boro-ma to the children, was much loved by all in the family's village home in Dhaka. One day, three months after the birth of their first son Sudarshan, the baby suddenly disappeared from his bed. The whole house was stunned even as the mother started crying. After some time, the baby's cries began mingling with his mother's. He was under the bed! My father—he was about five years old then—proudly announced, 'I have put him there. Why should he sleep beside Bouthan every night?' No one scolded him but they explained to him gently that the baby's neck was still tender and that it would be terrible if someone were to drop him. Imagine how Bouthan would cry then. 'Will Bouthan start crying? Like she was just a while ago?' Baba asked. He never laid hands on Sudarshan again. As they grew up, they became like two buds on the same stem.

Baba's Bouthan was good-looking, sweet-spoken, charming, and the most talented of all the women in the house. She said one day while she and Jogamaya, her sister-in-law of the same age, were bathing at the pond, 'Well, my dear, say what you will about other men but I know for sure that your Dada will never take another wife if I die.' She broke into peals of proud laughter as she said this and fell into Jogamaya's arms. Her sister-in-law embraced her lovingly and replied, 'God forbid, don't say such things, Bouthan. You're in the flush of youth, why should you die?'

But people do die young; and why such a thing happens is hard to say. Boro-ma, who was young, hale and hearty, with three sons and a daughter, a husband and a loving household, suddenly departed one day with hardly a few hours' notice. The grief-stricken family was shocked when Jetha-moshai brought home a second wife within six months. Thakur-da was no longer alive and Boro-jethamoshai was the master of the house. In village society, this wasn't surprising. He was a man after all; of course he would marry again. So what if his children were all grown? A woman who lost her husband had to remain a loyal widow all her life. But if a man's wife died, he was not expected to remain an abstinent yogi. No one had ever heard of such a thing. But still, Jetha-moshai's children bowed their heads in shame. The mourning period cast a longer shadow over the Sen Gupta family. The new Boro-ma never received the respect that was her due. It was as if she was merely a usurper, with no real right to the throne. She was not as good-looking or as clever with words, or as gifted as her departed rival. All day she looked guilty and diffident. And yet, she had been brought into the household after a proper marriage and was not to blame in any way. I feel sorry for her today, and for the unwanted and neglected life she had to lead.

Thakur-ma's eldest son, our Ranga-jethamoshai, lived in Allahabad. Ranga-ma would bashfully relate how she was married to my uncle twice. Once before puberty and a second time later. Ranga-ma had such a sweet way of talking. She was very thin and frail and unable to do any housework. Ranga-jethamoshai woke up early every morning, lit the coal oven, made tea for everyone, cooked two meals for the day, portioned out the vegetables into separate bowls and then left for office. Their daughter Manju, our Manju-di, cleaned the house, picked up and folded the dry clothes from the washing line in the afternoon. She tidied up the rooms and scolded her older brothers for leaving their rooms in a mess. They used to treat her with reverence and they all loved Ranga-ma. Ranga-jethamoshai, they avoided. One must know how to earn love. Ranga-ma knew it, Ranga-jetha did not.

Baba's middle brother, our Moni-jetha, lived in Bhowanipore in Calcutta. He was a brilliant student but joined a minor job in the Railways soon after he passed his master's. His salary was needed at home. Also, Thakur-da had left some debts behind. Moni-jetha gave his word, on Thakur-da's deathbed, that he would repay those debts. Thakur-da had four sons, yet the responsibility fell on just one—an unfair deal. Moni-jetha started working long before the others and consequently gave up all luxuries and indulgences.

Thakur-da had got Moni-jetha married but unfortunately, Moni-jethima died a few months later; even before they had had time to be properly acquainted. Her father Kalimohan Sen was an insightful man; he knew what a jewel of a son-in-law he had acquired. In fact, he was so fond of Moni-jetha that when his own daughter died, he found him another wife from the same village and he treated her like his own daughter. Such large-heartedness was only possible in the old days. We can't imagine it now.

Kalimohan himself was prosperous and so were his sons. Bhulu-mama, Raja-mama and Khoka-mama visited Moni-jetha's Bhowanipore home quite often. The minute one of them entered the house, he would call out for his adopted sister. Moni-ma, our second Moni-jethima, would come out to receive the guest with a gentle smile. Every year, during Durga puja, Kalimohan Sen would send loads of gifts. Saris for her, clothes for the children; sweetmeats of all sorts packed in beautiful boxes. As it turned out, Kalimohan's affections were not wasted. When he and his wife were grievously ill Moni-ma nursed them with heart and soul and at the end, Moni-ma was at their deathbeds, a faithful attendant to the last.

The house in Bhowanipore was the nerve centre for the whole family. I use the word 'family' for want of a better word. In fact, even 'clan' seems to be a poor fit. The house was almost like a public inn—free for all to stay in, month after month. Are you going to Calcutta on work? Don't worry, there's Rakhal Sen Gupta's house. Got a job in Calcutta with no place to stay? Why not put up at Rakhal Sen Gupta's? Jyoti-da, Khepu-da, Sukhomoy-da, Gouranga-da, Rasamoy-da, Moni-da, Khokon-da, Kanu-da, Phul-da, Phul-di—the list is endless. They all stayed at various times in the big room on the ground floor, slept there and bathed in the single bathroom that was in the house. On a pallet bed in one corner of the same room lived Thakur, a great-aunt of ours—Thakur-da's older brother's widow, the mother of our Boro-jethamoshai. She was old, immobile and decrepit. Yet I never heard anyone object to her being there. Everyone happily shared that one room. The second room on the ground floor served as a sitting room during the day and a bedroom at night if there were too many guests. One room upstairs was for Moni-ma and Moni-jetha and their children. The second room on the same floor was for his brothers and their families whenever they wished to come. There was no end to the comings and goings. One left, another arrived; a continuous flow of people. Not one of them felt unwelcome and, funnily, nobody ever asked how such a large household was kept running.

Let me give you a few examples of how they managed. Moni-jetha walked to his office every day, all the way from Bhowanipore to Garden Reach and back in order to save on bus and tram fares. He carried a small briefcase with his midday tiffin of handmade chapati and dry molasses, along with a few official papers. When he came back home at eight in the evening, he looked tired, dark and drawn. Moni-ma came upstairs and gave him a cup of tea and two biscuits.

Moni-ma herself never looked tired or vexed. No quarrel or sharp words ever came from her. Service and forbearance was her motto. She wore a plain-bordered coarse cotton sari in the Bangla style and cooked in the vegetarian kitchen. She served food on the veranda in bell-metal plates. We sat cross-legged on piris placed on the floor. Coarse parboiled rice, thin lentil soup, a handful of mixed vegetables and a watery fish soup with a piece of fish so tiny you needed a microscope to see it. Tapati and I both agreed that Moni-ma was really tight-fisted. We never bothered to find out what this miser herself ate or did not eat. Yet the woman we thought of then as being small-minded now holds an exalted place in our memory.

Her children, my first cousins, are far away from Calcutta now; settled in Canada, London and Bangalore. Only Chhor-di lives in nearby Kalyani with her daughter Jhuma. Chhor-di is needed there. Jhuma fell in love with the boy upstairs and married at a very young age when she had just passed school. Chhor-di and Jamai-babu could not say no to their only child and consented. One evening, fifteen years later, Jhuma, now a mother of two children, was cooking in her kitchen when she heard a knocking at the front door. She opened it to find her husband standing there. Beside him stood a young married woman with a newborn babe in her arms. He said, 'This is your younger sister, Jhuma. Welcome her in.' Jhuma stood aside. The young mother walked in with her child and went straight into the bedroom. Jhuma went back to the kitchen. Half an hour later, the girl came to the kitchen door and said, 'Didi, baby wants milk.' Jhuma warmed some milk and poured it into a feeding bottle. The next morning some boys of the locality came and checked in on Jhuma. 'Do you have any problems, Didi? You can tell us.'

Jhuma smiled a sweet smile and replied, 'Of course, you are like my brothers. Whom should I tell but you? But I don't have any problem right now.'

They asked her, 'Who's that girl who came here last night?'

'A sister of mine,' said Jhuma. She picked the baby up and showed them. 'My sister's son. I'm going to bring him up.' The boys went away.

Jhuma started looking after the baby. Every evening his parents left him in Jhuma's loving care and went out to enjoy themselves.

When I heard of all this I asked, 'Isn't this a bit too much?'

Jhuma said, 'What wrong has the baby done, Bharati-mashi?'

I was a little disconcerted. 'That's true, but the girl quite knowingly . . .'

Before I could finish, Jhuma said, 'The person I loved with all my heart for fifteen long years, the man whom I trusted, has betrayed me. How can I blame the girl?'

I still ventured some advice. 'Don't take this lying down, Jhuma. It's because women accept their husbands' wrongdoings without a word of protest that they have been ill-treated through the ages.'

Jhuma's answer, given with her head held high, was eye-opening: 'What will I do? Go to court? Where's the money? Where's the time? Should I borrow money from you people to do that? Should I inform his office? If he's sacked, what will we eat, Bharati-mashi? How will I feed my two children? I don't even have my parents' house to turn to. Where would I live with my boy and girl?' I realized then that advice is easily given. How can one really know what another woman has to suffer, or the problems she has to deal with, if one hasn't been through the same trauma oneself?

Jhuma wouldn't leave her husband's home despite the help I offered. Where in this wretched country is there a respectable place for an abandoned wife to live? Jhuma found a niche for herself in one corner of the house. She found a job and became economically self-sufficient. She is raising her two children on her own. Her father, our Jamai-babu, passed away many years ago. She has no siblings; her sole recourse is her mother. Chhor-di stays with Jhuma. Who else will take care of the children when Jhuma is at work?

Moni-jetha and Moni-ma are long gone. So is Baba's Chhor-da, the youngest of his three older brothers. He used to live in Dhaka, in the Gandaria area. He was an affable, jovial, outgoing, witty man of refined tastes, fond of cigarettes and paan. He was a good conversationalist and perhaps could have won an award for his public relations skills. His early years were full of joy and pleasures but in later life he suffered. He lived with his elder son. His son and daughter-in-law did not neglect him in the least; in fact, they tried to do more for him than they could afford, but these days, old parents never feel that they are really welcome in their children's homes.

Baba's sisters were all much older than him. When Moni-jetha retired and gave up his place in Bhowanipore, our home became the family's meeting place. My aunts loved visiting Baba, their darling little brother, and they came quite often. When one of them arrived, she would inform the others. What a hubbub the visits created! I never saw the oldest of my pishimas because she died many years ago. The second one, Mejo-pishima, was a frequent visitor. The way she rolled with laughter, even at the age of seventy-five, was something to be seen. This ever-smiling lady never seemed to have even a trace of anger in her whole body. Only once did I see a different side of her when I visited them in Krishnagore. Her husband had made an uncalled-for remark which made Mejo-pishima so furious she straightened her bent back to stand upright, drew her torn sari round her shoulders and scolded him in the manner of a haughty queen. 'What did you say? How dare you utter such unjust words?'

When Mejo-pishima visited us, Chhoto-pishima, the third sister, would come from Kanpur. She was a gentle creature as sweet as sugar. At one time she had been fat but then lost weight all at once; her skin was thus loose and wrinkled, a source of unending wonder for us two sisters because all our other aunts had taut skin like young women. Moni-pishima, the youngest of the sisters, came from Tollygunge. Sundar-pishima, widowed at a young age, stayed with us in any case. This gathering was of great delight for us for it meant an unending supply of snacks and savouries—Bori bhaja, amshi, tentu-er achar, home-made chirey, muri and khoier mowa—delicacies made with molasses and puffed rice—and the two most delicious items of them all: chirey-jirey and gangajol. These can't be described in words and need to be tasted to really understand what I mean. Gangajol was a type of coconut sandesh, fine as face powder, soft and smooth. Chirey-jirey looked like tiny cumin seeds. When our aunts foregathered, there would be special cooking sessions in the vegetarian kitchen. Ma did the main dishes and our aunts made snacks, giving Ma a helping hand now and then. They had a truly magical touch; just some herbs and vegetables into the brass pot, stir in a few spices and voila! Will those days ever return?

And yet food was but the most minor of the attractions of these visits. It was actually the chat sessions that were the centrepiece of the day. Every afternoon after lunch, they would sit on the bed with their legs outstretched and cut betel nuts with intricately designed nutcrackers. They would then talk and talk. There was such charm in the way they spoke; the language they used came straight from the heart, the voices had a fascinating lilt, and the peals of laughter that punctuated the conversation wiped away all sorrow. We loved their stories even more than our favourite fairy tales. Yet the things they spoke about were ordinary: reminiscences of their own life experiences, their childhood, their village home, the days when they all grew up together under the same roof. We didn't want to get off that bed. Ma would call out now and then, 'Go finish your arithmetic first. Then you can come back again.' Our pishimas would smile at us indulgently and say, 'Let them drop their studies for just a few days. We feel so happy to have them around us.' What could Ma say to that? She had to let us be.

It wasn't just us who couldn't bear to come away from that room; Baba would come back from his office, hurriedly take off his shoes and come straight to sit on the bed to join his sisters, without even freshening up. His sisters held out some snack or other. Baba would sit on the bed and eat—something that was forbidden in our house normally—like a little boy. He would munch and chat. Our aunts, however, simply drank milk at dinnertime. Baba rushed through his evening meal somehow and came back to join them on the bed. They chatted till late at night, creating a magical atmosphere. Their childhood days, hidden in the dim shadows and light, came alive once again. We two sisters went back with them across the Buriganga river and saw in our mind's eye that fascinating little village called Bera of which we had often heard but which we had never seen. When we were forced to go to bed, we continued recreating images in our minds. 'Close your eyes, Tapati,' I would say. 'Can you see Thakur-ma cooking in the kitchen with her head covered?'

Tapati would say, 'Thakur-da is counting his prayer beads in the small room. And Boro-jethamoshai is standing quietly by the door.'

I would say, 'Look how fast little Baba swims in the Buriganga!'

Tapati would add, 'And Moni-pishima is playing hopscotch under the tamarind tree.'

Moni-pishima was Baba's favourite sister, partly because they were closer in age as compared to the other siblings and partly because Thakur-ma had told Baba, 'You have to keep an eye on her.' Just that one sentence was enough. Baba always kept a watchful eye on his sister.

Moni-pishima was married into a family of very ordinary means. Her husband, our Moni-pishemoshai, was a pharmacist. They had seven children and two or three dependants too, as per the custom of the times. Their house was in Dhaka city and the expenses were high. Moni-pishima did all the housework single-handed—she cooked, cleaned utensils, swept and mopped the house, washed clothes and looked after her sick mother-in-law. And she did everything without flinching. She wore a big red vermilion dot on her forehead, tucked away a paan in her mouth and went about her work all day, smiling and talking constantly. A bolt from the blue changed this picture of happiness to an image of sorrow. The Hindu–Muslim riots that rocked India before and after Partition, inflamed Dhaka too numerous times. Many lost their lives, many women were violated and children maimed, many families lost everything. The numbers were so great that no accurate record has yet emerged. History books record events in broad outline and offer impersonal analyses. Only a few writers and filmmakers have tried to give us a closer picture of the searing human tragedy that overwhelmed the subcontinent.

In February 1950, the massacre of Hindus in Dhaka was of a different order from the earlier riots. It was the Pakistani government of the time that encouraged miscreants from outside the state to commit atrocities in order to drive all Hindus out. The revolt in East Pakistan and the subsequent creation of an independent Bangladesh happened much later. It was 7 February 1950; an uneasy calm prevailed, like before a storm. Moni-pishemoshai was sitting at home at around two-thirty in the afternoon when he heard people running. He looked out and saw a group of young men chasing one with open knives in their hands. He knew all of them, having seen them grow up in the locality. He came out and shouted at them, 'Hey, what are you guys up to?' The men stopped, startled. The one they were chasing ran away. The attackers, having lost their prey, turned their vicious rage on Pishemoshai. They stabbed him again and again in his chest, his back and his stomach. Moni-pishima heard his screams and came out. She begged them, 'Come and kill me too.' The fellows went off, grinning.

Violence in the name of religion or politics can make men lesser than beasts. Violence and death have but a common characteristic. When life comes to an end, death lays equal claim on all of us without distinction. So too on the level field of violence, there is no difference between Hindu, Muslim, Christian or Jew. All are equally cruel, equally beastly.

Pishe-moshai's third son Chandan, seeing the boys armed with knives, rushed off to the Hindu stronghold right across the Dolai canal. He informed Santosh Gupta, the police officer in charge. With his help, Chandan got hold of a small truck to evacuate his family. He came home and saw his father's body lying on the road disembowelled. They spread out a mat on the truck and laid the body on it. The truck drove off. That was the last the sons saw of their father. The fire they could not light for his funeral pyre still burns low within their hearts. With Santosh Gupta's help, the family was moved under the cover of darkness to a safe area. Santosh Gupta had tortured many freedom fighters during our independence struggle. After independence, he stayed back in East Pakistan (now Bangladesh). He gave shelter to young women in his own home and risked his life many times to help those whose lives were in danger. 'I'm doing penance for my sins,' he used to say. With his help, Moni-pishima and her children managed to move to Calcutta with only the clothes on their backs. Her old mother-in-law came too. Baba had just been transferred to Calcutta. He was staying in Bhowanipore with Moni-jetha. Moni-pishima told him in a broken voice, but with not a tear in her eyes, 'I've come, with my brood of children, to be a burden on your back. I didn't have the heart to leave my poor old mother-in-law behind. Please see what you can do, Byomkesh-bhai.'

Something was done. Baba and Moni-jetha found a one-room house for them in Entally in central Calcutta. Ma was surprised. 'You put them in a separate house? Couldn't we have stayed together? She has borne such great grief; being with all of us could have helped soothe her a little.'

Baba said, 'No. While it makes no difference to us brothers and sisters, there shouldn't be any differences among our children and no adverse comparisons. One who is beholden to others feels bad enough anyway. Didi's children must not suffer from any inferiority complex. There'll be less chance of any clash with our children if they stay apart.'

There was no clash amongst us at all. We stayed in different houses in the same city for many years. There was cordiality, friendship and sympathy. Those feelings still survive. Our cousins all grew up in good time. They gave up their tiny place in Entally and moved to a large house in Tollygunge. The girls got married one by one. Later, each of the brothers built a house of his own. Moni-pishima's family was among the few that managed to do well after the devastating partition.

Moni-pishima is no longer with us. She was a woman of sharp intelligence and strength of will just like her mother, our Thakur-ma. Her sons adored her and competed for her affection. If she stayed with one of them for too long, the others would pout like two-year-olds. Once when she was staying with her eldest son, the second son's house was burgled. Instead of calling the police, the first thing he did was run to his mother and complain, 'What are you doing here? If you were staying with me, my house would never have been broken into.' What can anyone say in answer to a charge like that? Even her daughters-in-law were equally competitive where she was concerned. I asked her jokingly one day, 'What secret spell have you used, Pishima, to make everyone so devoted to you?'

She answered, 'There's only one secret. See all, hear all, say nothing.'

That was only partially true. Pishima did keep her eyes and ears open and she didn't hesitate to speak up if she thought it necessary. She knew exactly how much to say and when, when to keep silent, when to persist, and when to let go. If you asked her, she would give advice but she wouldn't venture any opinion unasked. Only once did she reprimand me of her own accord for my lack of interest in household work.

'What is this I hear?' she said. 'Don't you pay any attention to housework in your in-laws' home? Remember this old saying we have: "Work is everything. Work is your husband, work is your son. Without work, you are nobody." Work sincerely, Bharati, work hard for everyone. Take pains and use your brains. Only then can you keep control over all of them.' Moni-pishima had mastered the art of running a home so well that she won all hearts. Our four hearts undoubtedly—that is, Tapati's and mine, our sister Pronoti's, who is ten years younger than me, and our brother Abhijit's, who is twelve years younger than Pronoti.

The story of Ma's family is incomplete without Pronoti and Abhijit. I wonder how it is that I didn't mention them earlier.

I have always loved Pronoti deeply from the time she was born. I was very proud of her too. I told my friends, 'My little sister is so pretty, she sings so well, and she's so very caring. You should see how she looks after our old Pishima.' But I was a wee bit jealous of her too. That's because Baba loved her so dearly—perhaps more than me. This was something that pained me. But that little trace of envy too vanished soon. How could it not? Pronoti is now the central figure in the family; a companion when you need one, an assistant if there is any work to be done and an adviser for when there are problems. She was first an editor with Oxford University Press, then with Ananda Publishers. She married Arkaprabha Deb, an officer in the IAS, a choice she herself made. He was known to be a brilliant intellectual. They have a son and a daughter, Arjun and Joyee, as brilliant as their father and as compassionate as their mother. I find it quite amusing that Arjun looks exactly like his father and Joyee is a spitting image of Pronoti when she was her age.

I got married when my brother Abhijit was hardly two years old but I met him every time I visited my parents, which was pretty often. He grew up looking and behaving more and more like my father. Abhijit went abroad for higher studies many years ago. He taught in the USA, Canada and Australia, and married Janice, a lovely person. Our links remain strong as ever. He always and repeatedly invited me to his home to spend time with him wherever he was; his behaviour still reminds me of the old days.

We brothers and sisters are like the strings on a sitar.

IN THE OUTSIDE WORLD

Truth be told, it was not one of the great interests of Ma to be an excellent housewife. Of course she would be very hurt if we told her that. But it is true that Ma never plunged heart and soul into her assigned domestic role. She did everything that was necessary quite dutifully. She also gave everyone his or her due. But the idea of making household duties a religious vocation was not something she was enamoured with. If I may use that well-known Vaishnava philosophy in a more mundane context, Ma followed the principle of 'bathing without touching the water'. She did her duty without excessive love; she worked but without routine; she had a large house but it was not orderly; she managed, but she was not well organized.

Ma was an extrovert and what truly appealed to her was the outside world. As a single girl, she enjoyed sports and games, she loved to swim and to cycle to college. At the time of her marriage, Baba was a deputy magistrate and later became an IAS officer. Not many Indians were appointed to such prestigious posts under British rule. '*Deputy babur Ginni*', the highfalutin wife of the deputy magistrate, was a mocking way of referring to the airs and graces that these officers' wives put on. There's an amusing book by Kailasabasini Devi, *A Housewife's Diary*, which describes how these grand ladies behaved. She writes that when she was due to board a big, fashionable river boat, a bajra, everybody from her 'baboo' husband Kishorichand Mitra, to his secretaries, clerks, guards and right down to the boat hands, would be on tenterhooks. Again, when she was due to disembark, double rows of light boats lined up all the way from the bajra in midstream to the landing stage. She would step from boat to boat, laughing and swaying.

Of course, Kishorichand was a government servant in the mid-nineteenth century. My deputy magistrate father did not, in the 1930s, have the thunderous might that Kishorichand did. But he was much respected for his integrity and competence. Ma herself was entitled to at least half of that respect; after all, she was his 'better half'. And she was, unlike Kailasabasini, a gentle person with no real desire for the limelight. She was frequently invited to be the chief guest at school functions, music soirées and prize distribution ceremonies. The smile on her face when she distributed prizes was a sight to behold. We would wonder who looked happier, the ones who received the prizes or the one who was handing them out. She spoke little but her speeches were well organized. She held a graduate degree after all, that too from Delhi University. She spoke fluently in English or an Urdu-inflected Hindi, and excellent Bengali of course. Such a 'Deputy Babur Ginni' was hard to find. I still remember clearly the way people would surround her after her speech and praise her to the skies. Ma simply smiled shyly without a word but I could tell how happy she felt inside. She looked forward to such occasions, though she never said so in so many words.

Ma used to accompany Baba on his official tours; I have mentioned this before. There was nothing she liked better than excursions. Baba loved travelling too. Whatever little they saved, they spent on holidays, which, however, were only possible once every three or four years. It was on those holidays that Ma would prove that she could be superbly organized too. One large wicker basket plus sundry other smaller ones as well as suitcases were all packed neatly with everything she would need. We never ran short or brought anything back. Our first holiday was in Kashmir in September–October 1941. Kashmir was so different then; no terrorists frightened us, this heaven on earth hadn't been torn apart by wrangling neighbours. First, we took a train from Calcutta to Rawalpindi. We had to carry blankets for the train journey because it was quite cold at night. At Rawalpindi, we pulled on thick sweaters and started on a long journey by bus. We crossed one mountain peak after another, watched over by the green hills on either side, and accompanied by the occasional sound of rushing waterfalls, till we arrived at Banihal Pass. We stopped at a nearby rest house for a meal of thick Punjabi roti with potato-and-tomato curry. After a short rest, we started out again. For the first part of the journey we had been so excited about everything that the strain of riding the mountain roads had not affected us. But after the hours of driving, and with our stomachs full, the minute we boarded the bus, Tapati and I started retching in turns. I would bend forward, vomit a little bit, look up and ask, 'How many times, Tapati?' Then she would bend forward, do the same and ask, 'Didi, how many times?' We reached Srinagar at dusk and our stomachs stopped churning immediately and our fatigue disappeared. We got out of the bus and Baba started jumping in joy. Ma was jumping too, and so were Tapati and I, jumping for sheer joy. I was seven, Tapati six, Ma twenty-six and Baba thirty-three.

We hired a houseboat in Srinagar called Noorjahan. Noorjahan floated about most happily on Dal Lake opposite the path leading up to the Shankaracharya temple. A light rowboat, a shikara, ferried us between the boat and the land. We stood at the lake shore and hollered, 'Bring the shikara, Siddiqa.' At once Siddiqa, a smiling, rosy-cheeked, fair-complexioned young man wearing a long coat and colourful cap, came down from the houseboat. It was his job to row the shikara. His mother used it in the early morning to sell flowers. His father looked after the houseboat and they lived in a small boat next to ours. We saw his mother sometimes cooking, grinding spices and washing utensils—all with water from the lake.

One had to take a little leap from the shikara to get on to our medium-sized houseboat. As one entered it, the sitting room came first. It had three single sofas and one double one. I think the covers were a red Scottish plaid design. In the centre of the room stood an ornate wooden table of Kashmiri design. It was carved all over with representations of fruits and flowers and covered with a glass top, similar to tables that one can see at the Cottage Industries Emporium or Kashmir Government Emporium these days. The dining room windows were hung with heavy silk curtains. For a dining table we had an oval walnut wood table with four chairs, their backs carved in a chinar leaf pattern. Against two walls were long walnut wood sideboards, also with chinar motifs. On one, decorative pieces of papier mâché plates and boxes, a timepiece and a large framed picture of the Mughal Gardens were placed. We sisters were more interested in the other sideboard where there was a large wooden boat loaded with walnuts. A nutcracker with wooden handles and brass jaws lay beside it. Ma had forbidden us to chew nuts before meals so we hurriedly went through our rice, dal and tomato-red fish curry, and looked greedily at the nuts. Ma cracked them one by one and handed them to us. Even as I write this, the taste of the walnuts lingers on my tongue. I also think of Jogen-bhai who accompanied us there. Baba was sixteen when Jogen-bhai first came to work for the extended family and then he chose to stay on with Baba. He and Ma had become great friends. When Ma sat down with the nutcracker, Jogen-bhai would order Siddiqa in a peculiar mix of languages, '*Siddiqa, oikhan thon pellet le ao.*' (Bring the plate from over there.) Ma would say, 'Jogen, drop the Hindi and speak in Bangla instead.' Jogen would laugh and reply in his old Noakhali accent, 'How can you say that? They don't understand, unless I speak Hindi.' Ma said nothing in response, merely smiled.

Once out of the house, Ma became a happy housewife—dusting, wiping, cleaning things up, even when everything was in order. One evening when we came back to the boat with some guests, Ma saw a paper bag lying on the table and hurriedly crushed it and threw it into the lake. She forgot that her bunch of keys was in the same hand. The Dal Lake has always been covered over with vegetation. In those days too, the plants stood tall above the water. As you looked into the water, you could imagine the vast underwater forest beneath the surface. But now we were stuck; without the keys we couldn't enter the rooms. Where were we to find a diver? Two relatives had been invited over for dinner: Bhulu-mama (our first Moni-ma's brother) and his wife. She turned to Bhulu-mama and said, 'If I had done something like that, you would have thrown me into the lake.' This was a dig at Ma because Bhulu-mama was extremely devoted to his wife and would not make a move without her permission. Ma looked woebegone; Baba looked terribly displeased. Jogen-bhai came to the rescue. He ordered Siddiqa in his Noakhali Hindi, '*Siddiqa kya dekhchcho? Oi panir thon Boudika chabi uthaiya le ao.*' (What are you gaping at, Siddiqa, go fetch Boudi's keys from the water.) Siddiqa jumped into the lake, long coat, pantaloons and all. After half an hour in the water he surfaced finally with Ma's bunch of keys triumphantly in his hands, the keys looking fresh and shiny after the long bath. I wasn't old enough to appreciate this great feat. Being soaked in fairy tales like *Thakurmar Jhuli*, I imagined Siddiqa was really a fish who had disguised himself as a man!

So many tales of Ma's exploits come to mind, I can't relate them all. There were horses available for hire beside the huge Srinagar racecourse. Ma insisted she would learn to ride. For the first two days the training proceeded well enough. On the third day Ma made up her mind to try galloping. She used to be so good at sports, she could swim so well, taming a horse was hardly a challenge. So she leapt on to the horse's back, put her feet into the stirrups, sharply cracked the whip and instructed the horse, 'Chalo, run along.' The horse didn't understand her words, but knew well the crack of the whip. He charged off. After about three lengths, Ma fell flat on the ground. We two girls stared in stunned surprise as we saw our mother being dragged along the ground. How she managed to get her feet out of the stirrups I don't know, our eyes blurred with tears. On the way to the doctor, Ma clutched her aching feet with both her hands and said, 'I know how a shuttlecock flies, but I was not familiar with the horse's motion, which is why I fell. Now that I know, I won't fall tomorrow.' All Baba said was, 'Hm.' Before Ma could take a second shot at horse-riding, Baba took us away from Srinagar to Gulmarg.

The chief attraction of Gulmarg in those days was its extensive green meadows. We didn't see that many gul, flowers. But ah, such grass—softer than velvet. We two sisters rolled around on it. We put grass on our faces, rubbed it on our cheeks and touched it lightly on our eyes. It was smoother than cream and greener than you could ever dream of. We used to stare in wonder at the golf course—reported to be the highest course in the world at the time. We had never seen a game of golf before and we watched spellbound. But what we liked most were the pine trees. They used to speak to the two of us—Ma said they spoke to her too. They called us to play hide-and-seek with them. If we slipped on the pine needles as we ran, they would laugh. We wouldn't accept defeat but carried on running. Ma ran too. She was a different person then.

Gulmarg is higher than Srinagar; eight thousand feet above sea level, like a mountain vale surrounded by high peaks on all sides. A fourteen-mile-long walkway for tourists circled the town. We wore thick woollen sweaters and mittens knitted by our mother and went out for long walks with our parents hand in hand both in the mornings and late afternoons. We lost our way quite often. Tapati would laugh whenever we were lost. Ma would look at Baba and quote a line from Rabindranath Tagore's romantic poetry, 'We two float with the wind that flows.'

'Let's go home,' I would say in a tired voice.

'We've lost our way,' Ma would reply. Baba said nothing but tried to find the right direction with a worried look. There was absolute calm on Ma's face.

Ma had this habit of wanting to go to the most inaccessible places. One day she said to Baba, 'How can we go back from Gulmarg without having seen the Alpather lake? Let's go to Alpather.' So horses were hired. We woke up at first light, shivering in the cold and wearing heavy coats on top of our sweaters, rode to Khilanmarg. We rested there under the open sky. A few locals sitting under two tents refreshed us with glasses of tea. We continued on horseback and finally reached Alpather. The lake had been birthed by the waterfalls from the ice-capped mountains all around. The water was very cold; just a touch could give you chilblains. The sky seemed so near that I thought I could easily leap up and touch it. I tried several times and realized that it wasn't so easy. So I settled down on a rock instead and ate home-made tomato-and-cucumber sandwiches and drank hot tea from a flask. The sandwiches had grown lumpy in the cold. 'Haven't you brought any rice, Ma?' I asked. 'That's the thing to have when you're hungry for lunch.' She said, 'We started so early, I couldn't cook anything. Besides, the rice would have been quite cold. I'll go back and give you hot rice with butter.' Though disappointed for the time being, I cheered up at the thought of hot rice topped with butter. Ah, delicious!

From Gulmarg we went to Pahalgam. We hired two tents and pitched them on the not-so-wide shore between two streams—Seshnag and Leder. There were two rope-strung cots in one tent for Ma and Baba. In the other tent, one cot was for the two of us and another for Jogen-bhai. There was a mini-tent which served as a kitchen, and a tiny one as the lavatory. There was not much cooking to be done—simple rice, dal and vegetables cooked at one go on an Icmic cooker, a useful utensil for cooking with steam. After that we roamed the mountain paths, taking in the beauty of the pine trees and listening to the song of the rushing streams. Ma would break into song now and then in her not-so-musical voice, *I can lose myself wherever I wish . . .'*

'Please don't. You're forbidden! Don't get lost or fall into the gully,' Baba would respond. Baba was cautious, Ma, daring.

When we came back to Srinagar, Baba asked Ma if she would like to go shopping for Kashmiri shawls and saris. Ma quickly responded, 'If you have money left over, I want to see the Kolhai glacier. I don't need to buy anything.' Baba agreed on one condition. We would go on horseback but she was not to try galloping. Ma conceded and we started out on a three-day journey to Kolhai. It was a tough journey over rocks and ice; we had to get off our horses several times and make our way carefully on foot before we reached the glacier. I was cold and tired. Why did we have to go through so much trouble just to see a huge chunk of ice, I wondered. I much preferred the safe little trips by shikara on the Dal Lake to the Charminar island or the grand Mughal Gardens. Another reason I was unhappy was that Ma was not paying us any attention at all. She ran in the snow with a stick in hand; she made snowballs and chucked them at Baba even as he laughed out loud. I turned to Tapati and asked, 'What's so funny?' 'Of course it's funny,' she said and she laughed too. I was the only one with a glum face wondering where I could sit down. Not on the snow certainly; so I stood there holding a stick and grumbling to myself. 'Jogen-bhai is clever so he dropped out of this. Why couldn't I be as clever as him?' I think I must have been a little bit stupid. If not, how could a thing like that have happened on our way back?

From Srinagar, we went to Lahore, Thakur-ma's brother's place. This uncle of Baba's, Professor Surendranath Das Gupta (not the reputed philosopher), was very popular and respected among students. After his death, former students had built a new college in his name and Ma and Baba wanted to see that college. Lahore was a beautiful city in those days. It was spick and span, roses of many hues wafted their fragrance through the city air, and the architecture was a mix of Mughal and British influences. The place had a special culture all its own. I remember Lahore very well as well as the night journey back. The train was a little late, I think. Baba, in a reddish brown jacket, was looking for the right compartment reserved for us. I was walking beside him. The station was crowded and everyone was running. I suddenly realized that the brown jacket I was following was not my father's. I stopped the gentleman and asked, 'Where's my father?' He answered disinterestedly in Hindi, 'What are you saying?' I can't blame him; the train had already begun moving. A busy railway station is an apt reflection of the world—it is every man for himself. The gentleman found his coach, switched off his torch, and jumped in. I did the only thing left for me to do—I started crying at the top of my voice. My aunt would often scold me for my high-pitched voice. 'You will never get married. Even if you are, they'll send you right back in no time. No girl should ever speak so loudly.' But at that time of crisis, my unfeminine voice proved very useful. And, sure enough, the person whose ears a child's cry reaches first heard me. Baba had found our compartment by then. Ma said, 'Bharati is crying. Where is she? She was with you.' They left Jogen-bhai and Tapati on the train and started running in two opposite directions. But they didn't have to run far. That bellowing voice of mine echoed forlornly like drums on the last day of Durga puja. Ma picked me up like a nestling fallen from the nest and got into our compartment. She asked me a little later, 'Were you very scared, Bharati? What did you think?'

I replied, sobbing, 'I thought I was lost. But why couldn't I see Ma and Baba one last time before that?'

My mother's eyes filled with tears; I was so surprised. We had never seen her crying before. We sisters used to say, 'Ma's eyes are not meant to shed tears. That's why she gets a headache when she wants to cry.' Then why did Ma cry that night?

After that trip to Kashmir, it was quite a few years till Baba could take us on another holiday. We sisters were more grown up by then and our baby sister Pronoti had arrived. We went to Nainital and Ranikhet. I remember Ma happily rowing a boat on the Naini lake. In the lonely hills of Ranikhet, Ma would sing quietly to herself the words of the poet Kazi

Nazrul Islam as we walked: '*Let's march forward to the beats of drums.*' In the evenings we played the board game Ludo together. Ma was a good bridge player but Baba was not that keen and we two didn't know the game at all. So we played Ludo and Snakes and Ladders. These two were much better than bridge in that they were family games. Baba and I would team up against Ma and Tapati. Pronoti stuck close to Baba and watched us play. Ma and Tapati won every time. I would lose my temper sometimes and overturn the board. 'You people must be cheating! Or else, how can you win all the time?' We squabbled. Pronoti laughed. There was one other game that didn't make us quarrel. We called it Word-making and Word-taking. The smarter name for it is Scrabble. However, we didn't buy the board, or the pieces, in any shop. Ma cut out the pieces from cardboard, coloured them on one side and wrote down the letters on the other. It was such fun! Isn't it unfortunate that parents don't find the time these days to play such family games?

We went back to Kashmir again for our next holiday in 1955. At that time I was studying for my master's degree. We went again to Srinagar, Pahalgam and Gulmarg but the second time is never the same as the first. There was no Siddiqa; the pine trees did not talk to us any more. We had also lost the habit of losing our way. The main attraction the second time was a visit to the Amarnath cave. Baba asked Ma once again, 'Would you like to go shopping, or to Amarnath?'

Ma's answer was, 'We can buy all those things in Calcutta, but will there be an Amarnath back home?'

Exactly what Baba was hoping to hear. The right time for the strictly pious pilgrim to visit is the Sravana Purnima, a full moon night in July–August—we were a month away from that. Baba said, 'Every day is auspicious when you're visiting the lord.'

Ma said, 'I never believe in almanacs anyway. So let's go'.

We found out that though the road had been declared navigable—after the winter snows—just two days ago, no pilgrims had started out yet. Baba said, 'We will be the first visitors this year. There won't be any problem, I'm sure.'

Ma looked him in the eye and quoted a line from a famous Tagore poem, 'What if there is? We will face death knowing you and I are together.'

'And what about us? Aren't we there too?' I piped up in mild protest.

Ma looked at me and said with a confidential, and a little mischievous, smile, 'One has to say such things.'

Getting horses was a bit of a problem. We were looking for horses that had been to Amarnath the year before so that they would be familiar with the roads. On perilous mountain roads, humans have to rely mainly on the animals' instincts, their 'horse sense', literally. After a few days, the right horses were found. I changed into a dark green 'frock' (that's what we called dresses then) and black pantaloons. I won't call it a salwar and insult the fashionable salwars of today! If my stylish daughters saw those clothes, they would burst into laughter. But poor taste in fashion apart there was hardly anything that could beat this bold daughter of Bengal on horseback, with her hair pulled back high in a long braid!

We started out from our tent in Pahalgam and reached the Chandanwari snow bridge: one that has been constructed by Mother Nature out of pure ice. Muddy feet and hooves had covered the white ice with a brown layer. We crossed over and rode forward even as the giant mountains surrounded us. Tall evergreens and tufts of ferns covered their sides. As we gradually climbed, the tree cover thinned out. Huge, craggy slabs of rock heaved into view. It got colder. Suddenly we saw a rather strange sight. A young man with a bedroll on his back was briskly walking up the rocky footpath all on his own. We were on horseback and already feeling tired. Baba called out to him and he stopped. He said that another group like ours had started on the way but had decided to turn back because of the cold and lonely road ahead. The groom the young man had hired was reluctant to leave the group so he had decided to proceed on his own. He was determined to see Amarnath. Baba said, 'Why go alone? Come with us.' Harish, the young Punjabi man, agreed happily. Two young unmarried girls and one intrepid young man were thrown together and the inevitable happened. We sisters were smitten and so was he, though he seemed to prefer Tapati more. We reached Seshnag in the evening. A fierce, icy wind was blowing over the mountain peak where a travellers' inn was perched. The local name for Seshnag is Wabjan, meaning windy heights. Seshnag lake lay below; from there the Seshnag river flowed. Waterfalls from the mountainside splashed into the lake. White cascades fell into emerald green waters—nowhere else in the world have I seen such a sight. We spent the night in a tiny room in that travellers' inn, shivering with cold. A Sikh gentleman, who owned the local eatery, brought us some thick Punjabi rotis, pea curry, and stir-fried vegetables on steel plates. Long live the Sikh community! Their bravery and resilience in hardship are quite remarkable. This gentleman from some remote village in distant Punjab had set up a business of his own in this frosty, friendless place. The money he earned supported his family back home. I have nothing for him but praise. After the hot meal he served, we felt a little less chilly. We spent the night there, woke up early next morning, had a quick wash and a steaming cup of tea, and set out again. The way ahead was covered with snow and there was no sign of any road. We had to repose all our faith in our horses. We could see nothing but ice and snow in front, behind, right and left. Ice-capped mountains loomed above us, not 'leaning against the sky in sleep' as an old song suggests, but very much alive. They stood, heads held high, ever restless, ready to fly off through the sky in search of outer space. Majestic is a word you don't quite comprehend until you see them.

We reached the Maha Ganesh peak. It is 18,000 feet above sea level but we didn't have any breathing problems. The air was so clean and clear, with a slight breeze blowing. The sunlight on the ice radiated such heat, we had to take off our sweaters. Our eyes were dazzled by its rays. We had to get off our horses often in order to ease their burden for some time. They walked on ahead, showing us the way. We followed. They seemed to have a sixth sense that warned against any danger. At one point the first horse in line stood stock-still, then turned at a sharp ninety-degree angle and started running. We followed. Ten minutes later, we heard a thundering sound and saw a huge chunk of ice hurtling down behind us. It fell right down to where the rushing Amarganga river leaped over the rocky mountainside to the gorge below—only to find more rocks waiting. That horse saved us from certain death that day.

From Seshnag we reached the next stop, Panchtarani, at around ten in the morning. After a short rest we started out for the Amarnath cave. A little below the cave, the grooms asked us to descend from our horses. We were to climb the rest of the way on foot. The rule for most temples is just that: whether you travel by car or on horseback, you are to approach the gate only on foot.

Inside the Amarnath cave is a Shivalingam that is made of ice. It retains its full shape for a few months in the year and vanishes completely for some months. As I entered the cave, a few icy drops of water fell on my head. I felt there was a scientific reason for the mysterious behaviour of the Shivalingam, connected to the presence or absence of sunlight within the cave. In other words, on the summer and winter solstices. When I first set eyes on that crystalline marvel in the magic half light of the afternoon in the freezing cold and lonely cave, with two doves cooing softly somewhere, I was so overwhelmed by so many thoughts that I find it difficult to talk about it coherently. All I know is that when we entered the cave it was twelve noon by the clock. When the horsemen shouted for us to return, it was four. I have heard of the relativity of time in outer space—I wonder how time functioned in the eternal solitude of that wondrous cave in the high mountains.

We spent the night at Panchtarani and came straight down to Srinagar next morning. Our new friend Harish came with us. Harish kept us company in Srinagar as long as we were there, except for a few hours at night. He looked exactly like Dilip Kumar, the matinee idol of Bombay films. They could have been identical twins. He was not only brave but also a great conversationalist and a lover of good literature. He was a high-ranking government official and a bachelor. A few months after we returned to Calcutta, Harish came to our house and asked Baba for Tapati's hand in marriage. If he had approached Tapati in private and declared his love, who knows what would have come out of it. Asking Baba had no positive effect. It is one thing to approve of a gutsy young man in the remote mountains of Kashmir, quite another to accept a dal-roti-eating, Hindi-speaking son-in-law in the family. Harish disappeared from our lives. We still have a picture of him in our old album, walking to Amarnath with his bedroll on his back.

After 1955 we went on a Himalayan holiday one more time with our parents. I was married by then. Our little brother Abhijit was two years old. Ma and Baba decided to go to Kedarnath and Badrikashram. I tagged along. We were five and a half of us at first—Ma and Baba, three sisters, and half a person, Abhijit! Then Didi-ma and Dadamoshai came from Berhampore and joined us. Didi-ma could be counted as another half with Abhijit because she was to travel by dandi, a sort of palanquin, with Abhijit on her lap. The six of us would travel by foot. A 135-mile trek. For the first few days we covered six or seven miles a day; later, when we got more used to it, we could aim for twelve miles. We mapped out the halts accordingly. We would take one guide along who would also double up as a cook.

We went to Haridwar by train. The Ganga there is a thing of beauty. We bathed at the Har ki Pauri ghat. In the evening we floated oil lamps on leaf boats on the river, like the other pilgrims and tourists. Thousands of lamplights flickered and shone like stars in the night. From Haridwar to Rishikesh, and from there to Rudraprayag, we went by bus. That was as far as any wheeled transport could go in those days. We had to walk the rest of the way.

Not being used to trudging such long distances, we tired easily at first. But we took it in our stride. The whole experience thrilled us—walking along the banks of the Alaknanda river, absorbing the beauty of nature and looking at the countless pilgrims, all moving the same way. Little children, old men and women, the sick and the disabled, the poor and the wretched. We had everything packed with us in Ma's inimitable style. She had taken along her famous wicker basket, quilts, blankets, bedding, sets of clothes for hot and cold weather, stove, kerosene, grinding stone for spices, bonti for cutting vegetables, water bucket, mug, soap, towels, shoes and socks, right down to Baba's handkerchiefs. And we still worried that we might run short over the month. Yet there were so many others travelling with just a little bundle on their shoulders or a few clothes wrapped in a towel. As if they were going from Calcutta to nearby Murshidabad. What were they looking for? What great boon that could come unwanted, or perhaps with much earnest prayer? They chanted. Some voices were musical, others out of tune, but they were all devoted hearts and their lives were dedicated to the feet of Lord Ramachandra and Lord Shiva. We walked all day until it was dark. The guide unloaded our bedding from the horses' back and laid them out and we dropped flat out on our backs. Ma had the most energy. She started cooking along with the guide: rice and dal from her basket, and potatoes bought from the local shop. For one month that was our fixed menu. We had pumpkin one day and gourds on another—vegetables we normally turned up our noses at in Calcutta. To know how delicious they can taste, you have to walk to Kedarnath. After dinner Ma packed her basket again while Baba chalked out the plans for the next day. Didi-ma sat on the bed counting her prayer beads while Dadamoshai tried to guard our bed. In those days, full democracy operated in the makeshift inns. Anyone could walk over your bed or spread a towel right next to you and settle down to sleep. There was no question of rent or reservations. Dadamoshai would sleep at one end of the bed and Baba at the other. The guide slept near our heads—being a Brahmin, perhaps. The rest of us slept peacefully in the middle; like Sita within her protective chalk circle.

We reached Kedarnath and spent three nights there. We had to. We had fallen sick. Let me explain how. Dadamoshai had been eating street food all the way—singaras, pakoras, sometimes chhole-puri. He completely ignored all official warnings—'Do not eat cut fruits, sweetmeats and other food fried in the open street.' Spoilt by Didi-ma's cooking, he could not settle for simple rice, dal and potato curry that we all ate. He would tempt us, 'Want some singara and jalebi?' We looked at the mouth-watering stuff but shook our heads and refused. Baba was dead against eating food sold on the roadside. It was perhaps to avoid his displeasure that Dadamoshai often fell back from the group and enjoyed those delicacies in peace. He did this all the way to Kedarnath but none of us joined him. Ironically, though, Baba was the first to get an upset stomach and the rest of us followed. Dadamoshai carried on merrily from one mountain peak to the next and from one singara shop to the next. Another item was later added, besan laddu, sweetmeats made with powdered gram. He would say to us, 'If you lock your body in a glass case the organs will stop working. Unlock it, let it free.'

From Kedarnath we crossed several mountains and finally reached Badrikashram. It was a terribly crowded place. Even at that time it seemed as if it was developing fast into far too showy a place. To my mind, the place disturbed the peaceful Himalayas. The whole town was decked up gaudily; loud music and the chanting of hymns could be heard all day. It all looked out of sync.

We came back to Calcutta a month later. That was the last time I went on a holiday with my parents. And it wasn't as if Baba kept going for those long and exotic holidays. He retired and could not afford them. And then, one day, Baba passed away leaving us dazed and inconsolable for a long time. It was a loss too deep for words.

After Baba's death, Ma's travels did not come to an end. In fact, she went abroad which didn't happen while Baba was alive. Abhijit started working overseas and he took Ma with him to many countries—Canada, USA, Australia. His wife Janice took great care of her, much beyond our expectations, in fact. Janice—god bless her—loved our mother. They took Ma to many interesting spots: the Niagara Falls, the Fisherman's Wharf in San Francisco, a Shakespeare play at Stratford, the Times Square in New York, the Covent Garden in London and the Australian outback to see kangaroos in the wild. Ma saw and loved it all and gave them her blessings. Yet a husband and a son are not the same. Nor can age twenty-six compare with age sixty.

Ma also had a world of her own outside her own home—a world that her children, and not even Baba, could reach. It was the All India Women's Conference or AIWC. An Irish woman called Margaret Cousins had initiated it way back in 1927, of course, with the help of many Indian women. Without the support of Indians, how could so vast an organization have come into being? Maharani Chimanbai Gaekwad of Baroda became its first president. Begum Sharifa Hamid Ali, Hansa Mehta, Kamaladevi Chattopadhyay, Sarojini Naidu and Vijayalakshmi Pandit were some of the others who pitched in. The AIWC is an organization of middle- and upper-class women, but in those days it was the leading light in the field of women's development. In the pre- and post-Independence years, the AIWC played an important role in women's empowerment and in the enactment of laws to establish women's rights. It continues to do so even today. Ma became a member of the AIWC in the 1950s. She was encouraged by the eminent social worker Asoka Gupta. They started working together while Baba was still alive. After his death, Ma devoted herself to this organization completely. She loved working there and loved her fellow workers and the indigent women they helped. She started a new branch of the AIWC in the newly developing Lake Town area where she lived. She was immersed all day in the activities of the basic training school and capacity-building programmes, and rose from secretary to president of the local organization. It could be said that the reason why she lived was the AIWC. Then she stepped down from her post and invited the wife of a high-ranking government official to become president in her place. She would continue to work as secretary. The idea was that the two of them together would make a stronger team. The new president arrived and instantly removed Ma from her post. This is a very old game in power politics but Kalyani Sen Gupta, being an absolute amateur in political manoeuvres, was extremely hurt. She felt cheated. A person who had remained calm all her life was as agitated as a little child. She could never be reconciled to the idea of being out of the AIWC.

By now her health started degenerating slowly. Baba had left. Her daughters were married and her son lived abroad. She was lonely. It was a well-laid ground for Parkinson's to set in. Gradually she became bedridden; her speech slurred, the doctor had to be called in often and nursemaids became her constant companions. Luckily, her physician sister Urmila, having lost her own husband, decided to move in. They could keep each other company. Urmila herself was an acute diabetic. The love for and the dependence of the two sisters on each other kept them both alive for quite a few years. Kalyani Sen Gupta's octogenarian years continued to flow; a thin, placid stream.

ADIEU, MA

Ma sometimes used to try her hand at drawing and painting. She wasn't very good at it but very keen. And some of them turned out quite well. There was one she did in black pastel that was framed and hung in our sitting room. I can't say it decorated the room because the picture didn't smile, it wept. The painting was of a dark, black, leafless tree holding out a few thin and bare branches in the twilight. It evoked some unknown sorrow that made your heart heavy. At the bottom of the picture was a caption in rounded letters: 'Time to go'. I used to say, 'That caption spoils it all. Why did you have to give it a name? The viewer could use his or her own imagination.'

Ma replied, 'Yes, one could. But I drew it with "Time to go" in mind, because all life, even a tree's, comes to an end.

That is true. And since all life must end, Ma's did too. It was morning and we had just taken our first sips of tea—Abhijit, his wife Janice, and me. There was a phone call from Calcutta Hospital. 'Your mother's condition is not good. No, you don't have to hurry. But you should come.' We left our breakfast and jumped from our chairs. I put on my slippers somehow and we rushed to the hospital, afraid that we wouldn't be able to meet her for one last time. We knew, of course, that the phone call could arrive any time. Ma had been in the intensive care unit for a month. The doctors and nurses took great care of her but they also reminded us that people did not live forever.

As we were standing in the lift, my brother said in a low voice, 'I don't want her to die now.'

I stroked his cheek and said equally softly, 'Let her go, Abhijit.'

I need not have said that, because the minute we entered the room, Abhijit took one look at her and said, 'She's gone!' She must have died before we received the phone call. Abhijit and Janice looked helpless and grief-stricken. Ma's foreign daughter-in-law was truly fond of her. They had wanted her to live a little longer. But I, stony-hearted, didn't want that.

My son Khokon came to the hospital when he got the news. He didn't say a word, just took me to the office and made me sit there. He dealt with all the paperwork and payments. Then he arranged for her to be put in an ambulance and took her home to Lake Town. My two sisters Tapati and Pronoti went with them. I went straight to Gariahat Market in south Calcutta to buy a Benarasi sari. I wanted to send her off like a queen. Luckily, I found just the right sari, one that Ma would have adored. It was a light cream silk with tiny flowers of fine gold threadwork all over. The border carried a gold floral design. By the time I reached Lake Town, they had finished dressing her up. I gave Pronoti the sari. She did a neat job. The gold-worked anchal came over her shoulders to the front. Ma looked beautiful. Why didn't I give her this sari before? I knew she would have refused to wear it even though she would have liked it. She would have only smiled shyly and said, 'How can I wear something so gorgeous?' But she would have been pleased, I know. If we had insisted, she might have worn it just for half an hour on the last day of Durga puja. I imagined how she would have looked. I remembered that pale yellow wedding sari of hers with minakari flowers all over, and the muff chain and ruby necklace and the ruby danglers she wore with it—how beautiful she looked!

Ma loved to dress up. A midnight blue georgette sari, which was a wedding gift from Sejo-mama, was a particular favourite. She had an eye for good saris and fine jewellery but she didn't buy any. Not even when her wedding trousseau looked old and worn did she go for expensive replacements. We were always short of funds for such indulgences. Ma had a tough time keeping a balance between what Baba used to earn and the necessities she had to spend on for the household and for Baba's guests and needy relatives and acquaintances. Moreover, in our conservative family married women normally stopped wearing colourful saris after forty. That apart, how could Ma have the heart to dress up when there were two widows living with her—her mother-in-law and her fabulously beautiful sister-in-law? They wore no blouses or petticoats, no ornaments at all, just plain white borderless white saris. My tender-hearted Ma couldn't bear to dress up in front of them. Once we sisters started earning, we bought her many saris, but they were all white. Why didn't I ever try to make her wear other colours like that pale yellow silk she wore on her wedding day? I'm sure my father's departed soul would not have been troubled in any way.

When I saw Ma for the last time, her arms were not stretched upwards; they lay lifeless by her side. She was covered in garlands and bouquets. Her face was serene and not at all melancholy like that painted tree of hers. She departed like a queen in all her majesty. Not in the dim light of evening but in the glorious sunlight of the afternoon.

I thought at first that I wouldn't go to the crematorium but I changed my mind. They carried her out of the hearse and put her on a makeshift bed. Abhijit sat on the ground holding her hand, never taking his eyes off her. What was he thinking? That he hadn't done as much as he wished to do for Ma? He lived abroad, so he couldn't give Ma the warmth of his constant presence, something she surely missed. Or was he thinking of his boyhood, her kisses, her scolding and their tiffs at play or at studies? Tapati wept all the way. Pronoti, with tearful eyes, was exchanging a few words with those who had accompanied the hearse or had come to the crematorium to bid Ma farewell. Khokon was attending to the formalities; he had taken charge of all the practical things involved. Sukhendu, my husband, was sitting beside me. My mind was a blank. I didn't think of the past. I didn't feel any pain. There was just an inert emptiness inside, a void that could not be explained, nor ever be filled. A certain something I had, that was now gone. A source of strength that flowed out to me in secret had gone dry. A beautiful warm light had flickered out. There was nothing now. No hope, no trust, no love, no creation, no existence, nor destruction perhaps. All that remained was an inevitable, harsh and cruel end. Suddenly Ma's bed started swaying. It seemed to move forward. There was a loud clanging noise. The bed seemed to jump a foot high. For a second or maybe less, a door opened up in front. Fire, bright, flaming, searing, dazzling, hungry fire, all-consuming, all-destroying, the primal source of all creative energy. Ma went smiling, bedecked in flowers and her pale cream-and-gold sari. Or was she crying, or wholly detached, I couldn't quite tell. She entered the fire. The door closed in the blink of an eye.

I came home. Without a word, without a sound. I knew for sure that the biggest chapter in my life had come to an end.

Did I love my mother very much? I didn't realize it while she was alive. From the time when Tapati and I were just toddlers, we had divided our parents between us. Baba was mine and Ma was Tapati's. All my kisses and cuddles, my childish demands and my adoration were reserved for Baba. For Tapati, it was always Ma. I think Ma loved Tapati more. She was thin, dark, sickly and cried easily. I was always the favourite of our huge joint family. To make up for that, I used to love Tapati with all my heart. I kept her under my wing and tried to protect her from all harm. But why should Ma be biased towards her? One day stands out clearly in memory. We lived in Patuakhali then. Ma was making a red striped shirt and matching pantaloons for Tapati. Ma was a competent tailor. I watched her sewing with such care. I felt that all Ma could think of was Tapati and Tapati alone. She finished stitching a lovely new suit for Tapati. I couldn't stand it any more. Ma stepped out of the room, and I used this chance to cut an inch off Tapati's new shirt. Ma came back smiling, ready for Tapati to try on the new shirt. Her smile vanished and her face grew dark with anger. I had never seen my ever gentle mother grow so livid with rage. She gave me one tight slap on my cheek and said, 'Chhi! You're jealous? Jealousy is a sin. It eats you up inside. It doesn't do you any good.' I was only six then. That was the first and last time that Ma laid hands on me. I froze on the spot. Ma actually hit me? How could she? I carried that hurt inside me for a long time then I forgot. Now, after so many years, my left cheek, which she had slapped, has started stinging again.

I was a disobedient girl. I did exactly what I felt like. There was forever a certain distance between the two of us. There were only three occasions when we came really close. The first two times were when my two daughters were born. There's a saying in Bengali which translates as, 'You can repay your mother's debt only when you become a mother yourself.' In other words, to understand both the pain and the pride of motherhood and to know what it really means to be a mother, you have to go through the experience yourself. Maybe that's true. I stayed with my mother for a long stretch of time after each of my two daughters was born. We were close, not just physically, but mentally too.

Mother–daughter relationships have always been strange all over the world. One is born out of the other. The same sex, the same problems of growing up and in the same way. There has to be some similarity in the way both their minds work. And yet, there's always a certain underlying tension at the root of the relationship. Twice—each time with a baby in my lap—and once while I attended her final sickbed, I felt a common bond between us, a mutual dependence and a sense of trust that overwhelmed my heart and mind.

Eleven days after Ma passed away it was time for her last rites to be performed. Abhijit said he would do the very special Brishotsarga ritual in Ma's honour. A portion of the second floor of our Lake Town house was given a fresh coat of paint. The discoloured walls were covered with white cloth. Garlands of white tuberoses and golden marigold were hung in triple arcs along the walls, although coloured flowers are normally not used for funerals. Janice spent all evening drawing out the design in which the garlands were to be hung. A picture of Thakur-ma was placed below the flowers. Below it we kept a picture of Baba and under that, on a small table, a lovely picture of Ma, smiling her sweet smile. Pronoti hung rows of white tube roses down the sides of the table. On one side of the table was kept a new bed, and on the other side lay the offerings that were to be dedicated to the memory of the dear departed, and which afterwards would be given away to the priest. The room was full of brassware, lamps, sandalwood, flowers and leaves, rice, fruit and a dozen other items listed by the priest for the prayer rituals. In the centre was an image of the presiding deity, Narayan. A few chairs were placed in one corner of the room for those who wished to sit during the ceremony. Abhijit in a dhoti with a chador covering his bare torso sat cross-legged opposite the Brahmin priest and repeated the Sanskrit mantras after him with great diligence. He stopped once in a while to ask the meaning of a Sanskrit word, or request a repetition of a line if he missed the pronunciation. In an adjoining room, an assistant priest recited the Bhagavad Gita; in another room, a second assistant read from the Mahabharata.

The staircase of our two-storeyed house was wreathed in marigold. The ground floor walls were similarly decorated. A group of kirtan and bhajan singers were performing there. Against the main wall, the decorators had constructed a small temple-like structure made of flowers and leaves. There was a beautiful oil painting of Baba in his youth placed inside and beside it was a photograph of Ma when she was twenty. They looked great together. Maybe that's how they had looked when they got married. We hadn't seen them then. Outside the temple heaps of garlands and bouquets were piling up. Had my quiet, soft-spoken, gentle mother gained the hearts of so many? I hadn't realized how well beloved she was. People poured in—elderly women neighbours; older couples from nearby homes whom she had befriended; Ma's colleagues from the AIWC; her sisters' close friends; many local ayahs and domestic workers who called her 'Mashima' and had turned to her for help and advice. We served them vegetarian food. We were fortunate that those who came seemed to relish what was served.

In the little garden outside, Abhijit was to perform the ritual. Below a wide canopy, on a broad and high platform, four Brahmins chanted mantras in unison. Beside the platform, a clay image of a bullock had been placed. It was a handsome fellow. Our clay modellers are so gifted and yet so neglected. The chief priest had had it specially made by a Kalighat potter. But a clay bull was not to every-one's satisfaction. So the local milkman's son produced a bull calf. The poor little fellow stood there for more than an hour. Everyone stroked and petted him. But no one had thought of providing him fodder; so he went back unfed.

The rituals upstairs being over, Abhijit came down and sat on the canopied platform. The sacrificial fire was lit. The smoke made his eyes water—or was it just the smoke? He repeated the unfamiliar mantras in a hoarse voice. This time he didn't stop to ask their meaning.

The rituals were started at seven in the morning; they ended at nine-thirty in the evening. By then the guests had all left. The Brahmins and the chief priest accepted their dues, showered words of blessing on Abhijit and took their leave. In the empty room, filled with wilted flowers, Baba and Ma remained standing side by side—just pictures in frames.

I came upstairs and told Janice, 'Now our ties will be loosened. Whom will you come to visit every year?' She said, 'I will come to see the three sisters.' Janice is such a lovely person. She did so much for Ma. She tried to anticipate and meet Ma's every need. And the answer she gave me was also sincere. But I knew that it would never be the same. Still I couldn't feel that, 'If it's over, it's over'.

I don't believe in rebirth. Baba had said once that the concept of rebirth is one of the pillars of the Hindu faith. I think of myself as a Hindu but I can't accept the concept of rebirth. Even if I did, how would that help? If I were reborn, Baba wouldn't be my father again. Ma wouldn't come back in the next life as my mother. I wouldn't be their eldest child.

The physical body does not remain after death. I don't know whether there really is such a thing as Atma; and even if there is, is it really immortal, changeless? I don't know. I have no proof of it and no inner realization certainly. In that empty room, the only thing my tired mind and exhausted body felt was that Ma was gone. Baba was gone. My old self was also gone. The loud laughter that was part of my very nature had lost its pitch somehow. My face that was modelled on Ma's had lost its charm. My mind had lost its inner strength.

Bharati Sen Gupta has left forever, and just Bharati Ray stays behind.

ME

CHILDHOOD

To write about oneself is far more difficult than writing about others. When the subject is someone else, it is easier to use judgement to select or reject facts, to think about what will appeal to the reader and what will not. But when the subject is the self, then ego stands in the way; a huge obstacle. All valuable, ego-less details are lost. As if one's own life is the most precious thing in the world. So many homes may not have light but all the self cares about is the little lamp that burns in its own backyard. Millions of hungry, homeless people may desperately hang on to life yet all that the self cares for is that its own life should be strewn with flowers. Thinking only of oneself is a self-diminishing act. It alienates you from the rest of the world. Yet let me write about a very tiny, narrow, insignificant life stream that is mine.

As I look back, my mind races to my childhood and adolescent years. The brilliance of Presidency College is lost in the sal woods of Jhargram. The joyous experiences of teaching and research are swept away by the enchanting waters of the Karnaphuli river in Chittagong. The Teesta-Karala rivers of Jalpaiguri make me forget the mighty Ganges and beckon me with an amazing love.

My first memories go back to Jalpaiguri. We lived there till I was three and a half years old in a small single-storeyed house that I still remember very well. Three steps led up to the front veranda. From the tiny sun-bathed courtyard below, you could see the Himalayas in a grey haze in the distance. Baba would sit me on his lap and sing in a tuneless voice, '*Hills, hills, you can see the hills.*' Six decades later, that voice and that song sound so melodious now. When Baba left for office, I would sit in the courtyard and call to the mountains, '*Aay, aay, aay.*'

Once, a mountainous elephant stood on his four fat legs in our little courtyard, steadily swaying his huge trunk. A mahout sat on a howdah on his back. He touched the elephant's ears lightly with a hooked stick. The animal at once folded his legs and knelt. Even then he towered over me. The mahout asked if I wanted to ride the elephant. I shook my head vigorously and refused. Just then, Baba came out. He was wearing khaki knee-length trousers and a sola hat. He had a canvas bag on his back. He said to me, 'I'm riding this elephant into the jungle.' I was worried sick all day. Suppose some tiger ate up my Baba! But when he came back safe in the evening, I began liking the elephant. After all it must have been him who had killed the tiger and brought my Baba safely back home. So now I told the mahout that I wanted to ride the elephant. He gave me a big smile, picked me up and sat me on the howdah. He got up behind me and held me with one hand. With the other he slapped the floppy ears of the elephant and the beast stood up. I was wonderstruck. How did the elephant know what to do? But the wonder soon vanished. As I looked down from that height, I was so terrified that I started crying and the mahout had to help me get off again. That was the first and last time I rode an elephant.

After Jalpaiguri we went to Patuakhali. Then Kusthia, Jhargram, Chittagong, Kurseong. All the numerous little incidents crowd my mind with black-and-white scenes and my imagination lavishly adds colour to them. Which should I pick out, how much should I say, how will I sift fact from fiction?

As children my sister Tapati and I were like two buds on one stem. There were no indulgences in our lives but there was contentment. Our life was simple, our love for each other deep and we were a peaceful family. We didn't go to school till we were quite old. Ma taught us at home. We were very proud of our mother's BA degree in economics and mathematics from Delhi's Indraprastha College—as proud as children are these days of mothers with D.Litt. and D.Sc. qualifications. Ma's rule was that we had to do ten sums every afternoon. I would beg for the first ten sums from the set of questions in the maths book, which are usually the easier ones. She would choose five sums each from the end of two sets of questions, the most difficult. She thought that by doing this, we would be occupied all afternoon. Tapati and I rushed through lunch and finished the sums as fast as possible. Who could hold us back then? There was an open field waiting for us outside and a big, leafy mango tree to climb. There were sweet and sour jujube berries. The white wax apple fruits lay thick on the ground, waiting to be gathered. However, the biggest attraction for us was a gulancha vine covered with white, scented flowers. We sat among its leaves and played our favourite game. One of us would say the first line of a poem; the other said the next line. The whole poem, thus, would have to be recited, line by line, in this manner. Each line carried one point; if you missed a line, you lost a point. This game was a passion with us. We secretly memorized poems all the time.

Another thing we all really loved doing was running in the open field. We ran, just plain and simple. And as we ran, we laughed and tossed our heads, we let our curly locks swing in the wind, we ran for no reason, for the pure fun of it and with no competition in mind. Then we chatted for long hours, with each other and with our friends at home. These friends were the flowers in our garden. Tapati and I had divided them between us. The roses in the garden were mine and the dahlias were Tapati's; the kalmi flower bush was mine and the aparajita creeper was Tapati's. Of the two easy chairs on the veranda, one was mine and the other Tapati's. The left side of the bed was mine and the right side Tapati's. We talked to our friends, told them our favourite stories. They cried with Kakanmala and rejoiced with Kironmala when I told them the story from *Thakurmar Jhuli*. As I repeated the Mahabharata and the Ramayana to them in rhymes, committed to memory by repeated readings before Thakur-ma, they seemed to be spellbound by Karna's bravery and terrified to hear of Hanuman's arson in Lanka.

While these friends were ever present, the dominating factor in my life was my love for my grandmother. I did love my parents and my sister but the person I was closest to was Thakur-ma. This illiterate woman kept us enthralled with her keen intelligence and her spirited personality. As soon as I learned to read, barely one letter at a time, she ordered me to read aloud to her from the Mahabharata and the Ramayana. It was from these epics that I learned to read the more complicated diphthong letters. And if I got stuck after the first letter, she would simply supply the whole word from memory. That's how I learnt to read Bengali. At age six—we were in Kushtia at the time—when I finished reading out the 585 pages of Krittibas's *Ramayana,* and Kashiram Das's 1086-page *Mahabharata*, Thakur-ma made sandesh for me with her own hands as a reward and also treated some of my friends.

In 2003 my friend Shamsul Alam, principal of a college in

Dhaka, invited me to his city for his son's wedding. I happily accepted and requested, 'Shamsul bhai, can I ask you for a favour? You own land in Kusthia, I hear. Can you take me there for just one day?' Dear Shamsul Alam; may he live long! After the wedding festivities ended, we left for Kusthia by car along with a few friends. Unfortunately, it started raining very hard as soon as we began. The journey involved crossing the Gorai river en route but in that bad weather there were no boats prepared to ferry the car across the river. Others in our group said, 'How shall we go then, Didi? Should we turn back?' I stood there looking quite distressed. Then a tall boatman with a jet black beard and a gamcha tied round his head came forward. 'Leave the car behind, I'll take you across.' We all climbed into his boat and soon we were crossing the Gorai river, my eyes full of tears! Luckily, it was still raining, so I was saved embarrassment. We got off on the other side and took cycle rickshaws to Kusthia. The rain had let up for a bit by then. We went to the Kusthia Court Station and I searched for our old house. I asked the locals, 'Where is the sub-divisional officer's house? The white building right opposite the station. Don't you know it?' No, they knew of no such house. The new sub-divisional officer had a dazzling new house and the Kusthia Court Station had been completely revamped, and rows of hawkers' stalls stood opposite it. I decided to walk down the road to see if I could spot the house. A little way ahead, I found a huge iron gate near the place where I remembered our house stood and impulsively stepped in through a little gap in the gate. There I saw what I had come to see—our old house, now dilapidated and empty. The beautiful semi-circular steps were still there, and the veranda too. I stood transfixed, a deluge of memories flooding my head. Beyond the large front room I saw what used to be

Thakur-ma's veranda and mine. It was a corridor really; five feet by four feet at most. I saw Thakur-ma sitting with her bare back against one of the walls and gently waving a hand fan. I was sitting by the opposite wall reading the Ramayana: the big heavy book clutched in my small hands. Thakur-ma's lips moved slightly as she chewed on cloves after her lunch and her eyes gazed steadily at my face.

The vegetarian kitchen beside that passageway was where Ma and Thakur-ma would do their cooking. The utensils, the grinding stone and the spices would be neatly arranged on one side. Thakur-ma would sit down on the other side for her meals. On Ekadasi, the days on which Hindu widows traditionally fasted, she ate raw, soaked sago and milk in a heavy black marble bowl. I sat by the door watching her eat and asking her sometimes to give me just a little bit. She would pour some into my outstretched palm. It was heavenly! Where is that black marble bowl now? I haven't seen it at Ma's place in a long time. Did it break, or did we lose it? From the kitchen, or from life too?

A little distance away was the regular kitchen where Jogen-bhai held sway. I have already talked of how fond Jogen-bhai was of us two sisters. We never thought that we were plaguing him or disturbing his siesta by running into his room in the afternoon with our petty problems. I see him clearly now, squatting in front of the open fire and toasting bread which we munched happily. The picture that sprang to my mind was so vivid that my mouth started chewing of its own accord. All at once I began thinking of the time Calcutta was gripped by the scare of Japanese bombs. Moni-jetha had brought his family over to the safe refuge in Kusthia. My cousin Shotu and I used to quarrel over who would take the first piece of hot toast from Jogen-bhai who said he wouldn't give it to either of us if we kept squabbling like that. He would give it to Tapati or Runu, Shotu's sister, first. So we promised to stop fighting and he agreed to serve us before the other two. But if he gave Shotu the first piece, I would say, 'I'm your Boro Kuncha, how can you give it to her first?'

If he gave me the first piece, Shotu would say, 'I've come from Calcutta. She stays here but you gave it to her first?'

'See, this is what I mean by quarrelling,' Jogen-bhai would say. 'I'm not making toast for any of you.' So we had to beg and plead before he began toasting again. Toast made on a wire frame over an open fire is never as crunchy as the ones made in electric toasters. It gets crisp on top and remains soft inside and has quite a unique kind of taste. Shotu is now settled in England. Jogen-bhai has passed away. But the smell of his cooking still hung in the air of that kitchen in Kusthia. Walls so easily capture human smells and human memories within their bricks and mortar.

The guava tree outside the kitchen was gone; gone were the raw green guavas we loved to chew on. The well under the tree was dead. We used to peer into it when no grown-ups were around and see our faces clearly reflected in the water. This trick had been taught us by Moni, the son of Baba's clerk Baidyanath Mukhopadhyay. 'We don't need any mirrors. We can see our faces in a clear pond or a bowl of water or even a well. Look how beautiful it is,' Moni said. I realized that indeed my face looked much better in the reflection than in a mirror. It was a mysterious play of light and shade. Baidyanath's room in our Kusthia house still stood intact. I wondered where those people could be now.

Baidyanath Mukhopadhyay cannot be easily forgotten—a man perennially dressed in his long coat and a red peaked cap. It was over him that Baba and Thakur-ma had a run-in

for the first time. Thakur-ma had arranged for some puja to
be performed. Everything was ready but there was no sign
of the officiating priest. Baba had gone off to work. Ma and
Thakur-ma paced the floor anxiously. Then the appointed
priest's son came running to inform that his father had high
fever and would not be able to come. This was indeed a bind:
the auspicious hour for the puja to be performed would soon
pass. Thakur-ma called for Baidyanath. 'You're a Brahmin,
please perform the puja for me.' Baidyanath changed out of
his uniform and sat down with great pleasure to play the
role of priest. He didn't think it necessary to inform Baba.
Everyone knew that Thakur-ma's word was enough and no
one else's mattered. The puja was duly performed. Ma blew
the conch shell. Thakur-ma touched Baidyanath's feet and
handed him a fee. She mixed parched rice and curd in the
black stone bowl and doled it out as prasad. We all ate it
happily. However, Baba was very displeased when he heard
of all this. He explained, 'I'm angry not because he is my
clerk. But you don't know his background, Ma. He's a very
dishonest man. I could have sacked him but I didn't want him
to starve. Instead, I keep a very strict eye on him. Now that
you have made your obeisances to him, he'll think no end
of himself. Merely being born in a Brahmin's house doesn't
make one a true Brahmin. '

Thakur-ma's reply was curt. 'If I have to keep track of
all the Brahmins whom you have saved from starvation and
refrained from sacking, I will never find a priest to do my
puja.' The dispute caused the atmosphere in the house to hang
heavy for two whole days. Then the air cleared naturally, as
it always does.

Beyond Baidyanath's room was the sub-divisional officer's
office. Between the office and our house was a sort of an

outer corner room. In 1943, during the man-made famine, long queues of men and women stood before the room. Ma measured out bowls of uncooked rice for each person and Thakur-ma gave it away. I learnt later that Baba had to argue hard with higher officials to get some relief for the people in his area. When Baba was transferred from Kusthia, the people were in tears. They even wrote a long poem for him: 'Dear friend, will you really leave us in this time of distress?'

I strolled around outside the house, revelling in the old memories. There used to be an iron ladder which led to the roof. One day I was so mad with Ma—because I thought she didn't love me at all—that I decided to kill myself. I would jump from the rooftop. I climbed up three or four steps and stopped. The ladder was visible from Baba's office window and he was inside, working. Going up to the roof was absolutely forbidden because it had no parapet. I kept sitting on the fourth rung of the ladder for a long time. Baba didn't come out of his office. At last I lost patience and abandoned the idea of suicide. That wretched ladder that had made me a promise-breaker was not there any more. But I looked for it and managed to spot it a little later. It was lying in the grass near a pond—all rusty and broken but not lost.

Nothing has been lost: Baba and Thakur-ma, Jogen-bhai and Baidyanath, the Ramayana and the veranda, the guava tree with its raw green fruit and the well to see our faces in. Perhaps they may not be visible, yet they remain inside my eyes and my heart.

Before I came away I asked my companions to take a picture of me sitting on the steps. They did but the picture, as was only natural, came out looking blurred. The real pictures are the memories of light and shade that reside within us. When it was time to leave, I came up to the gate of our Kusthia house and looked to my right. One night, many years ago, Ma had escorted Thakur-ma and me up to the jamrul tree near the gate. Baba, carrying two bags, was taking us to the station. I was going with Thakur-ma to our village home for Durga puja. Thakur-ma's sons and many of her close relatives were now earning fairly well and the family was better off. The village puja was to be held in our house. Thakur-ma said, 'Come with me to see our ancestral home.' The prospect made me very excited. Ten times each day I counted down the days when we would set out together. I would leave my parents but I didn't care. Thakur-ma asked Ma to make four new dresses for me to wear on the four main puja days. I could wear one for the journey; that would be enough. Ma suggested mildly that I might need an extra one in case my dress got dirty on the way. Thakur-ma said, 'There is no need; I will wash it. Just add another undergarment. And don't forget to add a pair of slippers.'

I said, 'Then you should buy slippers too.'

Baba said, 'Ma, let me buy you a pair of cloth slippers at least. Journey by train and steamer and walking on paved roads would hurt your feet.

Thakur-ma refused. 'Just listen to the boy. Do village women ever wear shoes?'

Baba tried to argue. 'This is not a village; it's a town. Do village women travel at all? You're taking a train.'

Thakur-ma's answer was prompt. 'Yes, I am. But my feet will still remain mine. They won't belong to the train.'

Thus Thakur-ma's little tin trunk held a few borderless white cotton saris that Hindu widows used to wear those days. Two of them were new meant for Mahashtami and Bijoya Dashami—the two important puja days. Her prayer beads and her shalgram shila, the black stone that traditionally symbolized

Lord Vishnu, wrapped in a red cloth and a volume of the Bhagavad Gita were carefully packed. I had a leather suitcase with four new dresses, one undergarment, four underpants and two storybooks—Abanindranath Tagore's masterpieces, *Nalak* and *Rajakahini*. Thakur-ma warned me not to take them. I wouldn't have time to read there and I would lose the books. I didn't listen to her but later realized how right she was.

How do I describe how thrilling it all was? I and the person I loved most in the world were travelling together. I spent the night with my head on Thakur-ma's lap. In the morning she fed me puffed rice, bananas and the crunchy brown sugar candies called batasha that we offer for puja. She managed to buy a little milk. And when we got on to the steamer at Goalondo, why books, I forgot about Thakur-ma even! The water was so deep, the beauty of the Padma–Meghna rivers majestically sweeping both the banks was so stunning, the people on the steamer wore such an amazing variety of clothes and spoke an even more amazing variety of dialects. I could only stand and stare.

Once in Dhaka, we hired a boat to cross the Buriganga river—a canal leading off from the Buriganga was to take us to our native village. The swaying boat made me feel so sleepy that I clung on to Thakur-ma and nodded off. When I woke up the boat had reached our private ghat. Relatives and neighbours were gathered to receive Thakur-ma. She got off the boat and I followed. We entered the house, which I didn't like much; but I liked all the people I met. A sweet housewife, nearly as old as my Ma, came up to me with her head covered and said, 'You are my aunt-in-law; should I touch your feet?' I was taken aback. How could I be the aunt-in-law of a woman so much older than me? I knew that Thakur-ma was Ma's mother-in-law.

So I said, 'Not me, it's Thakur-ma who is your aunt-in-law.'

But the woman still insisted. 'Not at all. It's you who are my shasuri. Because you happen to be my husband's aunt. Come to my room, I'll give you chirar moa.' Now that's one sweet I really like, so I readily agreed. She laughed. 'Haw! Now that you are an old woman, no wonder you crave for food!' I took my fill of chirar moa and when I went home I asked Thakur-ma how it was that the woman called me her aunt-in-law. She explained that the entire village was on kinship terms with us. The people who lived in the village had ties with us from my grandfather's time or even from two generations before. She was also certain that everyone would be fond of me. Thakur-ma didn't have time to explain any more; she was busy making arrangements for the puja and I was busy too, visiting all those houses where I was so welcome. I played with the children on the banks of the canal under the tamarind and mango trees, my dusty, unkempt hair flying loose in the wind. I would run to the place where the puja was to be held, off and on, to take a peek at the work in progress. The images of the deities, Durga, Kartik, Ganesh, Lakshmi, Saraswati, all grouped under one arched frame made of pith, looked divine. The demon, lying at Goddess Durga's feet, was pierced by her spear, and, at the same time bitten by a snake and clawed by the lion which the goddess rode. His mouth was wide open, screaming in agony. The entire village crowded into the puja venue but what held my interest was the raw tamarind hanging low on the tree outside and the few small boats on the canal. Some boats were open—meant only for men—while others had little roofed shelters for families. I saw two or three women with babies in their arms. I wondered where these boats came from and where they were going. How did the people on the boat sleep and what did they eat? Thakur-ma had instructed me to attend the puja during the anjali ceremony when we all prayed together. I would quickly ask the goddess for her blessings, 'Give me brains, give me knowledge,' and then hurry back to the canal. But in the evenings when the priest performed the beautiful arati ritual, marking the end of the day's festivities, honouring the deity with lighted lamps even as two drum-beaters played their massive drums, and people danced with clay pots filled with smoking incense, I would be quite mesmerized. I then felt an indescribable longing to own something, or to be taken away somewhere—it was a strange feeling, one I could not define.

Can four days pass in the blink of an eye? They do during Durga puja. The last day arrived; and it was decided that the immersion of the images, the traditional method of bidding farewell to the gods for the year, would be done from a boat. Thakur-ma didn't want me to go along but I insisted. So my cousin Phul-dada held me by one hand and a newly discovered distant cousin who had become a great friend in the last few days held the other and I jumped into the boat merrily. But soon all joy vanished at the thought that such a beautiful goddess was to be cast away into the water. An immersion makes everyone heavy-hearted. It's the pain of bidding farewell to the daughter who is leaving her parents' home.

I turned to my newfound cousin and asked him to give me Goddess Durga's crown as a keepsake. He retrieved the crown from the water without anyone else noticing and kept it on the roof of our house to dry. 'Put it in your bag later. And come again next year,' he said. At the last minute before I left I forgot the crown and I couldn't go back again the next year either. How could I? Thakur-ma herself passed away.

We had just left Kushtia and gone to Jhargram where my father was transferred. Thakur-ma didn't come with us to Jhargram; she had fallen ill and had to be in Calcutta for treatment. My mother took me and Tapati to her natal home at Berhampore since she was expecting her third child. All at once, I fell ill with a severe case of typhoid when our youngest sister Pronoti was born. I heard later that Baba had said, 'If Bharati doesn't survive, I don't want this new girl.' Well, I did survive. And Pronoti, whom Baba had spurned, became his most favourite child. There really is no point being jealous. Going purely by her human qualities, Pronoti is certainly the best of Baba's children.

Ma took one-month-old Pronoti and convalescent me to Calcutta to be at Thakur-ma's bedside. Thakur-ma didn't suffer too long. One morning in the Bhowanipore house, all of Thakur-ma's children were sitting around her—except for her eldest son, our Ranga-jethamoshai. She opened her eyes wide and looked around, as if looking for him. The eldest always has a special spot in a mother's heart. Moni-pishima called out to her, 'Ma, how are you feeling now?'

'Don't call out to me any more. Let me go,' Thakur-ma said and turned over to face the wall.

Moni-pishima wept. 'If you turn your face away, to whom shall we turn, Ma?'

Thakur-ma must have heard this but she didn't reply. Hours passed. Late in the afternoon her sons lifted up her bed and placed it out on the veranda and Thakur-ma breathed her last in the open. Thakur-ma had an amazing capacity for being loved and losing their eighty-two-year-old mother made all her children and their spouses, aged between thirty-five and fifty-five, feel like motherless three-year-olds. Baba held her hand between his palms and wept silent tears. My soft-hearted sister Tapati sat beside him and stroked his back and wept. Chhoto-pishima said, 'Don't cry, Byomkesh bhai. You've lost one mother but another sits beside you.' Baba put a hand on Tapati's head. I did not cry. Like Ma, I don't cry easily. I watched Thakur-ma as she lay there, quite still. She had no fan in her hand; her mouth which constantly moved as she chewed cloves, was still. Her eyes did not rest on me as they did when I read the Ramayana. The borderless white cotton sari wrapped her and a *namabali*, which is a piece of ochre cloth with lines of prayer printed on it, was spread over her. A little of her bare shoulder was visible, and a little of the black thread she wore round her neck.

Evening approached, and her sons carried her out on their shoulders. Thakur-ma was gone; and with her my childhood left.

FORMAL EDUCATION

My first school was in Kushtia—the Charulata Girls' School. It had classes up to the sixth form only. Baba secured help from the government and local people to advance the school up to Class X. He got us two sisters admitted and we studied there for four months or so. Our favourite teacher was Bela Datta Gupta who is now a sociologist. She had just passed her MA then and was slim, fair and sophisticated. I still remember the big shouting-at we got from her. She had asked us, 'Whose class is it now?'

'Kishkindhya babu's!' we shouted together.

'His name is not Kishkindhya, it's Krishnendu,' she told us sternly. 'You must talk respectfully about your teachers. Don't you know that Kishkindhya is the mythical forest abode of monkeys described in the Ramayana?'

We bowed our heads in shame. We really did not know his proper name because everyone called him Kishkindhya. It is remarkable how awkward names stick to some people!

There was a girl in Tapati's class who was blind from birth. We used to feel sorry for her but she appeared unconcerned about it. The teachers didn't treat her differently from the rest, although they must have kept an eye on her. Chhabi Chatterjee in Tapati's class wore skirts and blouses. We two were wide-eyed in wonder. Only English girls dressed like that, not Bengalis, surely? 'Chhabi Chatterjee is so smart, Didi,' Tapati used to say and I nodded in agreement.

Tapati was in Class III; they wrote with pencils. I, in a higher class, was permitted to use pen and ink. There were no separate desks for each girl as they have in many city schools now. Five girls shared a long bench and a long desk. There was a hole in the desk in front of each girl to hold ink pots. My mother made ink for me at home. She borrowed an empty bottle of Quink ink from Baba, filled it with water and dropped in it an ink pellet bought from the local stationery shop. I had a wooden pen with a slit at one end where I fitted a shiny gold-coloured nib. I would take that nib out ten times a day and fit it back again proudly. After all, I wrote with a pen while poor Tapati still used a pencil!

We had joined the school in the middle of the year. On the first day in history class I saw the picture of a headless bust of King Kanishka. The picture put me off history. As for geography, I had to trace out a map of India, colour the different provinces with crayon and rub blotting paper on it to smoothen out the wax. How could I manage without Tapati's help? She was the one who was good at drawing. But yes, I did manage to go one up on her when I crocheted a little bag in class. It was orange with a matching orange button clasp. Tapati was quite impressed. I didn't have the heart to use it; I put it away like a precious thing.

I visited Kushtia and my old school in 2003. It is a fine big school now with a new name: Kushtia Government High School for Girls. The headmaster, who knew I was visiting, was waiting for me. He welcomed me warmly and called his best student over to meet me. I was really gratified. Bangladeshis are well known for their hospitality. He fed me sandesh, singara, minced mutton fried inside a potato casing done in the Bengali style, and cordially asked, 'When will you come again?'

There was no school in Jhargram where Baba was transferred after Kushtia. Ma taught me at home as she had always done. But when Baba was transferred to Chittagong, we were admitted to Nandankanan Girls' School, Tapati in Class VI and I in Class VII. The school was a half-hour walk from home. Kamala-didi, the school ayah, arrived around nine and called from the gate, 'Khuki-i-i.' We came running for she would scold if we were late. School ayahs had to go from house to house to collect the girl students because in those days society frowned on girls walking through the streets unescorted. That was the only concession to convention that Nandankanan School made. In all other matters, the school had a modern outlook. Hindu girls wore saris as well as dresses. Almost half the girls were Muslim; some of them wore saris but most wore salwar-kameez and their heads were uncovered. There were no burqas to be seen. Noorjahan-didi ranked first in Class VIII. In Class VII, I came first, Reba second and Maleka Azam, my best friend, came third. In Tapati's class,

Seba Som and Kamal Akhtar were strong rivals for the first position. All this was happening in 1946. The whole country was seething with political turmoil which affected the school students too. Frequent strikes were called; senior girls made passionate speeches and related with great pride and emotion the valiant tales of Kalpana Dutta and Pritilata Waddedar, women revolutionaries from Chittagong. That is when I first heard the names of Lila Roy's student organization, the Dipali Sangha of Dhaka, and the Mahila Atma Raksha Samiti of Calcutta. I also heard there that incomparable song sung in the name of Khudiram Bose, the young eighteen-year-old revolutionary who was hanged to death: 'Let me go, Mother, I prithee. I shall wear the noose with a smile for my countrymen to see.'

In spite of all the excitement and political awareness, when classes were held, the teachers taught us conscientiously. They were extremely generous in their affection towards us. The lady who taught us Sanskrit was known as Sadhu-ma. She once gave me twenty-four and a half out of twenty-five for a class test. In my childish arrogance I opened the grammar book and challenged her, showing that I had made no spelling mistake. Sadhu-ma smiled a little and said that there was a printing mistake in my book. 'I can't give marks for spelling errors, no matter whose error it is.' There was such charm in the way she taught us and in the way she spoke that I fell in love with Sanskrit. And that love remains with me even today. A Sanskrit sloka makes me feel peaceful and content.

Sudha-didi taught us English. She had a beautiful voice and a perfect accent. Her only fault was that she favoured me too much. In one exam paper I had confused a quote from Rani Durgaboti with Chandbibi and written the story of Chandbibi instead of Durgaboti, which I should have done. Sudha-didi said, 'Bharati has caught the spirit of the words very well. So I've given her half the marks instead of a zero.' I said nothing. Perhaps I didn't want to embarrass her. It could also be that I happily accepted the bonus marks however undeserved I knew they were.

Nandankanan was a good school. Nevertheless, Ma shifted us the next year to the famous Khastagir Girls' High School. The high standards it maintained would be rare in any part of the world. Let me choose a few examples. I was admitted to Class VIII. In my first Bengali class, Moyna-didi—in Khastagir we called our teachers by their nicknames; Moyna-di's proper name was Jyotsna—came in and wrote on the board a subject for an essay: two lines from a song by Tagore! Roughly translated:

> Spring has come to the forests,
> Splashing colour in leaves, fruits flowers and trees.

How could I, the daughter of a mother who knew English and Hindi, tackle a subject like that in Bengali? The next week Moyna-didi chose two other tough lines of poetry for an essay on the advent of the monsoons. A rough translation:

> New monsoon clouds have gathered in the east
> Sounding thundering kettledrums.

Moyna-didi returned both the essays with the comment: 'Bharati's Bengali is atrocious.' Which was actually quite true. But my love for the language began from Khastagir School. Our 'Rapid Reader' was the unabridged version of Madhusudan Dutta's *Meghnadvad Kavya*, that brilliant piece written in blank verse based on the Ramayana which made a hero out of the anti-hero Meghnad, Ravana's son. How beautiful it sounded when Moyna-didi recited the epic poem in her mellifluous voice. Even to this day, on some quiet evenings I seem to hear her reading Ravana's bitter-sad words of mockery addressed to the ocean that had allowed itself to be bridged by Rama's troops:

> How lovely that garland round your neck,
> O Ocean! For shame, O King of Waters
> Is this worthy of such as you . . .!

The low marks I got for Bengali vied with the low marks I got for needlework and 'drawing and painting' (the term art class was not commonly used then). Sewing was beyond me, no matter how much our teacher Renu-didi took me to task. How could I catch up with the Class VIII girls who knew complicated stitches like 'donthread', had learnt about dress-making and knitted wool at great speed? And as for art, I remember our teacher Buju-didi had asked us to paint a little girl sitting in front of a doll's house in a flower garden dressing her doll. We were to use proper shading to bring out the beauty of the flowers and the girl's dress. Oh hell! The only thing to do was to catch hold of Bonu, the skilled artist in our class. 'If you do my painting, I'll do your English précis, Bonu. But don't make it too perfect or Buju-didi will know.' Bonu obliged. I held up the painting for Buju-didi to see. She smiled sweetly and said, 'Very good. Now you've learnt how to sketch and paint, Bharati.'

I blurted out the truth without a second thought. 'I didn't do it.'

Buju-di's smile vanished at once. 'I know the drawing style of each and every girl in this class. This is done by Bonu. You confessed right away, so I'm not punishing you. You might get two extra marks by cheating for just one day. But the lie will stay with you for the rest of your life.' I bowed my head and went back to my seat.

I went back to Buju-didi a few days later. 'I'll never be any good at drawing, Buju-didi. I can't even draw a circle.'

This time she gave me an affectionate smile of encouragement. 'Let go of the circle. You start with squares. You're trying, so you will succeed.' Buju-didi's words didn't come true. I never mastered the art of drawing or painting or any form of art for that matter.

The sense of beauty and good taste that permeated Khastagir School spread like the soft glow of dawn and the gentle breeze that blows at that hour. The paintings and handicrafts put up on its walls displayed the students' talents; as did the dance dramas of Rabindranath Tagore which were performed annually. The school gym for physical training was run with equal care. The large playground was spotlessly clean, not a scrap of paper or discarded nutshells were to be found because Mini-di herself inspected the place during the lunch break. Mini-di, Suprabha Dasgupta, was headmistress at Khastagir School. She was extremely fair; her salt-and-pepper hair was knotted into a little low chignon, and she wore a sari with a brooch on the left shoulder to hold the train in place. This sari never creased or crumpled all day. She was neat and clean from head to toe, not just in looks but in her nature too. Mini-di taught us English comprehension once a week. She read out an essay for half an hour and the next day we wrote down what we remembered of it. Once she sent for me and asked, 'Have you read the Bible?' I looked down and shook my head. 'You come by the school bus—one of the first batch, I'm told. That's forty minutes before school begins. There'll be a copy of the Bible on the third table in the library. Read it to learn good English.'

We studied in Khastagir School for seven months before the partition happened. Baba was then transferred to Kurseong. We left Chittagong on the evening of 16 August 1947. We had put up an Indian flag at one window and a Pakistani flag at another. I salute Chittagong. In 1946–47, when Calcutta was embroiled in Hindu–Muslim riots, in Chittagong we walked to school safely in broad daylight—to Nandankanan earlier and later by bus to Khastagir. In the afternoon we participated in extra-curricular activities at Monimela, a well-known all-Bengal children's association those days under Kamal Akhtar and Ranjan Barua. At Nandankanan School, Maleka Azam and I shared our tiffin from the same box; at Khastagir we learnt about the Koran from Firdausi. Jainal Abedin-chacha and Sailesh Talukdar-meshomoshai came for regular evening chat sessions in Baba's sitting room. Communal fratricide did not dare raise its ugly head in the historic, firebrand city of Chittagong.

We were put into a school in Kurseong where all girls' schools were run by missionaries. We had to walk two kilometres each day over hilly pathways to reach St Joseph's Girls' High School. When the rains come in Kurseong and Darjeeling, it pours for days on end. We wore translucent plastic raincoats to school; mine was white and Tapati's blue. Sometimes leeches made their unerring way right up our legs up to our knees and sucked our blood merrily.

There were only four Bengali girls in my class—the rest were all Nepali. I really liked my Nepali classmates. They were so full of life, always smiling, and talking incessantly about their love interests. Who would not be excited at even a whiff of romance at my age? Besides, they were all very good at sports.

Especially Margaret and Kamala Subba could have been world class in basketball had they got an opportunity for proper training. Once they got hold of the ball, that was it. They'd charge the field like lightning and put the ball straight into the net. Mixing with those girls helped me pick up spoken Nepalese quite well. Whenever I met people I greeted them with a big smile and said, '*Ramro chha?*—Are you well? But I had one bitter experience. At the prize distribution ceremony at the end of the year, I got a first prize for every single subject. But the prize for best student went to a local girl. The next day I went to my class teacher with a sullen face and held out my report book. She snatched it from my hand, took eighty marks off the total and signed under it. 'Now you are second,' she said. How was that possible? I understood somehow that there was some other reason for this irregularity. That was my first-hand experience of the rising political tensions in the hills.

I left that school in disgust and went to my Didi-ma's place in Berhampore. Kashiswari Girls' High School was one of the earliest girls' schools in the district towns of Bengal. I was happy, the teachers were good, and my classmates were friendly. But I heard that Mini-di had become headmistress of a new government school in Jalpaiguri. I decided in a flash that I had to go there. I packed my belongings, sent a telegram off to Baba and boarded a train to Jalpaiguri. Mini-di was stunned to see me. 'What are you doing here? No one told me you would come.'

'I'm going to study in this school.'

'Not possible,' Mini-di said. 'This is a new school and has not yet been set up properly. There's no place for you to stay in our tiny makeshift hostel. You'll have to give up additional maths. Your career will be ruined. Just go back.' But I had not come all the way only to go back. I practically forced myself on Mini-di and the school. Thank god for that! It was one of the best decisions I ever made.

I have seen very few people like Mini-di who can live up to their ideals and love truth with their heart and soul. Our small school building, called Noor Manzil, was three-storeyed. Two tiny rooms on the top floor served as a hostel. One other small room there was for Mini-di. The afternoon classroom was used for evening study and the staff room doubled up as a dining room. Three other teachers had come with Mini-di from Khastagir: Moyna-di, Buju-di and Runu-di. Other teachers—they weren't from Khastagir—were Parul-didi for Bengali, and Anima-didi for English. They taught us so well and with such loving care that learning was pure pleasure. When school ended at four o'clock, the eight of us hostel girls sat down happily to eat our tiffin. A new item was served every day: fried beaten rice with grated coconut, puffed rice with fried groundnuts, spicy stir-fried green chickpeas, taal fruit fritters, semolina pudding. After that we went to the playground. Soon after, it was time for me to rush back upstairs to Mini-di's room. She sat on an easy chair and I sat at her feet. She read out from Rabindranath Tagore's works—poetry, drama, songs, *Muktadhara, Raktakarabi* and my all-time favourite, *Raja*. My love of Rabindranath is a gift from Mini-di. It was through her that I plunged into his works. One a creative genius, the other an ideal teacher.

Mini-di taught us gardening on holidays. We grew potatoes, cabbages, cauliflowers, spinach, aubergines, and tomatoes. When the potatoes and tomatoes came up strong and healthy, Mini-di told me one day, 'Never forget them; they have contributed to the greening of your life.' As we walked through the garden, she modified a line from Rabindranath's *Sphulinga* and recited, 'Remember the trees that gave you shade and also the grass that made your life green.'

One day I had not gone out to play. Mini-di found me on the veranda engrossed in a book. She said, 'Why are you reading in the afternoon? It's playtime now.'

I replied, 'I heard that a boy in the district Jalpaiguri school has done very well in the annual exam. I want to study a little harder. How many students would get high ranks and scholarships from the same district?'

Mini-di said, 'If you rank among the top ten in the university, I will be certainly very happy. My new school will get recognition. But what I would really like is that you build your own character and personality so well that when you visit someone's house or meet someone, the person will say, "I met Bharati today." Meeting you and talking to you should be a joyous experience. Spread a song of happiness wherever you go.'

In my matriculation examination—known as secondary nowadays—I was ranked among the first ten among boys and girls combined and first among girls in the university. Girls do very well in exams these days. In 1950, I was the first girl to have achieved such a distinction after many years. Mini-di wrote to me, 'You are the only one in my whole teaching career to rank among the first ten. I am delighted. The girls in the school are also very happy and wanted a holiday. I refused. Because, do you know, Chhaya in your class has failed? Can one person's glory assuage another's sorrow? Today I have gathered a flower and a thorn at the same time.'

What we now call higher secondary was then known as Intermediate Arts or IA. I studied for the exam at the Berhampore Girls' College, although Baba had been transferred to Calcutta by then. It was a mofussil college and there were not many students. But the teaching standard was good and Priti Gupta, the principal, was completely dedicated to the institution. Everything, be it studies, sports, acting or singing, was given equal importance. Nihar-didi taught us history, Bina-didi Bengali, Himangshu-babu English and Kalihar-babu—who had also been Priti-di's teacher—taught us logic. Nirmalya Bagchi gave me extra coaching in history for free. He came in the morning on holidays and would teach for no less than two to three hours. He was an inspired teacher, and it felt as though he led me by the hand to the Forum in ancient Rome, to the Parthenon in distant Athens and to the podium for Pericles's 'Funeral Oration'. We needed a long time to get back to Berhampore.

Himangshu-babu taught us English prose. Reza-ul Karim sahib taught English poetry. How can I describe this wonderful man? I have never met a Muslim holy man but I have seen Karim sahib. He had the innocence of a child and a heart full of affection, absolute magnanimity and pure love of humanity and a radiant smile that I believe can never be seen on anyone but a pir. He had a chronic pain in one leg, so he walked with a stick. I used to have mock quarrels with him. 'Karim sahib, I'm very upset with you. You love Karuna-didi more than me.' (Karuna Bhattacharya, who became later pro-vice chancellor, finance, of Calcutta University, was two years senior to me.) He smiled a toothless smile. The charge was true, so he said nothing. Can a pir ever lie?

Our crafts teacher was a man whom we all called Khuku-dada. Perhaps his mother wanted a daughter so she named him Khuku, or girl. It could also be that he looked like a cute, sweet-natured girl as a child, hence the feminine name. He was a talented, peaceable and charming person. Under his guidance, the girls, on festive occasions, would paint splendid alpana, which could be compared favourably with the artwork done by students of Kalabhavan in Santiniketan. The finest examples of art were to be seen on Saraswati puja day. Almost all of Berhampore would come to our college to admire the artwork that the students had done. In the evening, rows of finely decorated lamps were arrayed before the dazzling white image of Goddess Saraswati, poised gracefully with books and her many-stringed veena in her hand. In every corner of the room, marvellous alpana designs paid tribute to her inspiring presence.

The standard of the sports we played was not bad at all for a mofussil town. While we didn't have much by way of equipment or great training facilities, the girls were very enthusiastic. The best sportswoman amongst us was Satyavati, a girl who had come all the way from far-off Patna to study at the Berhampore Girls' College.

During my time at the college I stayed in the hostel and not at my grandparents' place. The food there was absolutely basic: tea and two slices of dry bread—without butter or jam, not to mention cheese—in the morning. At 10 a.m., before classes began, lunch was served which comprised rice, watery dal, a mixed vegetable dish and fish curry. After college, we had dinner at 6 p.m. Rice, dal and vegetables again. I don't remember if there was roti or not. The hostel charges were so low that they couldn't afford to give us anything fancier. Nowadays I hear that girls take turns to organize better meals; we tried nothing of that sort. The matron, whom we called Mashima, took care of everything. She was a thin, wiry widow with a cheerful smile. She tried her best, but unfortunately she wasn't very efficient. We all loved her dearly, though. If any of us had a specific complaint, she would look into it and try to find a solution. We were like her family.

I was friendly with all the girls in the hostel. One of my close friends, Gita, had a sweet singing voice. Her daughter Indrani reads the news on television these days and sings beautifully. Sati was another dear friend. Her father was a schoolteacher in Muragachha, then an insignificantly small town near Berhampore. I was a guest at their house a couple of times when we had a break of two or three days. We stayed up half the night, chatting. The next morning, for breakfast, we had hot puffed rice with grated coconut and groundnuts which her mother served us in bed. In the evening her father went out to teach at a student's house. We followed him with a lantern in hand. He taught. His pupil's mother brought him a cup of tea and two biscuits. She gave us one coconut laddu each. We nibbled at it with great relish. On the way back late at night, the lantern light on the narrow uneven path seemed to intensify the darkness all around us. It frightened us but there is fun in that kind of fear. Gita and Sati don't live in Berhampore any more but there are many others who still do—Niyoti, Bharati, Kona, Bhabarani, Nihar, Roma, Lakshmi. Their lives still revolve around the place; I try to see them whenever some work takes me to Berhampore.

From Berhampore Girls' College, I ranked among the first ten among boys and girls for my intermediate examination in University of Calcutta the, as I had done for my matriculation. This time, I was ranked higher which made Priti-di very happy. I moved to Presidency College, Calcutta, for my undergraduate studies. The trepidation with which I entered that great institution still remains with me. On the top of the building, a non-functioning clock perched on a tower. Yet, despite its apparent uselessness, it proudly announced its presence: 'Look, here I am.' I saw it from a distance, crossed the gatekeeper's room to my left and approached the portico.

Three steps led to the veranda beyond which was the majestic stairway leading to the first floor. It was impossible not to stop there once and think of the luminaries of the nineteenth and twentieth centuries who had walked that way—Henry Derozio, Madhusudan Dutt, Bankimchandra, Ramgopal Ghose, et al.

The mid-twentieth century, especially the decade of the fifties, was a golden era for Presidency College, both for the quality of its teachers and for the brilliance of its students. In our arts building, Taraknath Sen was a stellar presence in the English department. This department also had other renowned scholars like Subodh Sengupta, Amal Bhattacharya and Tarapada Mukherjee. In Bengali, we had Debipada Bhattacharya and Bhudeb Chaudhuri; in philosophy, the sage-like Gopinath Bhattacharya; in economics, the celebrated Bhabatosh Dutt and Dhiresh Bhattacharya. In the Sanskrit College, Gourinath Shastri reigned radiantly. Those who opted for Sanskrit had to walk across to Sanskrit College for their classes. Although I was not a student of Sanskrit, I went along with them and slipped into Gourinath Shastri's class as an intruder to listen to his lectures on Kalidas's *Abhigyanashakuntalam*. It was an experience to remember.

I studied for honours in history. The legendary Sushobhan Sarkar was one of our professors. He would pace the classroom as he expounded history in a measured tone. We traversed the barriers of time with ease and delved into the history of European civilization in the seventeenth, eighteenth and nineteenth centuries. The European Renaissance, the rise of the middle class, the significance of the French Revolution all came alive in his eloquent expositions. Though a fervent believer in communism, Professor Sarkar never preached politics in class. Nevertheless, the majority of his students embraced leftist politics.

One professor who was not overshadowed by the scintillating presence of Susobhan Sarkar was Mahmud sahib. Famous earlier in Dhaka as Bachchu-mia, a great sportsman and football fan, very friendly with students, he was a colourful personality on campus. He was a wonderful teacher too. When he vividly dramatized the failure of the Athenian expedition to Sicily, history took on the flavour of literature. I was quite close to him, as were many of his students throughout the years. My schooling had been in my mother tongue throughout; I was afraid therefore that I would find lectures in the English language a little difficult to follow. Who but Professor Mahmud should I confide in? The room echoed with his laughter when he heard me. 'Give it some time. Your fears will vanish. And there'll be fireworks, I promise.' How many teachers can reassure you and inspire you in such a fashion?

Bhupesh Mukherjee taught us the history of the Mughal period in India. When he lectured us on Akbar's reign, he would become so involved that stepping down from the dais, he would himself take on the role of the great emperor. When explaining the secular nature of Akbar's world view, and din-i-ilahi, the new moderate religion that Akbar innovated, Bhupesh Mukherjee would get very animated indeed. And the way in which he castigated fundamentalists, both Hindu and Muslim, was simply incomparable. Sashi Choudhury taught us the history of ancient India. He was a genuine scholar but it took me time to get used to his English accent. By the time I caught up, he had left Mohenjodaro and Harappa far behind and entered Pataliputra, the capital of Chandragupta Maurya's empire.

The professors who taught at Presidency College in the 1950s were all exceptional scholars. The students were no less worthy. When I entered the third year, spread over several subjects and several years, from the first to the sixth (you could do your Master's through Presidency, though classes were held in the Calcutta University building), there were brilliant students like Sipra Sarkar, Rathin Sengupta, Ashin Das Gupta, Sukhamoy Chakraborty, Amartya Sen, Benoy Choudhury, Barun De, Nitish Sen Gupta, Jyotirmoy Dutta, Partha Sarathi Gupta, Subir Dutta, Pradip Das, Mihir Rakshit, Meenakshi Bose, Meenakshi Chaliha, Arjun Sen Gupta, Alakananda Das Gupta, Dilip Bhadra, Jatikumar Sen Gupta. Within the next three years, more arrived—Amiya Bagchi, Nabaneeta Deb, Sabyasachi Bhattacharya, Sumit Sarkar, Tirthankar Bose and Mandakranta Rai Chaudhuri. It takes all my self-restraint to avoid the temptation of launching into tales about each and every one of them. But I must speak of at least three.

One was Sukhamoy Chakraborty in economics. Everyone called him a walking encyclopaedia. There was nothing flashy or flamboyant about him and he was widely respected for the depth of his knowledge. India is the poorer now for his untimely death.

Ashin Das Gupta was another—one of the finest historians of our time. Ashin was dark and quite ordinary-looking, but his eyes sparkled like diamonds and flashed with an ever-present sense of amusement. Many years later, when I was teaching in Bethune College and he in Presidency, we used to walk together on many a Saturday to a lane in Bowbazar where seminars were held at Professor Shibapada Sen's Institute of Historical Studies. Ashin-da would talk about history all the way—the teaching methodology followed in Cambridge; the 'Cambridge School' approach to historical studies; and his own thoughts on the captivating story of trade and politics surrounding the Indian Ocean. He was in the middle of an intense romance with Uma Ray at the time, an extremely attractive woman. In later years the way Uma took care of Ashin-da during his grave and protracted illness, I came to appreciate the rare qualities she possessed. Today she is widely respected as a scholar and a fine human being.

Amartya Sen was phenomenal—the way he looked, the way he spoke, his choice of words and his manner of delivery were so attractive. He never carried any books, only a thin notebook. You would think he'd come to college for a carefree chat with his friends. It was only when he spoke that one realized his total dedication to Saraswati, the goddess of learning. It was little wonder, then, that all the girls were in love with him and all the boys held him in awe. Arunava Das Gupta, then a first year student, and very talented, went so far as to compose a eulogy on him for the mural magazine *Deali*. A rough translation of the Bengali composition would read:

> A shining light wreathes his face,
> He speaks in a measured tone,
> He isn't fashionably dressed,
> Still more or less holds his own.
> ....
> At debate he's an ace
> The immensely popular Amartya Sen,
> Lights up this earth—alone.

I've forgotten some of the words in between. Amartya might remember. He hasn't forgotten his old college or his old friends, even after he won the Nobel Prize for economics.

In our time—I joined in mid-1952—girls were admitted to Presidency College only from the third year. We all wore saris. Jeans were unthinkable; even the salwar-kameez was not considered to be a viable option. Saris then were of average quality; very few girls wore matching blouses or even ironed their saris daily. No one wore lipstick, and no one carried fancy hairstyles. Only Meenakshi Chaliha put her hair up in a high chignon, which the rest of us envied. She taught Tapati how to do it but my sister didn't quite master it. The only concession to fashion was a little kajal, used to line the eyes; the most common make-up was lining the eyes with kajal, a red kumkum bindi in the middle of the forehead and face powder, which, in some cases, was rather excessive. We wore ordinary flat slippers. I don't remember seeing any high heels, except on Alakananda Das Gupta. Most of the boys wore ordinary shirts and trousers while some favoured the traditional dhoti-kurta. In class all the girls would sit on one side. We never thought of sitting alongside the boys and sharing textbooks with them like they do these days. What great opportunities we lost!

We didn't sit side by side, but that didn't hamper romantic give and take in any way. The first flush of youth is the best time for romance. To that the Uttam–Suchitra duo of the silver screen added a new wave of inspiration. Rathin-da and Jayati-di, Meenakshi Bose and Jyotirmay Dutta, Meenakshi Chaliha and Biswapriya Bose, Tirthankar and Mandakranta, how many more shall I name? Lalita Bhaduri passed her B.Sc. with chemistry and then re-joined the third year with economics honours, all because of Sukhamoy Chakraborty, who was a star pupil in the department. I had a touch of romantic leanings too, to be honest. So did Tapati. She took me aside and remarked once about Sujan Das Gupta, 'Fair-skinned men look a bit silly, don't they?' She married the same Sujan Das Gupta later and is still deeply in love with him.

The young men of Presidency College were not short on mischief. The girls didn't participate in their pranks directly, but enjoyed them from the sidelines and even goaded them on a bit. A new professor in the Bengali department was greeted with a line from a Tagore poem chalked boldly on the blackboard,

> All these days I waited, counting the minutes and scanning
>   the roads;
> Finally, my love, we get to meet in spring.

The lines weren't rude, the ecstatic song of a pining lady whose long wait for her absent lover finally ends. The professor, however, was very displeased. Writing these messages on the blackboard was a common source of fun. And quite amazingly, those boys knew exactly what remark would rile a particular professor. If some lecture got boring, all kinds of noises would be heard around the classroom and the third floor of Presidency College would sound like the Alipore zoo. The kingpin of all pranks was Sambit Chatterjee—elder brother of the renowned film star Soumitra Chatterjee. His most amazing talent was to convincingly feign a dead faint if he didn't like a particular class. An acting skill that could far surpass his brother's perhaps. Suniti Bose was another one. Everyone was a bit wary of this huge tall man and the remarks he made in a deep baritone. I didn't like him at all. But the funny thing is that I am pretty friendly now with those whom we considered mischievous—particularly Suniti and Sambit. Because I have realized that they have more vibrant life in them than the ones who never lifted their noses from the books because all they cared for was to get a first class.

In Presidency College, Sambit, Suniti, Barun and company were in opposition to me—that is, they were anti-left. Presidency College was then, as it is now, rife with politics. But nobody imagined that there would ever be such an unbelievably long Left Front rule in West Bengal. Nevertheless, the left was even at that time very vocal and gaining in strength. I was in the leftist students' group known as the Students' Federation of India or SFI. Sukhamoy, Amartya, Partha, Sipra Sarkar, Arjun Sengupta were all in the same group. Those who didn't support us we referred to as Anti-SFI, and in private as the 'La-re-lappa Dal', meaning, the generally frivolous party. Their leader was Suniti Bose, with others like Barun De, Pradip Das, Shakti Mukherjee and Pradip Sircar as followers. Ashin-da also supported this group. Strikes, speeches, agitations, setting up groups, expanding membership—that is what student politics was about. Murder and mayhem had not poisoned politics then; though there was a bit of physical confrontation occasionally. When strikes were called, SFI students would sit near the gate. Would anyone dare enter the college when there was a strike? Such a thing could never happen. Once Barun De was making a speech defending a student's right to attend classes if he so wished. People pushed him off the steps and threw him to the ground. Now he laughs about it.

The physics laboratory was the best place to engage in a battle of wits. Debates were held there every month before a packed hall. The razor-sharp logic of Amlan Dutta, Sudhangshu Dasgupta, Vishwanathan, Amartya's incisive analysis and Jyotirmoy Dutt's amusing extempore interjections were both pleasing and intellectually satisfying for the audience. Inevitably, whatever be the topic of debate, the audience would be split between pro- and anti-SFI. Excitement mounted and there was screaming and shouting during voting. Sometimes people came to blows but the violence did not go as far as sticks and stones.

Outside the college premises, the coffee house was an integral part of student life. Very few places in the world can offer such a marvellous ambience where, at times, one could spend three hours over a cup of tea or coffee. The famous pavement cafés of Paris would be beaten hollow by the second-floor coffee house where a dozen students could cram around a single small table. Granted that no Balzac or Sartre ever composed classics of world literature there or no Baudelaire wrote poetry, nor was any art movement engendered. But no lone coffee house can ever claim to have inspired as many youthful spirits with the flavour of life. As Professor Rajat Ray once reminisced, they served a heady cocktail of politics, romance, friendship and intellectualism. The coffee drinkers fell into three categories. One lot, like us, could afford to have coffee only; another lot, among them Biren Pal Chaudhuri, Pradip Sircar and company, ordered cutlets with coffee. The second categorization was gender based—there were separate tables for girls and boys. Of course, unspoken exchanges occurred, but from a distance. On one occasion a boy, who was eager to take a better look at a particular girl, had tilted his chair so far back that he fell right off and raised a gale of laughter from the whole house. Anadi, who was in our class, picked up a potato chip from Bithika Sen's plate and won a five-rupee wager (which was a lot of money in those days). The gender divide was breaking down gradually. Biren and Pradip would treat us now and then; we sat at their table and relished the cutlets they ordered.

But the real separation in the coffee house was between SFI and anti-SFI factions. Certain tables were earmarked for each group, which the waiters were aware of. At the leftists' table sat Partha, Sukhamoy, Amartya and the rest. At the other table sat Suniti, Barun, Pradip and their friends. Sometimes, Amlan Dutta would be their star attraction. The topics that the 'other table' discussed were actually a little mundane. As one of them laughingly recalls, 'We had three major topics. Number one was girls. Birendrakishore Roychoudhuri's daughter Rani was everyone's heartthrob. The number two topic was marks—who scored how much in each subject. And the third most important thing that we discussed was jobs—what offers we were likely to get. Most of us came from St Xavier's or similar schools. Our families were of the salaried class.' At the SFI table, there were two main topics—books and politics. From Kafka to Cuba, from Engels to Jibanananda, from Impressionism to Patua art, from US imperialism to the agony of Africa—there were heated debates on each of these themes. For a girl like me, from the mofussil, it was all very new. I used to think then that the students of Presidency were their own best teachers. Complex issues were thrashed out through discussion, debate and storytelling. We could build up reading lists and get to know about important articles in famous national and international journals. And we also learnt how to floor your audience by reading merely the blurb or a review of a book!

The left–right divide was bridged somewhat during the steamer parties held on the river Ganga once a year. In our time Pradip Das played a leading role in organizing the steamer party. He was anti-SFI. He pulled it off pretty well, with plenty of food, songs, entertainment and games. The annual steamer party is still held by Presidency alumni.

Another activity that put politics on the back burner was theatre. We staged *Sesh Raksha* once but we had to hire a theatre hall outside college because we were not given permission to put up a mixed cast of males and females! I played the role of Kamalmoni, with Jayanti Chakravarty as my playback singer. She is Gayatri Chakravarty Spivak's elder sister. It was a challenge for me to act in a play along with boys.

Baba had said, 'If you want to study in Presidency College, go ahead. Only, you must not mix with the boys.' But how could that be? If you didn't mix with the boys, half the charm of Presidency would be lost. You might as well study in all-girls colleges like Lady Brabourne or Bethune. Being a disobedient girl always, I didn't think twice about ignoring Baba's stricture. I simply adopted a stage name—Krishna Choudhury.

As is bound to happen if you're taken up with politics, theatre, debate, I managed to get a first class honours degree but I did not come first. The lure of Presidency made me enroll there for a master's degree from Calcutta University. Those postgraduate years were the two worst years of my life. The professors were fond of me, some classmates were close to me while politics, debating and studies were part of routine. Yet I have hardly any memory of the years 1955–57. My subconscious mind has deliberately wiped them out. A feeling of despondency had taken hold of me. Luckily, that agonizing phase did not last long. The dark night gave way to a new dawn in 1958.

ROMANCE, MARRIAGE, HOME-MAKING

My first love came in Chittagong when I was twelve. I can't call it love exactly. Perhaps it was just a little whiff of something. The boy's name was Badrul Hossain. Nobody would know of him, so perhaps there's no problem in mentioning his name. He was a young Muslim fellow from north-west India: fair, tall and slim He knew I liked pictures and so he drew a new one for me every day. He was in the army and when he went out on tour for short periods, he wrote me fat letters every day with elaborate sketches on the envelopes (how stupid!). The letters were intercepted by Ma and never reached me. As soon as Badrul returned, Ma told him in her usual quiet way, 'I am Bharati's guardian. Wait until she's twenty. You can contact her then.' She told me not to see him. I never cared for what Ma said but this time there was something in her expression that made me nervous. Badrul turned up many times after that day but he didn't enter our door. He stood outside on the street to gaze at me and I felt an urgent need at those precise moments to study sitting out on the veranda. And yet, sadly, Badrul did not wait. I crossed my twenty years many moons ago. Badrul did not attempt to contact me! Today after so long I suddenly remember the look in his eyes.

In the 1940s, lesbianism had not become a fashion or even a matter of debate. It was not an overt practice, but for sure the feeling must have been present through the ages. In the Khastagir School in Chittagong, my friend Gitu confessed that she 'loved' one of the senior hostel girls. Well, I couldn't very well admit defeat in this vital area of romance. So I said, 'Really? Well, I'm "in love" with Bijan-di.' Bijan-di used to teach us English at the Nandankanan school. There was no way for Gitu to verify this from the Khastagir School hostel where she lived so I made up all kinds of imaginary stories about what Bijan-di and I talked about and how her behaviour towards me made me happy or sad. I owe Bijan-di an apology; I made up stories about a respected teacher.

Class IX in Kurseong. In that place there was no need to stretch one's imagination in search of romance. The air was humming with it everywhere. But I was smitten by another tremendous love by then—ambition. I had left behind my life of swings on tree branches and wide open spaces of the open fields. My most intense desire was to be at once the best student and a fine human being.

I had Partha by my side. We met in Chittagong. Our families knew each other and it was their hope that our friendship would turn into love. We had hoped so too but by the time we were eighteen, we realized—it was Partha who realized it first—that we were close friends but not in love. The main ingredient that transforms friendship into love, physical attraction, was missing between us. We didn't discuss this at home or outside. We only talked things over between ourselves and then took our decision. Partha later married Narayani, a love marriage. I married Sukhendu.

I selected Sukhendu as my husband. Sukhendu married me on his mother's advice. Let me explain. When I had just passed out of school, Sukhendu was studying chartered accountancy in England. At my aunt Urmila-mashi's wedding, Sukhendu's uncle and aunt (his Natun khuri-ma, who was Urmila-mashi's sister-in-law) first noticed me. After Sukhendu returned from abroad, Natun khuri-ma landed up at our place one afternoon; we were her relations by marriage. She brought along her sister-in-law Gargi Ray. It is difficult to describe Gargi Ray. She was five feet four inches tall and about one and a half times the size of a normal woman; she had shoulder-length curly hair, her face was devoid of make-up, and a large vermilion dot, a bindi, graced her forehead. She wore a broad-bordered, hand-woven white cotton sari and leather sandals A paan was perennially tucked away in a corner of her mouth. But how can such a dry description convey a personality that was so great it could not be contained even within her enormous frame? She was not just one among many, she was the first among all of them.

Gargi Ray visited our house almost every day around teatime, coming by rickshaw from her house at Rashbehari Avenue to ours at Sarat Banerjee Road—the roads were not very far from each other. She brought paper bags full of snacks: singara, kachuri, dalmut, jalebi. She settled down in our drawing room. Ma, Sundar-pishima, the housemaid, all came and joined her. We shared the food, laughed and chatted and had a great time. She called on me one day—she must have spoken to Ma earlier, about which I didn't know—and said in a straightforward fashion that she wanted me to marry her son. 'Will you come and live in our house?' I was stunned. I was on my way to joining the IAS like Roma Mazumdar, our model. My exams had gone off quite well; I was preparing for my viva. Why on earth would I wish to marry her son? And so my outright refusal sounded rather harsh. Gargi Ray was undaunted. 'You're thinking that there's no reason why you should come to our house. We don't have a grand house, no car, no locker full of jewellery, no bank full of money. We are not moneyed people, but we are rich—rich in our hearts.' Her arrow hit the mark. I said I would like to meet her son and she went away happily. But Sukhendu did not agree to meet me. He argued: how could anyone get to know a person in one or two days? He was averse to meeting anyone with the obvious objective of marriage. But I wouldn't proceed without assessing things for myself. Ultimately, the whole Ray family decided to drop in for tea one day. The minute I saw Sukhendu I decided to marry him. My ability to assess people is something I've inherited from my father and it has stayed with me like a protective amulet all my life. I wore a yellow cotton sari with a thin red border that day. Tapati wore a deep blue sari with stripes all over. I preserved both for many years.

Sukhendu made a few things clear on that very first day. He was the eldest son of middle-class parents; his family depended on him so he would not be able to set up a separate home after marriage. When he heard I was going to Delhi for my IAS interview, he said his work and his family were in Calcutta, so he wondered if it would be convenient if I took up a transferable job. My face clouded over. But I had already made up my mind about him. I felt physically attracted to him. (A strange thing, this. There's no rational explanation why one person feels especially attracted to another. I saw Sukhendu and immediately realized he was the one for me.) I gave up my I.A.S. ambitions but I did say one thing. I knew women in the Ray family did not work outside the home, but I was going to find a job in Calcutta. No one should ever ask me to quit. Now it was Sukhendu's turn to look displeased. I am convinced that he never liked the idea of my being a working woman but he did accept it. At the end of it, both of us had reasons to be just a little angry. But the future is forever hidden. When we looked up at the silvery full moon on that summer night, neither of us knew that we were standing on the brink of a dazzlingly happy life together. Three days before the wedding I developed a high fever. I was anxious. Although we had met several times after that first day, I had taken the decision all on my own. Baba had not shown much enthusiasm. What if I had decided wrong?

There was no question of dowry. For my wedding, Ma gave me a set of red-and-white stone-encrusted jewellery—necklace, bracelets and earrings. I chose it myself from Guinea Mansion on Gariahat Road. Price: Rs 1050. Ma ordered a goldsmith she knew to make me a pair of thick makar-headed gold bangles, and a dozen thinner ones, six for each wrist. Didi-ma gave me a gold necklace costing Rs 200; my aunt Subhadra gave me gold earrings for Rs 75; and Urmila gave me a wristlet for Rs 100. I bought five saris. Baba took me to Indian Silk House on College Street to choose them. My wedding sari was a red Benarasi silk with tiny gold floral motifs all over and a half-inch wavy golden border. It cost Rs 84. For phulsajya I chose a green tissue sari with closely woven gold leaves and a one-inch gold border. Price: Rs 200; I thought it was very costly. For the day after the wedding, Baba bought me a lovely Kanjeevaram silk sari—light blue with tiny orange dots. I think it cost Rs 105. A mauve Mysore chiffon with a purple border cost Rs 65 and a deep yellow Mysore nylon with fine gold checks cost Rs 110. I mention the prices in detail because they sound so fantastic now. For the cost of a pair of gold earrings in those days we might buy just a plain cotton blouse today. Ma also bought three handloom cotton saris—I don't remember their prices—one for my mother-in-law, the other two for my two sisters-in-law.

Baba bought us two beds, a cupboard for clothes, a dressing table and an a wooden clothes stand from Nu-Built Furniture on Park Street. He had also ordered a sofa set. But Gargi Ray put her foot down. 'We'll buy the set ourselves. Your daughter will look prettier on a sofa bought by my son than on the one bought by you.' Baba was forced to cancel his order. He couldn't cancel the other pieces of furniture because the advance had already been paid. My father and Gargi Ray developed a close friendship later. He called her 'Didi' and she called him 'Gouranga Mahaprabhu Bhai'—Gouranga being the name of Shri Chaitanya and my father being a believer in Vaishnava philosophy spread by the guru. She brought a dhoti for him on every Bhaiphota Day, along with sandalwood paste for his forehead and bhapa doi and sandesh, popular Bengali sweets. Baba's death came as a great blow to her; she herself died six months later.

After the wedding I came to live in the huge joint family mansion at 148 Rashbehari Avenue. There were thirty-four members; two kitchens. The third floor was taken up by my elder uncle-in-law's family—he and his wife, their married son, daughter-in-law, a widowed daughter and grandchildren. We occupied the first and second floors. My father-in-law Kanak Ray, Shasuri-ma, their four sons, me, along with Sukhendu's deceased uncle's four sons—Tiku-da, Mana-da, Buro, Neltu—Mana-da's wife Aparna and their little flower of a daughter, Swati. Of the eight cousins, Tiku-da was the only one who was my bhasur, being older than my husband, the rest were my devars being younger. Tiku-da was a bachelor and an ace engineer. Mana-da ran an electrical goods shop called Service Syndicate in the groundfloor garage. Buro and Neltu were businessmen. Sukhendu's brothers, Kobi-da and Robi-da (Subhendu and Subir), had just started working. The youngest, Kallu (Soumyendu), was an apprentice cinematographer under Ramananda Sen Gupta. He left the house early in the morning and came back at 11 p.m., his face tired and dark as coal. Today he is one of India's reputed cinematographers, having worked with Satyajit Ray for years.

Shasuri-ma was right. They were all very rich of heart. Those who were the actual owners of the house, that is Tiku-da and his three brothers, never threw their weight around or ever showed a grain of pride. It made no difference to them as to who earned more or who brought home less. The eight cousins were close and relatives dropped in every now and then. Young friends of my devars livened up the place; food was in constant demand. I was no good at cooking in those days. In winter when hot green pea kachuri was to be served to the guests, I would be close to tears. Aparna rolled out the dough expertly and Bogoli Jha, the cook, fried them with equal speed. Poor me. Whenever I put in the filling, the kachuri would break apart in the pan. Aparna took pity on me and said, 'Why don't you sit and watch, you'll learn soon enough.' She took over the filling, and all that was left for me to do was to serve the kachuris to the waiting guests with a smile. Shasuri-ma would comment, 'Aparna has rolled them so thin and fine and Ma-moni—she would affectionately call me Ma-moni, jewel mother—has fried them into beautiful puffs.' The brothers and their friends would clamour for more. 'Keep up the supply, Boudi!' I was mortified but I couldn't contradict my mother-in-law in front of the guests.

Who would dare contradict her? Who could nurse the sick better than her? Who knew better than her how to ease their suffering—which way to sit if you had a backache, what to take for a stomach pain and how to give hot compresses on a carbuncle? And all this she did not only for her own family, but for anyone in distress, regardless of whether she knew them or not.

For relatives distant and near, 148 Rashbehari Avenue was a wedding venue to be used rent free. The large rooms on the second floor were cleared out for guests. The fourth-floor terrace was covered with a marquee to serve as a dining hall. The veranda and courtyard downstairs became an improvised kitchen. Mishti doi, sweetened curd, was the only item that was brought in from outside. My mother-in-law supervised every detail. Her resounding voice could be heard giving orders from the ground to the top floor, equally concerned whether people who used the place for the wedding were closely or distantly related.

'Nitai, keep the fish on the veranda, dear boy. Don't throw them on the ground like that! Cut large pieces for fish fry; for the curry cut the pieces from the stomach of the fish long and from the back side of the fish squarish.'

'Subrata, you're like a grandson to me. You'll get the catering order. See that you charge a fair price, don't slash their throats. They have come all this far to Calcutta to marry off their daughter. A daughter's wedding is an expensive affair, you know.'

'Mana, please decorate the place with your "Service Syndicate" stuff. They will feel happy if the house is well lighted.'

It goes without saying that Mana-da, Subrata, Nitai followed her instructions to the letter. The family, whose daughter or son was getting married, breathed a sigh of relief.

It's not that I liked everything my mother-in-law did. Women in a joint family have fun but they have problems too. I had taken up teaching at Bethune College a month before my wedding and I had to leave the house at 9.45 a.m. In a joint family, each one has specific assignments and I wanted to finish my duties before leaving for college. So I asked my mother-in-law to tell me the night before what I would be required to do the following day. What vegetables to cut and in what size—an important factor for Bengali cuisine—and how many paan I would have to prepare. Also, I wanted to know what I was expected to do after coming back from college so that I could plan my work schedule accordingly. Being systematic in such a large family is easier said than done. The vegetables arrived at 8 a.m. There was no knowing how many were to eat on a particular day and the menu too was not fixed. Each one had different demands—Sukhendu wouldn't like rice for lunch; he preferred grilled fish or corn on the cob, a raw vegetable salad and fruits. Kobi-da loved catfish soup, he would have it every day. Robi-da hated catfish. Kallu worked so hard; he would gobble two chapattis and some stir-fried vegetables and rush off early in the morning. If he didn't have meat for dinner how would he gain strength? Tiku-da was a lifelong ascetic; he didn't fuss about food. Mana-da was fond of fish and meat and didn't care for vegetables. Buro was like Tiku-da while Neltu liked meat. Aparna and I had to have rice and fish curry, mother-in-law was fond of charchori with spicy vegetables. She took a great deal of trouble over father-in-law's meals. At least seven or eight items would be laid around his plate. If I teased her about it, she'd come back with, 'A little poppy seed ball, you can't count that as one item, Ma-moni. Bitters can't be considered as a separate dish either!' The point was that there were multiple dishes but) and more items simply meant more things to chop up and prepare. And in the meantime, the clock moved merrily on. Shasuri-ma said—she actually didn't approve of my going out to work—'You carry on, go to college, Ma-moni. Aparna and I can manage.' Was it right? I felt the injustice done to Aparna, yet I had to leave; there was nothing else I could do.

Aparna was made to order for a joint family. She was older than me in years but younger in terms of protocol, since she was my younger sister-in-law. She had entered the Rashbehari Avenue home as a stunningly beautiful young bride of seventeen, a niece of my mother-in-law's—her cousin's daughter. My father-in-law at that time lived in Dharamjaygarh, a little town in a princely state, where he worked. He sent his children down to Calcutta for their studies. The family was really huge then. Two uncles, Natun-kaka and Chhoto-kaka, with their wives and children, doddering old Daku-di, who was the childless widowed sister of their grandmother, another widow, their sister, with her half-crazy son, and several cousins, all lived under the same roof. Kallu says, 'We were eighteen cousins, all told. Natun-khurima reigned supreme over all.' She was a kind-hearted lady. Once a thief was caught red-handed. The boys tied him up and were discussing what they should do—give him a good thrashing or call the police. Natun-khurima heard the commotion at dawn and came down to investigate. She poured cold water on their plans and said, 'Let him go. He's just a kid. It must be poverty that has driven him to thieving.' She turned to the thief and said, 'Wait, son. Don't go away without a bite. You must be very hungry. Let me give you some tea.' She fed him tea, biscuits and moa before sending him on his way. It was Natun-khurima again who in 1946 hid their Muslim washerman Birju (he had escaped somehow from his torched shack) in the attic room that six of the cousins used to share as a study-cum-bedroom. Natun-khurima, with her sweet and low voice, held the reins of that huge household firmly in her hands, sacrificing her own interests and those of her own children in the interest of the larger family. Chhoto-khurima was her assistant, rough-spoken and hard-working. These two sisters-in-law bore the whole burden of home management. With them they had the young newcomer, Aparna. They came downstairs to the kitchen at 6 a.m. and never packed up before 11 p.m. All her in-laws were very fond of Aparna. Her husband Mana-da, having married at a young age, felt shy paying about attention to his wife. Not everybody is good at romancing and I don't think Mana-da had the knack. He would be busy in his shop and their daughter Swati would move around from lap to lap. Aparna didn't feel deprived in any way, at least not until I arrived. When my mother-in-law, who was her aunt, shifted to Calcutta in the 1950s after her husband's retirement, Aparna was very happy. Then I arrived, special from the start. I had university education, I was working, and I was the apple of my mother-in-law's eye. I spent time laughing and chatting with my brothers-in-law and their friends, rushed off to college at 9.45 a.m. sharp and went out every evening with Sukhendu (which Mana-da and Aparna never did) to some place or the other. Why wouldn't Aparna feel upset? She never showed it. She was soft-natured, soft-spoken and soft-hearted. But I could understand how she felt and I felt a little guilty. I treated her gently, but I didn't give up my college or stop going out in the evening with Sukhendu. It was a kind of selfishness, I admit.

Three years later, Tiku-da decided to sell the house—they needed the money. Kanak and Gargi Ray's part of the family moved to a rented apartment at 55 Lake Place. The rent was Rs 550 per month. The second floor of the three-storeyed house was ours. The front door opened into a long corridor with rooms on either side. There were four rooms to the right. The first room was mine, next came the living room, followed by the parents' bedroom and then the largest room for the three unmarried brothers. To the left of the corridor were two bathrooms, a dining room, and a kitchen that was of a good size. Opposite the kitchen stood a large platform that took up the breadth of the corridor. On it were the kitchen chopper, vegetable basket, cooking ingredients and above all, my mother-in-law. She sat there all day, cutting vegetables, giving orders to the cook, entertaining relatives and friends. That platform was her domain.

The owner of the house was Pahari's father; Pahari was a close friend of mine from my days at Presidency College. I had ritually adopted him as a brother on one Bhaiphota day. He lived with his family on the third floor. Theirs was an amazing family, with not an ounce of discipline anywhere, something I've rarely seen. However, at the same time, I haven't seen so many talented and broad-minded people in one place. Pahari's father Suresh Sen Gupta had been a renowned professor of English in Barisal. And after he retired all he knew and cared for was books. His children adored him and I adored their mother. She seldom left the house, but when she did, her family would worry, not sure what she would do. She would bring home any beggar she saw on the road, feed him and make a place for him to stay below the stairs leading to the upper floors. The place was always crowded with little children, old women and disabled beggars of every description. Sen Gupta-mashima wore no ornaments except for two red glass bangles and thick white shell ones. How could she? She had given her gold bangles and her gold necklace away to someone somewhere. 'Gold necklace? That little thing? I don't remember whom I gave it to. What could I do? She had nothing to eat and nothing to wear, she was crying. How could I turn her away?' That was it, who could say anything to that? The children of such a mother were all extremely talented and compassionate. If one was a philosopher, another was a physicist; if one was a pianist, another was an exponent of Rabindrasangeet; if one was a doctor, another was an economist. Pahari escaped the terrible ragging meted out to the freshers at the Indian Institute of Technology, Kharagpur, simply by singing Rabindrasangeet. One can only imagine how well he must have sung. In Mashima's children's dictionary, it would have perhaps been impossible to find the words 'mine' and 'others'. It was no surprise then that when one of her grandsons, Kunal, returned from the USA with a Ph.D., all he brought back was a cloth bag in which he carried his thesis and a few fat volumes of rare books. 'Who wants to cart back clothes and stuff?' Whatever little he owned he'd given away to friends. He would borrow clothes from his brothers, Bapu and Apu, when he was home. This was the kind of family that we grew deeply attached to in our new home in Lake Place.

However, from the moment we shifted to our new home, differences emerged between me and my mother-in-law. It was a generational conflict, something almost inevitable in joint families. The issues may differ, depending on the context of a particular family. In our case, the issue was Isha, my daughter. Was she mine or did she belong to the family? This was a crucial question because the two generations had different opinions about child-rearing. Shasuri-ma wanted to feed the child only stewed apple and boiled catfish; I wanted her to learn to eat all kinds of different things. If Isha cried, Shasuri-ma would come running to pick her up immediately. I would say, 'Let her cry a bit, it won't hurt any.' Shasuri-ma would pile Isha with pretty clothes and toys. I worried that over-indulgence was not good for her. These petty differences, which were all too frequent, made the air heavy between us. Once I spent one whole night on the balcony, thinking bitter thoughts. Finally I told myself that after all my mother-in-law had brought up seven children of her own and that they were all pretty healthy and nice people. So perhaps I should let her bring Isha up? From the next day I stopped saying anything to her concerning Isha. There were no more quarrels; peace returned.

But a new problem arose when Isha got fever. Shasuri-ma said, 'Your daughter is ill. Don't go to college today, Ma-moni.' How absurd. Has any child grown up without falling ill?

'I have only ten days' casual leave; seven I have taken. I should keep at least three days in hand for some really serious problem. I have to go today.'

My mother-in-law made herself quite clear now. 'You've been going to college for so long. It's time you gave it up.'

I answered equally clearly, 'I am not leaving my job. I told you so before I got married. It was a condition . . .'

Before I could finish, she broke in, 'You said so. But you didn't have a daughter then. Does she come first or your condition?'

'There's no contradiction between the two,' I said, and proceeded down the stairs on my way out.

A graver crisis cropped up when I got admission to Lady Margaret College at Oxford to do my Ph.D. under the reputed historian C.C. Davies. I was determined to go. My mother-in-law put her foot down.

'You often talk of your condition. I don't think it included your leaving home and baby daughter for three years and going off abroad, did it?'

The rest of the family took her side. I was ready to walk out of the house. But hindrance came from an unexpected quarter—from my own mother. Ma said in a calm, hesitant, low voice—almost frightened to speak the truth, 'You're making a mistake, Bharati. To leave all that you have received here and go off merely for the fascination of Oxford would be a big mistake.'

When you become a mother yourself, you appreciate the worth of motherly counsel. For the first time in my life I set aside my wish and took my mother's advice.

No one can see into the future. Within the next year, my second daughter Tista arrived. Before her birth and for almost two years after, aches and pains, operations, hospitals and nursing homes were my constant companions. And another constant was the tender care I received from my Shasuri-ma. Fortunately, I had let her take charge of Isha earlier or else where would I be? Tista was put into ayah Narayani's lap under the close supervision of my mother-in-law. In my opinion, living in a joint family often means that one's desires and one's personality are curtailed. But what one receives in return is beyond all calculation.

When Isha was nearly three years old, Sukhendu and I, along with our two daughters, moved to his company flat at King's Court on Theatre Road. Leaving a family home you shared for five years through joy and sorrow engenders mixed feelings. I had tears in one eye and a smile in the other. King's Court at the corner of Theatre Road and Chowringhee was a premier apartment mansion. A pleasant breeze blew from the open ground across the road. It was a spacious apartment bathed in sunlight and fresh air, warm in winter and cool in summer, thanks to its thick walls, and fully furnished in the current style. I was thrilled, and why not? I had two new experiences at King's Court. One was running my own establishment. Another was coming into contact with an Indo-Anglian community.

My first problem was managing a household all by myself. I had no experience whatsoever. My mother-in-law came to the rescue. I called her up every morning to ask about what I should include in my shopping list, what menu to prepare, and how to cook which dish. On home décor, I would consult my young sister-in-law Babi—she was an artist, stylish and fashionable—about curtains and cushions and colour-matching and polishing brass, copper, silver, wood. The tips I picked up from her I would confidently relay like a know-all to my assistant Mahangi Keora. Luckily he was a very amiable man, and we developed a good understanding within a couple of days. He was twice my age, yet he addressed me as 'Ma' and I called him son. He preferred eating at his own place. 'I cook for you, yes. But I wouldn't be able to eat your kind of food. It is better that you pay me money for my meals.' I agreed. But I still felt uncomfortable about the arrangement. One day he agreed at my request to eat two pieces of the chicken he'd cooked for us. He took four or five Kashmiri chillies and a large onion, made a paste of these, added sugar and half a cup of oil, and cooked the chicken again. I shivered when I saw the final outcome. It was a thick, blood-red curry with the two pieces of chicken hidden somewhere inside. I thought we were lucky that he didn't eat with us; one spoon of that lethal stuff would have laid us out for a week!

Shasuri-ma visited us every day at 2.30 p.m. and stayed on till 7 p.m. She brought snacks like she used to bring earlier when she visited my parents' home before my marriage. She moved around the flat, inspecting every room, she chatted with the girls, and most importantly, kept Narayani in line. Keeping Narayani under control was necessary. Shasuri-ma had recruited her a week before Isha was born. Narayani laid certain preconditions before she joined. She must have fish every day and parboiled rice for lunch and dinner, and she would do her own cooking not on gas but on a kerosene stove. Shasuri-ma agreed; the conditions could be easily fulfilled. She told me in private, teasing me laughingly, 'Looks like my fate is to be held by preconditions!' Narayani kept her own clothes in the children's cupboard, used their bathroom, slept in their room. She was devoted to Shasuri-ma, and hated the sight of me. She plagued me, spoke rudely, and showed her temper. For example, one day I bought small mourala fish from the market for Narayani. She came from Dhaka and was an excellent cook.

Both of us had one thing in common—we enjoyed eating the smaller variety of fish. When that came, she cooked and I had a share. On looking at the fish that morning, she started screaming, 'You've bought rotten fish for me!'

I said, 'Not only for you. I will also eat that fish, as you well know. Here, take some money and go buy fish yourself!'

She shouted back, 'Why? The contract was that you would arrange for my meals. There was nothing about my going to the market!'

Another day, Narayani had gone into our bathroom for her big job. Sukhendu was waiting outside for her to come out. So I scolded her and said, 'I've told you to use the children's bathroom! Why are you here?'

She snapped back promptly, 'Why shouldn't I? Because mine smells and yours doesn't?'

That was Narayani. Yet, it wasn't just Shasuri-ma's bias that forced me to put up with her nonsense; it was much more than that. I had to go to college and Isha to school. Little Tista, left alone in the house, would be safe and sound under Narayani's care. I knew that this foul-mouthed, bad-tempered, childless, destitute widow loved Tista with all her heart. The one who gives birth is not the only mother; the one who takes care of the child is a mother too. I would often come home late at night and find Tista in Narayani's bed, clinging on to her with both arms, sleeping peacefully. On many an afternoon, I would find Tista in the kitchen, picking up grains of coarse rice from Narayani's platter and popping them into her mouth. She would greet me with a big smile and say, '*Muri bhaat.*'

Our precious Narayani left us suddenly after fourteen years. Her beloved younger brother took her away. I had seen Jogen-bhai being given a pension. I offered Narayani. But no, she wouldn't accept any. 'If you wish to give me anything, give it all at once,' she said in her usual rough way. So I did and that was a mistake. We lost Narayani forever. Her useless brother must have taken her off to some faraway place, or it may be that she died suddenly. We made every effort to trace her but in vain. Today even after twenty-five years mention of her 'Nani' brings tears to Tista's eyes.

In the King's Court phase of my life, Mahangi and Narayani were a part of the inner quarters. In the outer part was an Indo-Anglian social circle. I, a middle-class Bengali daughter and wife, found myself in the centre of the 'corporate world'. I took my decision: I would mix with them but would not be one of them. 'I'll bathe, but I'll keep my braids dry . . .' as the much-acclaimed philosophical *Vaisnab Padavali* verse goes.

There were twenty-four flats in King's Court. Two Bengali families, two Punjabi, two south Indian, one Parsi, and the rest were foreigners. John Hutton lived in the flat above ours. A Scotsman, he loved two things—golf and whisky. He woke up at dawn and stomped around in heavy boots for a while and went off to play golf. I peeped out of my window and saw him clasping his red tartan leather golf kit in both arms like a baby and loading it into his car. Every night he drank a great deal of whisky and sang Bobby Burns songs in a loud voice. Drinks did not hinder his morning golf. His wife visited him very rarely and he led an expatriate's life. He was an alien in two countries.

Sukhendu's boss Robert Ritchie was also Scottish. Scots are often called skinflints, unfairly I think. There was not a trace of thriftiness in his behaviour towards us. Robert went out of his way to keep Sukhendu happy. Either he was excessively fond of him or else, because he wasn't very good at his job, he tried to keep on friendly terms to make Sukhendu cover up for him. Robert's wife was German. She came once in a while and went on crazy spending sprees. She might have been a little off in the head and imagined herself to be the wife of the Kaiser himself!

On the topmost floor lived Paddy O'Leary and his wife. They were Irish with their typical fondness for talk, laughter and song. Mrs O'Leary was quite a bit older than her husband and talked about Ireland all the time. She dreamed of going back and buying a house in some village close to Dublin. The dream never materialized; she died of heart failure. Hardly three months later, Paddy married the young daughter of his dead wife's sister. The affair must have been going on for some time but when she was alive the first Mrs O'Leary never breathed a word. Her niece entered the flat as the queen of Paddy's heart and wiped away all traces of the earlier occupant. She changed the furniture, got new curtains and threw out all the old oil paintings. Marrying again after a wife's death is no sin, neither for the widower nor for his second wife. But why must people be so heartless?

The Bengali family that lived in King's Court was a true representative of Indo-Anglian culture. They were a strange blend of English style and Bengali orthodoxy. Their daughters learnt the piano as well as Rabindrasangeet. They were educated at Loreto House, the most prestigious convent in town, but were expected to marry in a traditional way. The parents were very modern but when their second daughter wanted to marry someone of her own choice, they turned deeply conservative. The girl simply walked out of the house and moved in to her would-be in-laws' home. She works at a foreign educational institution these days. Self-reliant, confident, full of self-esteem; it's a pleasure to see her.

Almost all the residents of King's Court used to go to the Saturday Club. They held good Western music recitals there and put up excellent plays; for sports and games there were billiards, tennis, squash; and there was ballroom dancing on the spacious polished wooden dance floor. I had no taste for alcoholic beverages, didn't know how to play cards or to dance and didn't care for dogs. I couldn't enjoy the club much.

After nine years at King's Court, when Sukhendu became managing director of his company, Guest Keen Williams, we moved to 2D Burdwan Road in the posh residential area of Alipore. 2D was a gracious old-style two-storeyed mansion. A giant pipal tree stretched out its leafy branches to the rear. In front we had a huge lawn surrounded by a lovely flower garden. We lived on the first floor while the ground floor was kept for visitors from other Indian cities and abroad. The place had a special character. The wooden staircase leading up to the first floor was an attractive old-time structure. The reputed film star Robi Ghosh directed his film *Sadhu Judhistirer Karcha* there. That day the kitchen in the house remained virtually shut as the two domestics practically went on strike. Outsiders crowded the gate to watch the shooting. They were taking shots of the driver. Why should they stay in the house? The two of them started milling around the cameramen. Unfortunately, they didn't appear on the cinema screen; only Sharma, the driver, was briefly seen. But they got passes to watch the film and were quite thrilled.

Satyajit Ray himself came to shoot. Mainly for the staircase, which he used for his film *Piku's Diary*. He worked with such intense concentration! His wife Bijoya and the two stars, Victor Banerjee and Aparna Sen, sat around chatting and sipping tea and going in for a shot now and then. Satyajit paid no attention to anyone; his eyes were glued to the camera viewfinder and the shooting area. I stopped near him on my way to college and said, 'I'm Soumyendu's elder sister-in-law. Please treat this as your own home and ask for whatever you need. I'm off to college.' He replied in a serious, half-distracted tone, 'I'll ask if I do need anything.' Today I regret that I didn't take a day off from college to observe how the great director went about his work.

The house on Burdwan Road was an abode of joy for the children and for us. It is replete with sweet memories of the best years of our lives. But that was also where I came very close to death. Not a normal death but murder! It's a spine-chilling tale.

One evening I was getting ready to go out with Sukhendu for a dinner. I opened my wardrobe and found two of my favourite saris missing. Sukhendu said, like all husbands do, 'You must have misplaced them, the way you keep your stuff all over the place.' I was sure I hadn't kept them anywhere else. But then, who could have removed saris from a locked wardrobe? I left the house with a disturbed mind.

The next morning I woke up with a strange sense of fear that snaked right through the centre of my chest. Sukhendu left for office at 7 a.m. and the girls went off to school at around eight. My son was to leave at 8.30. I couldn't hold myself any longer and told him, 'Don't go to school today.'

'Why, Ma?' he asked.

'I'm feeling frightened.'

Khokon looked surprised. 'But you always say one shouldn't be afraid. If you do, fear will take a grip on you. So why are you frightened now?'

That embarrassed me. 'I said it just like that. You better go to school, son.'

The minute he left, I locked the bedroom door and sat inside. I felt a peculiar, inexplicable fear, so strong I could hardly breathe. My heart was screaming silently inside, 'I'm feeling terrified!' I bathed and thought I'd go to college. There would be people there, my fear would go away.

I was getting ready when there was a knock at the door. It was Sarat, a new hand whom I had recruited to clean the rooms.

He said, 'Lokenath is here. He wants his salary; he won't work here any more.'

Lokenath was my cook. He had been with us seven years. He had taken three days' leave. Was he back already? 'I'm going to college now. I'll talk to him when I get back,' I said. My bedroom door had a Yale lock. I pulled it close from the outside and hurried down the stairs on my way to college. The car had hardly reached Theatre Road when my heart started beating faster than ever. Sukhendu's office, Guest Keen Williams, had a branch office on Theatre Road. I went in there and requested the secretary Miss Chandra Uttam, 'Please phone my college and tell them I won't be coming today. Two of my saris have been stolen; I want to report it to the police.' Uttam must have thought that I'd gone crazy. Whoever reported the theft of two saris? She looked at me sympathetically and said, 'You're looking quite distraught.' So I was; I realized suddenly that I was still wearing my bedroom slippers!

Having startled Miss Uttam, I walked out fast and asked Sharma, the driver, to take me back home. Usually I rang the front door bell when I got back. That day I just walked in distractedly and without ringing the bell unlocked the entrance door with my house key. As soon as I opened it just a crack, I thought I saw a shadow flitting into my bedroom. How come? It was closed and had a Yale lock on it. Thoughts travel faster than light and a moment is a mighty long time. In a split moment I noticed the kitchen chopper lying under the floor-length curtain, quickly pulled the front door shut and jumped down the stairs screaming, 'Sharma! Sharma!'

Sharma came running. 'What's the matter? I saw Sarat and Lokenath running down the spiral staircase and moving off towards the next house. What's the problem?'

'They've escaped then. Let's see what's happened,' I said.

Sharma and I went up and unlocked the entrance door together. The chopper was still glinting on the floor. We walked into the bedroom and stood there aghast. The telephone wire had been ripped out. Sukhendu's leather gloves were chucked on the floor. The wardrobes were wide open. Apart from books, shoes and glassware, everything, including our two passports were bundled up in a cloth and placed on the bed. It was the quick work of expert hands. Sukhendu rushed back, so did Shasuri-ma when they were informed by phone. Shasuri-ma held me in a close embrace and wept.

'What if you had gone in unawares, Ma-moni?'

By then the reptile gnawing at my heart had run off. I laughed and answered, 'As you often say—whom the lord protects, nothing can harm.'

Sukhendu was supposed to take the evening flight to Bombay. He was hesitating. I said, 'There's nothing to stop you now. The danger's passed. You can relax and carry on.' Sukhendu went off. When Baba came later in the afternoon, he was quite displeased. 'Our experience with criminals teaches us that they usually come back to recover their booty which they were compelled to leave behind.'

On his advice an extra security guard was employed for that night. I don't know whether the criminals came back but the police came with their sniffer dogs. It was no use. Sarat and Lokenath could not be traced, even though the police searched their village homes. The only one to gain was me. I gained an invaluable experience!

We spent twelve years in Burdwan Road, then Sukhendu retired. After a short stint at Tivoli Court on Ballygunge Circular Road we moved to our present home in Sonali. This is a small flat which we own in an apartment complex run as a cooperative society. Pritish Nandy, now a reputed media personality, who once was Sukhendu's colleague at Guest Keen Williams, and is a dear friend to us, found this flat and arranged for us to buy it—a kind gesture I will always remember. The society is basically middle class, but has many well-known personalities as occupants. The artist Paritosh Sen—a tall octogenarian with a youthful, ramrod-straight back—used to live here for years. Sadly, he passed away in 2009. He could stand at his easel and paint for seven to eight hours at a stretch. He went for walks each morning and evening and practised yoga. His wife Jayasree is a retired professor of economics. She was happy leaving her husband to run the house and feels very lonely now. The economist Ashok Mitra lives here. He was once finance minister of West Bengal and spokesperson for the Left Front at large conferences. Now he writes regularly for the *Telegraph*. His wife Gouri Devi shopped basketfuls of vegetables and fish for the many guests they entertained regularly—she too died in 2008. Dr Mitra is childless but owns an enviable collection of books. Jyoti Malik, son of one-time vice chancellor of Calcutta University, is a non-resident Indian who lives in Holland but spends four winter months in Sonali every year. Aparna Sen used to live here for years and shifted to an apartment beside Sonar Bangla Hotel on the Eastern Bypass recently. She is nationally and internationally admired as an actor and film director. I know Aparna, the daughter–sister–mother. Her father Chidananda Das Gupta is a filmmaker and film critic. It's remarkable how well Aparna looks after her parents! What tender loving care she devotes to her sick younger sister! I was amazed when I went to her flat one evening for dinner. There she was, surrounded by a happy throng: her present husband Kalyan—a delightful human being—two daughters from two earlier marriages, Dona and Konkona, Dona's little daughter and Aparna's parents. In the midst of conversation she told me, 'My family is my sustenance.' That is so true.

The residents of Sonali are on the periphery of my life here. Among those who are in the centre of my life, stands Kumar. Achinkumar Pal is his full name. He has been my right hand for all the twenty years that I've been here. Quite unknown to me and perhaps to himself, he has gradually taken over the responsibility of running my home. On his request I put his only child Reetika into an English-medium school, St Thomas' Girls' School. As a child, she used to ignore everything I said and waste time watching television. She became clever and mature as she grew up. She passed her Class XII higher secondary exam in the first division and secured a bachelor's degree with honours in English from New Alipore College. She was thrilled when she scored the highest marks in her class. 'I have tasted success. I don't want to let it go,' she told me. She's a bright girl and talks with self-confidence. 'I want to be an air hostess, Dida,' she once told me. 'Then I can see the world—the Taj Mahal, Niagara Falls—and meet so many different kinds of people. I want to have wheels under my feet like my Dida.' But her plans changed. She is now working at the call centre of the HSBC bank in Vishakhapatnam, sharing an apartment with two of her colleagues. We are so proud of her.

If not quite as bright as Reetika, Mampi is intelligent, studious, sober and ambitious. She's quiet, gentle and well mannered. Mampi is Reba's only child, Reba being the part-time cleaning woman who worked for me for an hour every day over the last five years or so. Mampi passed out of Chetla Girls' School with a first division, did her B.Com. at New Alipore College and is now working for a construction firm for Rs 3000 a month. Mampi says she wants to be an interior decorator. 'They don't pay me much, I know, but they allow me to go to the field and study architecture. If I want to be a good interior decorator, I should know about architecture, don't you think?' Four days a week, Mampi doesn't come straight home from office but goes to teach kathak two days a week at a school and gives two days' private tuition as well. What she earns from these dance lessons is enough to cover her own expenses. The salary she earns from the office goes straight into a bank as savings. Reba thinks the money will come in handy for Mampi's wedding; Mampi dreams of taking an advanced interior decoration course.

Not everyone's story is so inspiring. Jamuna was another woman who worked part-time for me before Reba. She was a quiet, middle-aged woman and I rather liked her. She was trying to get her younger daughter married. 'Don't give any dowry!' I warned her. Dowry demands are very much on the rise these days—even in poorer homes. After much searching she found a suitable boy. 'He wants just a bicycle, Ma. If I don't give anything, my daughter will never be married.' So I consented and the marriage was arranged. Why not give the poor girl a little trousseau, I thought. Surely Jamuna would like that. Mother and daughter were both very happy with what I and my friends gifted the bride. But Jamuna's older son-in-law was terribly displeased. 'Your mother didn't give so many things to *you*!' he complained bitterly to his wife. Some days later Jamuna informed me with a wan face that her elder daughter was burned to death because the kerosene stove burst in the kitchen. They couldn't take her to the hospital in time. I was stunned. 'You should inform the police,' I told her. Jamuna shook her head and refused. She didn't want her two grandchildren to grow up with the shame of having a father who was a convicted murderer. Jamuna's health broke down. She gave up all her jobs and now lives on the pittance of a pension she collects from her old employers.

Another of my favourite girls is Tumpa. Both her parents work as cooks in two flats in the apartment complex. Tumpa is a slim girl with a sweet face who loves mixing with boys. And why not? She's old enough, well past twenty by now. I became friends with her when she got together a dozen children from the apartment complex and organized a sit-and-draw competition. I saw that being poor hadn't taken away her thirst for life. She failed her secondary exam and gave up studies. I advised her to join an open university course and offered to pay for it but she wasn't willing. 'Don't ask me to study, Dida. I don't have the time. I give singing lessons in two houses and tutor two kids in another. If I stop earning, it'll be a strain on my parents. Besides, I want to bring up my younger sister properly.' So that's what she's doing.

What will Preeti do? She's Chilu's little girl, very naughty. Her mother works as an ayah in the flat above ours. Preeti runs around the compound with her curly hair in two plaits tied with red ribbons and two butterfly clips on top. She goes to school and is exceptionally smart. When she cocks her head, gives me a big smile, stretches out her hand and says, 'Good morning, Dida,' my heart simply melts. Preeti could be trained to join politics, why not? All these girls are not strictly part of my household but how can I leave them out from my story?

Today my home runs pretty smoothly. There are no quarrels, no raised voices, no untidiness or disorder. Shasuri-ma would have been pleased to see it. Then again, she would perhaps be unhappy to see her son eating just a one-course or, at most, two-course meal day and night. She might have said in her usual way, 'You've won, Ma-moni. Everyone is healthy in your family. But food is not only to keep you physically fit; it's for enjoyment too. And that's what you have killed.' The allegation would be true, so I wouldn't protest. I would refrain from putting up a self-defence like, 'When working women took up home management, the whole system had to change. Time was limited—we had to deal with both home and workplace. There was less time to devote to caring for older people and children and for elaborate meals. If the men of the house don't come forward to help, then that's the way it will be.' I would not tell Shasuri-ma, 'We working women often seek entertainment outside the home; in plays, music, cultural programmes and social gatherings.' If I did tell her, would she have understood? Our two generations have different perspectives.

Sunanda Ghosh taught political science at Bethune College. She told me once, 'I do the whole week's shopping on Sunday. I divide the fish and vegetables into seven portions and pack them into the fridge. Then I can take out a packet each day and cook.' I used to live in Shasuri-ma's household at the time, tasting her seven-course lunch and dinner. So I thought, Sunanda overdoes it. Is she the only woman who teaches in a college? Are such extreme shortcuts necessary?' Who knew then that I would almost follow her example one day?

All this talk has brought me right up to the present. Can women ever stop talking about their homes? And yet, home management was never central to my life. I was always attracted to the working world outside. It drew me like Lord Krishna's flute drew Radha. Nothing could hold me back.

Therefore, I shall go back from the present to the days when I first started working—to 1958.

IN THE WORKING WORLD

If the year 1958 could be brought back again, I would hold it fast to my chest and never let it fly away. I joined Bethune College that year; my first step into the working world outside my home. It was a government job for which I was selected after an interview by the Public Service Commission. The salary was Rs 200 per month—the usual starting salary for college teachers those days. But I had earned it and I was simply thrilled.

I remember that first day clearly. 1 February 1958. I passed through the tall gates of Bethune College at 10 a.m. sharp and walked up the high staircase to the first floor. Bethune is an old college—the first women's college in Bengal—with a glorious tradition, but to me, everything smelt new. The stairs, the walls, the broad corridor, everything seemed new, as if all the heritage lay behind a fresh coat of paint. The corridor was full of girls in colourful saris—some wore their hair open, others wore long plaits; some wore glasses and some did not. They looked at me curiously. My curiosity was no less than theirs. I took a good look and then went into the staff room. I picked up the roll register. One staff member asked, 'You picked up the register right away? Aren't you feeling nervous about taking your first class?' That's when I realized that I wasn't nervous at all. I felt like I had been teaching for a long time. As if that was what I was born to do.

I climbed up to the second floor with quick steps. It was an intermediate arts first-year class—Class XI by present-day reckoning. There were two hundred girls seated in the huge classroom which was like a gallery. I got up on the lecture platform and looked at them. They looked back at me. The first meeting of eyes was an auspicious moment. I was charmed. They, too, seemed to like me much, which I gathered from the whispering that spread all over the class and entered my ears like a loud hum of welcome. Instead of proceeding with the roll call, I started laughing. They burst into laughter too. There were two hundred girls of seventeen or eighteen. I was past twenty-three. What a bond of friendship there can be between seventeen and twenty-three!

I taught the history of England to the intermediate students and Greek and European history to the BA honours class. I loved to teach them, they loved to listen. I can freely admit today that every morning I practised my lectures until I knew them almost by heart so that I wouldn't get stuck anywhere. I had excellent relationships with my students and at a personal level with a good many of them. Once a girl begged me to come home with her to persuade her mother to consent to her marrying the boy she was in love with. We talked it over for a while and I felt that the girl had made a bad choice. Finally she did accept my advice, but I don't know whether she found happiness later in life from the marriage she ultimately entered into. With hindsight I regret having interfered. Who was I to try and regulate the course of anyone's life? I remember another girl who was a classic beauty. Two months before her BA honours exam, she unexpectedly got married. Couldn't she have waited just two more months? I sent word to her to see me. 'You will stay at your parents' place for the next two months. You have to get honours marks,' I said. A month later she told me she was living with her parents but not making much progress with her studies. Why? She gave me a big, embarrassed smile. 'What can I do, Didi? My husband comes every day and stays all evening.' What could I say to that? How could I obstruct the delights of newfound love?

The students of Bethune College won my heart and so did my colleagues. The staff room was like a huge extended family. All personal problems were openly discussed and quite often solutions were found. Who but women can appreciate the problems any woman must face in her daily grind as a home manager? During recess the staff room would hum with animated conversations. Usha Bhattacharya of the philosophy faculty would proclaim her opinions loudly on every subject under the sun. The ever-youthful Karabi Bhattacharya of the Bengali faculty would burst into laughter at the slightest. Juthika-di who taught Sanskrit had a voice as sweet as sugar. The nationalist journalist Ramananda Chattopadhyay's granddaughter Ishita Datta recounted stories of the old days and brought to life the exciting times when her grandfather was editor of the influential journals *Prabasi* and *Modern Review.* Manisha-di supplied us with all kinds of new recipes. Kind-hearted Kamala-di of the history faculty would give me a mild dressing down, 'Can't you move at a slower pace? You are always running.' We all teased Sujata Chaudhuri of the

English department about her brilliant son Sukanta. 'It's prize distribution day at your son's school. You better take the day off today, Sujata-di, or how will that young boy carry home all those prizes by himself?'

The teachers of Bethune College were mostly first-generation working women. Women had started working from Kadambini Ganguly's time and female education had been under way from the middle of the nineteenth century, Bethune School was established in 1849. Still, many of my colleagues at Bethune College had to struggle hard to pursue higher studies and work outside the home. When Chameli-di had joined an undergraduate college wishing to study science, her grandmother had been livid. She walked straight into the principal's office. 'You're an old maid, you want my granddaughter to be an old maid too?' Chameli-di had to shed tears at home and apologize to the principal before she finally got her way and took up physics honours. Usha-di was an only child. Her doting father didn't stop her from studying but wouldn't allow her to join the famous Eden School in Dhaka where they lived. 'It's too far away. Study at a local school.' Usha-di said, 'I ranked fifth among all the successful candidates in the matriculation examination. If I'd gone to a good school like Eden, I could have come first.' In those days, girls from Brahmo families were generally ahead of girls from average Hindu families in terms of education. Roma-di, Manisha-di and Ishita-di, who belonged to the Brahmo community, had full approval of their guardians for higher education. But none of the mothers and grandmothers of my colleagues in Bethune College had been salaried workers. Roma-di might have had in her extended family a few aunts who were working women. Ishita-di's two aunts Shanta Devi and Sita Devi were both schoolteachers, one honorary, the other paid, but her mother and grandmother did not hold down jobs. However, her great-grandmother, the famous Manorama Majumdar of Barisal, was one of the first salaried schoolteachers in Bengal. She had taken part in the freedom movement at a very young age and she had even conducted Brahmo services as a priest. But she was an honourable exception. None of my other colleagues had such ancestry to boast of or lean on. They had to step out boldly on their own.

The principals of Bethune College are equally worth talking about. The first principal I came across was Mrinalini Emerson; a member of the family of Womesh Bonnerjee, one of the first generation of nationalist leaders of India. She wore her sari rather clumsily, like a novice, and couldn't speak Bengali too well. Although not very efficient as a principal, she had a big smile and a heart as large as the ocean. She taught English and the word 'malice' she kept out of her dictionary. Her husband Lindsay Emerson worked for the *Statesman*. People said he was a bit of a bohemian. Whenever his name came up in conversation, Mrinalini would say in a loving way, 'Poor Lindsay!' It sounded so sweet. After Mrinalini came Nalini Das. She was Satyajit Ray's Nini-di, his father's sister's daughter. Nalini edited the children's magazine *Sandesh* which their grandfather Upendrakishore Ray Chaudhury had established many years ago. Nalini-di was an able administrator, an orthodox Brahmo and a woman of strong principles. We all enjoyed talking to her and listening to her talk. After her came Dipti Tripathi, a famous dancer of yesteryears and later the wife of historian Amales Tripathi. She was a vivacious character and a central figure in all cultural programmes organized by the college.

The cultural programmes at Bethune were of a high standard, particularly the plays that were staged. There were two big events held every year. One was the prize distribution ceremony and the other was the reunion of the alumni. The teachers shared duties and responsibilities. A major part was managed by Dipti-di, Ishita-di and Karabi-di. Ishita-di designed costumes for English plays, Karabi-di taught singing and Dipti-di took charge of direction. The stage décor was superb. A palanquin was brought in once; another time, a huge wooden horse was constructed for a tribal dance of Madhya Pradesh. Not bad for a medium-sized undergraduate college with budget constraints. The students' acting was of the first order. I remember a dance-drama based on Rabindranath Tagore's story *Dalia* that they staged once. The proud hauteur of Meenakshi Ghosh in the role of Julikha, the spirited vigour of Kajal Sen as Dalia and the romantic ardour of Bharati Mukherjee as Amina. How can I ever forget them? They were part of my youth.

Nevertheless, it was while I was in Bethune that a new infatuation took hold of me—research. I was sitting on the veranda of our King's Court apartment one day way back in 1968–69. I saw by the roadside a big kinshuk tree laden with flowers. People passed by without paying any attention to it. A host of questions came crowding to my mind. For how many years had I been staring at that same kinshuk tree? How many years had I been teaching at Bethune College? And when did I pass my MA? Fourteen years ago! A sharp shock passed through my body and I almost began to tremble. I had been sitting around for fourteen years without studying anything new! I just put on my shoes, called a car and practically ran to the Darbhanga building of Calcutta University and straight into the office of Amales Tripathi, head of the history department. He was very surprised to see me. We had a long discussion and I settled on doing research on Hyderabad. Historical research had made rapid strides over the last fourteen years but not much work had been done on the former princely states. Hyderabad was geographically the largest among them and was centrally situated in India.

My life took a different turn. Hyderabad got under my skin and I forgot about everything else. While teaching Greek history in class, instead of the Parthenon, the Charminar came floating to my mind. Elaborating on the Renaissance in Europe, I thought of Dewan Salar Jung constructing the railway lines in Hyderabad. I was becoming short-tempered at home. Anything that was unrelated to Hyderabad made me lose patience.

The only place where I could find some mental peace was at the National Library. My daily routine changed. I would reach the library before nine o'clock. From there I would go to Bethune College and after classes come back to the library again for as long as it was open. Such tranquillity, such happiness lay there. I would sit in the reading room at one corner of the long table, which used to be the banquet table of the British viceroy in the colonial days. I made notes on ruled papers in long hand in big letters—no computers in vogue then! Nor was photocopying of rare documents permitted. I became friends with the library staff. They treated me respectfully; seldom did they delay in issuing the books I wanted.

After I'd finished with the National Library, I went to work at the National Archives in New Delhi. Shasuri-ma had stopped me from going to Oxford but now she held out a helping hand. I would go to Delhi every vacation and she would move in to King's Court to look after the children. This is a debt I can never repay.

In Delhi, I stayed with Sej-da and Sej-di, that is, Santosh and Sita Sen. They dropped me at the Archives in the morning before nine. Sej-di packed sandwiches for me—though I could never eat them for lack of time. I worked there until it closed in the evening. This was not the National Library of Calcutta where people would oblige me and hurry simply because I needed the books. At the National Archives I had to requisition the files I would be working on the following day in advance the evening before. One day I got fed up waiting for a file I needed and spoke in exasperation to myself in Bengali, 'Oh, I cannot stand it.' A little later two young men came up and asked in Bengali, 'Are you Bengali? We see you here every day and are quite amazed. You work all the time without breaking for tea or lunch.'

I replied, 'I don't have the time. I've left three little children at home and I have to finish my work fast. You people are young; you can take your time. And your research will be better if you do.' They were a pair—Gopal and Sukumar. They forced me to take twenty minutes off every afternoon. They had tea, made good use of Sej-di's sandwiches and made me eat some. In later years Sukumar became director of the National Archives. Gopal got a good job in Lucknow.

After Delhi I would have to go to Hyderabad to look at the material available there. I booked accommodation at the Osmania University hostel. Bina-di of the mathematics department in Bethune College said, 'Why will you stay in a hostel? Kaku, my father's younger brother, lives there; he'll be happy to put you up.'

Sukhendu was delighted when he heard this. 'Since Bina-di has made this offer on her own, stay with her Kaku.' Spoken like a true husband. His wife must stay under his care or under the care of another respectable gentleman. Unless a woman is under someone's protection, men can never feel relaxed.

Bina-di's uncle came to pick me up from the airport in

Hyderabad. His house was being repaired so he had arranged accommodation for me at a friend's place. I was dejected. After all, I didn't even know the man and here he was expecting me to stay with friends. I went along anyhow, thinking that I would shift after two or three days without giving offence to Bina-di or her uncle. It was past evening and the living room in the house of his friend was dimly lit. The couple was at home but there was no sign of them. The clock ticked on. I felt a little humiliated. I can't possibly stay here, I began to think when a woman drew the curtain aside and entered the room. To me, she looked as if Kamal-lata from Saratchandra Chattopadhyay's popular novel *Srikanta* had come alive! I was floored. She wore a sandalwood paste tika on her forehead, held a plate of fruits and sweets in her hands and said apologetically, 'I was saying my prayers, so I was delayed. Please have some sweets.' I picked up a sweet and asked, 'Where shall I keep my suitcase, Didi?' It did not take me a minute to decide that I had arrived at the right place in Hyderabad. I enjoyed my stay at Didi's enormously. Bengalis who live outside Bengal have a way of making even an unknown fellow Bengali feel very much at home! But Didi was someone special.

The record-keeping in Hyderabad was disorganized in those days. All the historic letters that Dewan Salar Jung received from well-known people from India and abroad as well as office copies of the replies he sent were all bundled up together in red cloth packages without cataloguing (now they are properly arranged, I understand). I would open these bundles one at a time and select the most important ones to read. Most of them were written in English. My research topic was British paramountcy and these letters were invaluable for viewing British politics from a Hyderabadi perspective. There were many documents in Urdu and Persian but I don't know these languages. I made friends with one of the employees who was familiar with Urdu and Persian. He was a benevolent soul. In the evenings after office hours and also in the mornings on holidays he would pick out important portions of relevant documents and explain them to me in English. I would take notes. When I told this to Didi, she looked grave. 'You don't say! All the other researchers had left, and you were alone in his room? Not done, Bharati.' I loved Didi but I continued with my work and my friend continued to help.

I finished my work in Hyderabad, came back to Calcutta, submitted my thesis and breathed a sigh of relief. Now I could go back to my normal life. Yet it was not possible to do that because research had become my new passion. When I finished one book I felt dispirited until I could get on to the next. Till I found a theme that interested me, the world seemed different to me, like life held no meaning. Research is still the one thing I enjoy most today.

Meanwhile, I got an offer from Calcutta University—Amales-babu asked me to join as a part-time lecturer. I was happy to accept. Those who were my teachers once, whom I had looked on with respect from afar, would be my colleagues now. The first day I entered the classroom I saw the girls and boys all seated together side by side. That was not how it used to be in our time. Times had changed and I liked what I saw. But somehow I felt nervous; something I had never felt even on the first day at Bethune College. Being all strung up I rushed through my lecture and finished in half an hour what would normally have taken one hour. I sat there dumbfounded for a while, and then I started laughing. The students started laughing too and we became friends. All was well thereafter.

Some time later I joined the university as a full-time reader/ associate professor in the history department. I bade a tearful farewell to Bethune College. Fortunately, I didn't have to cut myself off completely. A few years later they invited me to be president of the college governing body and today I am still happily in touch with my old institute.

History classes at the university were held on the fourth floor of the Darbhanga building. The department did not have its own office or staff room. The common staff room of the arts and commerce faculties was on the second floor of the Ashutosh building. It was a large hall. A couple of non-teaching staff sat at one corner—they handled bills and letters for the teachers. In the middle of the room several medium-sized tables were joined together to make one big seating arrangement with rows of chairs on either side. Teachers sat there, drank tea, held discussions, talked politics or simply chatted. The room was always buzzing with excitement.

The history department didn't remain in the Darbhanga building for long. It moved to Hazra Road next to the law college. All the hassle of shifting files and books and ordering new furniture was borne by the young teacher Bhaskar Chakraborty. It was a three-storeyed building; the first and second floors were earmarked for modern and medieval history and the ground floor for Islamic history. The teachers' rooms were on the first floor on two sides of a long corridor. Two teachers shared a room. The head of the department, Professor Amales Tripathi, had a separate room in the middle. The new building created a sense of intimacy among the members of the history faculty.

The department was full of brilliant teachers, young and old. Amales Tripathi was a noted historian. He spoke and wrote excellent English and Bengali. Nilmoni Mukherjee had a D.Litt. and was a man of few words and high scholarship. Arun Das Gupta was enthusiastic about everything, especially tracking new fields of research. He was the one who suggested I take up women's studies. Among the younger colleagues, we had Hari Vasudevan, Gautam Bhadra, Shekhar Bandopadhyay, Rudrangshu Mukherjee, Suranjan Das and Bhaskar Chakraborty. In my opinion they were all brilliant. Rudrangshu is a successful journalist. Shekhar is a well-known professor in New Zealand. Hari is a widely respected specialist on Russia. Suranjan is vice chancellor, Calcutta University, and Bhaskar Chakraborty, currently director of the Centre for Social Studies in the department of history, reigns as the main pillar of the department.

Many good students came to study history. Suman Chattopadhyay is a media man today, Tapati Guhathakurta is an art historian, Kumkum Chatterjee teaches in Pennsylvania, Nandini Gooptu teaches at Oxford, Sudeshna Banerjee and Jayanta Sengupta are at Jadavpur University, Suparna Gooptu is looking after the Gandhian Studies Centre, Calcutta University, and Samita Sen is director of the School of Women's Studies at Jadavpur University. They were all top students of our department. They were all very well behaved and I was personally close to quite a few. But all of them didn't necessarily follow my advice. I remember one girl in the first-year MA class. I thought she would make an excellent officer in the IAS. I sent for her and suggested that she prepare to sit for the IAS exam. She looked upset. 'You want me to join the IAS? Are you saying I won't be any good at research?' I was taken aback. What could I say? I had just thought to myself that if all our best students decided to become academics, that wouldn't be right. We need our brightest students to enter the all-India services—administration, police, army, aviation, communication.

That was how I was biding my time in the history

department, centred on research and teaching. One fine morning Asish Ray, a leading organizer among university teachers, turned up at my house. He said they were on the lookout for a suitable person for the post of pro-vice chancellor (academic) of Calcutta University. It was a post just below that of the vice chancellor; this person was meant to assist him and stand in for him in his absence. The pro vice chancellor was also to supervise the entire undergraduate education programme of the university. The governor makes the appointment on the advice of the vice chancellor and the minister of higher education. If I were agreeable, my professor friends would propose my name to the vice chancellor. I agreed. I had once wanted to join the IAS so I thought I would enjoy being part of the administration.

Two days later, on 7 March 1988, I was summoned to the Raj Bhavan to meet the governor. I went there in the evening. Governor Nurul Hasan held me back for one hour. He didn't bring up academic matters or the affairs of the university. He simply heard me talk. Those who haven't met Nurul Hasan have missed something. He was a rare personality, both gracious and graceful. He was enormous in size, walked with a swaying gait yet he dripped with style. On the one hand was his aristocratic background and on the other his leftist ideals; on the one hand his immense scholarship, on the other his experiences as a statesman. What was actually happening was that the governor was interviewing me for a job but not for one moment did it feel like that. It was only when I came back home that it occurred to me that I hadn't said any of the things I had wanted to say.

Three days later I saw my picture in the front page of a newspaper—I don't know where they got it—with my name. The media gave me plenty of coverage as the first woman pro-vice chancellor of Calcutta University. Some of them asked, 'What is your politics?' I said I believed in two things: justice and efficiency.

I took charge on 14 March 1988. And once again the course of my life took a different turn. I plunged into an ocean of work. I say 'work' for want of a better word. Actually, I never thought of it as work. I was a woman from an ordinary middle-class family who had been given an opportunity to help thousands of young people. That year the number of undergraduate students in colleges under Calcutta University was nearly two lakh and roughly a lakh was to be added every subsequent year. Could I make a positive impact on so many young lives?

The first thing was to see that the examination results came out in time. The BA honours results were taking ten months to be published. This meant that in effect, students in West Bengal were losing a whole year. I decided that the honours results had to come out in three months so that students might apply to other educational institutions outside West Bengal in other states in India or abroad without missing a year. This was not something one could do alone. The staff of the university and the professors extended their full cooperation, particularly Professor Anil Bhattacharya, a teacher in an undergraduate college, and a member of the Syndicate, the policy-framing council of the university. I can't count the number of times he sat with me in my office helping me chalk out a detailed plan for this project. The deputy controller of examinations, Arun Kiran Chakraborty, helped as did the assistant controller, Onkar Sadhan Adhikari, currently the controller of examinations. Gopal Banerjee was the controller at the time, an intelligent, efficient and colourful personality. He could have opposed me if he had wanted to but he didn't. Consequently, the

BA honours Part II results were declared one day before the completion of three months after the exam. The results have kept to the schedule ever since, so I understand.

I turned my attention next to the system of awarding Ph.D. degrees. Postgraduate exams were under the direct supervision of the vice chancellor. In my time the pro-vice chancellor took charge of the Ph.D. programme with the approval of the vice chancellor. When I entered the Ph.D. office, I was horrified. The cupboards were filled with stacks of unexamined theses! They had been submitted by researchers but not forwarded to examiners. I knew that the university had been in turmoil for several years but did that mean that the submitted theses would lie in such neglect? Should dreams lie locked up in dusty cupboards? Work started in full swing. The Ph.D. department personnel put in commendable effort and the one who worked hardest was Jyotibhusan Datta. He is someone I still remember; bespectacled, fair, intelligent and honest. He worked till nine or ten o'clock in the evening day after day. With the combined effort of all these people, I was able to clear the backlog. Before I left the university, Ph.D. results were routinely declared within one year of submission, barring ten to fifteen controversial theses.

The person whom till now I have not mentioned was the vice chancellor Bhaskar Ray Chowdhury. He did not exactly welcome me with open arms as the first woman pro-vice chancellor. Frankly, the first time I met him I thought he was arrogant, discourteous and garrulous. We had many differences, even outright arguments on matters big and small. Once while addressing the Syndicate, he kept using the word 'man'. I objected to it and said, 'You must say man and woman.'

He glared back at me and said, 'Man includes woman.'

'Then in that case you must use the word woman. Woman also includes man. Notice the spelling.'

Bhaskar Ray Chowdhury was not one to be put down. He ignored me completely and continued using the word man. Another serious difference arose when I wanted Sukanta Chaudhuri, at the time a professor at Presidency College, to be selected for a prestigious chair in the English department. According to Bhaskar-babu, Sukanta had not shown any interest or even submitted an application. 'On what basis is he to be selected?' he asked.

'On the basis of his well-known academic excellence. The university rules permit professorial selection without an application,' I replied. Ultimately, Bhaskar Ray Chowdhury and the selection committee did not accept my recommendation. Sukanta joined Jadavpur University.

The power struggle between the vice chancellor and the pro-vice chancellor (academic) of Calcutta University had a long history. One was head of the university; the other kept in constant touch with the huge body of undergraduate students and professors. One presided over the Syndicate; the other was present there. The pro-vice chancellor presided over three undergraduate councils: one, arts, commerce and science; two, medicine; and three, engineering, in which the vice chancellor had no place. It was easily conceivable that tensions could exist. But the tension between Bhaskar-babu and I did not turn to outright antagonism because I respected the man. He was dynamic, he was blunt in speech, but he spoke his mind and had a big heart and his one desire was to improve the university.

As pro-vice chancellor, I had announced right at the start that I wished to open a women's studies centre. Calcutta University being rather old and orthodox, no one was keen on the idea. In fact, they were against it. Bhaskar Ray Chowdhury and feminism were poles apart. Still he did not oppose the idea. He only asked, 'Who will finance it?'

'The University Grants Commission. But they need your signature of approval,' I replied.

He gave his signature. We received the grant and organized a big inaugural ceremony. Chief minister Jyoti Basu, finance minister Asim Dasgupta and famous social worker Phulrenu Guha attended. The two best rooms on the second floor of Darbhanga building were allotted to the Centre for Research in Women's Studies. The furniture arrived fast. The assistants I selected—first Sarvani Gooptu, later Supriya Guha—were given appointment letters by the vice chancellor, no questions asked. Sarvani was sincere but she had to leave soon; Supriya was intelligent, capable and gifted with a winning personality; the Centre started running extremely well. Teachers arrived from undergraduate colleges, so did students. Research projects on various subjects were taken up. Field research was done on scheduled caste women in three villages of West Bengal. Several eminently successful seminars were held. I would send Supriya and our research students to conferences in other states whenever I myself received any such invitation. They received compliments, felt encouraged and wrote books and articles. I devoted my attention to editing a historic women's journal, *Bamabodhini Patrika, 1863–1922* in two volumes.

Now I come to a later phase; even though it seems like a deviation from chronology, I won't get an opportunity to deal with it later. While I was pro-vice chancellor and also later, I took some time out to pursue research on women. I have written or edited eight books on the history of Indian women. This has brought me in contact with the women's movement. But it is also something I have inherited from

Sundar-ma, Didi-ma and Ma. They had all worked for various women's groups which are an integral part of the women's movement. The character of the women's movement has changed considerably since then. Earlier, most of the women's organizations were middle class. We have learnt now that gender is a social construct, not a biological one. Therefore, to break down gender discrimination, it is not enough to build women's groups and women's studies centres. We must connect with other social movements that are combating other forms of social discrimination. Moreover, in our country the role of men in advancing women's 'development' is a matter of record in the history of the nineteenth century. That initiative must be rekindled today.

I used the word 'development'. Notions of what development signifies have changed too. In earlier times, women leaders would shed tears for the miserable status of women and work for their 'upliftment'. Amartya Sen in his book, *The Argumentative Indian,* has, in connection with such an approach, used the word 'patient' for women to be 'uplifted', as if the aim of development was to nurse ailing women back to health. Nowadays we look at women not only as victims, but as agents of change. We demand women's empowerment to enable them to exercise agency in determining their own lives. We believe that when women are empowered, it will benefit not only women themselves but men, children, and indeed, the entire society. It is the Centre for Research in Women's Studies that helped me formulate my ideas and approach to research. None of this would have happened had Bhaskar Ray Chowdhury opposed the institution of this new discipline and a new centre.

There was one big project that Bhaskar-babu and I undertook together. Calcutta University owned a treasure trove of ancient scrolls and manuscripts—at least twenty thousand in number. Arabic, Persian, Bengali, Hindi, Oriya, Sanskrit and Tibetan writings and illustrated scrolls were stacked in five or six different places without any system of classification or cataloguing. Some of them lay in cloth bundles in a room marked 'Manuscript Division'. When I went to inspect this room in my capacity, I was aghast. Bhaskar-babu listened carefully to what I had to say and agreed to take up the initiative. A new room was built and appropriate shelves put in for the manuscripts to be stored in one place. The day this newly furbished Manuscript Division was inaugurated, I was so happy my feet hardly touched the ground!

Bhaskar-babu completed his term of office and retired. Rathindra Narayan Basu came in his place. There are some people in this world about whom you can have nothing either good or bad to say. Rathin-babu was such a man. I continued working under him. After the first four-year term I was reappointed for a second term. My work as pro-vice chancellor continued apace.

Was there no inner conflict, no tension or at least some impediments that I had to face in my work? Indeed there were, and in full measure. The first problem was the vice chancellor himself—both Bhaskar-babu and Rathin-babu. As I have mentioned earlier, there were some innate problems in the very way that our jobs were defined. Inequities in the power structure made rivalry inevitable. One had to adjust and accommodate. Moreover, there was a good deal of tension between me and the controller of examinations, Gopal Banerjee. This was aggravated by me, he was not to blame. I was interfering far too much in his area, switching around positions and responsibilities in his department as and when I thought it necessary and holding meetings with officers who worked under him. He had every right to be displeased. I was constantly on guard in case my efforts were sabotaged from within but he did no such thing. I must thank him for that. I was a woman—their first female boss—and on top of that I had something to say about everything. It must have been very difficult to stomach. In executing my job, another area that I had to pay special attention to comprised the teachers' associations in the university and its affiliated colleges. Two organizations, the West Bengal Calcutta University Teachers' Association (WBCUTA) and the Calcutta University Teachers' Association (CUTA) were extremely powerful. Without their cooperation it would be impossible to run the university. The Syndicate was another body whose advice and criticism one had to accept without protest, whether one agreed with the venerable members or not. I was fortunate that I managed to keep on their right side, more or less. They would come to my office quite often to discuss with me their forthcoming agenda. Fortunately, political leaders who were outside the university did not come to see me. Why should they? I was only 'number two'. They could always approach the vice chancellor straight, if needed. There is always a certain fascination for being the top boss anywhere, but there are some advantages in being second-in-command.

My real problem lay within my own family. Sukhendu did not like my post as pro-vice chancellor. The phone would ring day and night at any odd hour and there was no knowing when I would be back home and when I did return, my mind would be completely preoccupied with university affairs. I hardly had time to meet friends and relatives, exchanges with Sukhendu were brief and an unspoken strain in our relationship—more powerful than anything spoken, as we all well know! No quarrels took place, interestingly—had become a part of my daily life. My two daughters were overseas. My son Jishnu was studying at Jadavpur University and I could spend hardly any time with him. Although I didn't feel guilty about it—I believe that one cannot do everything one wants to—sometimes there was a secret pain within my heart. Nevertheless, I enormously enjoyed my work as pro-vice chancellor. And there was the sweet taste of success in the results I achieved.

I prefer to live by the rules, by and large. Though I profess openly that 'Laws are made for people, not people for laws,' in my heart of hearts I believe that following rules makes for a sense of discipline. Making exceptions opens the way for malpractices and corruption. Does that mean that I never bent the rules in my role as pro-vice chancellor? I cannot say that. Let me give a few instances.

A well-known college in the city was not allowing a BA honours student to sit for the final exams because he didn't have the minimum requisite class attendance as per university rules. How could he? He was playing cricket all the time! I saw the boy who looked bright, quite serious and was very well behaved. I was impressed. Sports are a part of education, I reasoned. Since he was playing for the state cricket team, there was an excuse for his not attending classes. I gave him special permission and it was ratified by the Syndicate. Happily for us, the boy justified our decision by doing well in the exam. His name: Sourav Ganguly. Who knew then that the boy would one day be captain of the Indian cricket team?

On another occasion, I had gone to the Academy of Fine Arts in order to view an exhibition of Paresh Maity's paintings. I was standing in rapt admiration before a large painting of a Rajasthani woman. A young man came up to me and said, 'Do you like it? If you do, please take it.' How absurd! Where would I get the money to buy such a painting? 'You don't recognize me? I'm Paresh,' the young man said. He had passed out of the Government Art College in Calcutta and gained provisional admission for further studies at the Delhi College of Art. But because the graduation results of Calcutta University were being delayed, his name was likely to be scratched from the Delhi admission list. Paresh had come to see me then, and now he reminded me of how I had requested the controller of examinations to forward his mark sheets confidentially to Delhi. A young boy from Bengal should not lose his opportunity due to any delay on the part of our university, I had apparently told the controller. And so, his results were sent. It was because of me, Paresh said prettily, that he could pursue postgraduate studies in Delhi and realize his ambition. I told him, 'You offered to give the painting to me; that in itself is gift enough for me. Thank you, but I don't have space to hang such a large painting in my small apartment.' I have met Paresh many times since then. Rakhi Sarkar has opened an art gallery in Calcutta called the Centre of International Modern Art (CIMA). There's another gem of a girl. She has set up this marvellous place in such a short time. CIMA exhibits Paresh Maity's canvases quite often. I go there, admire his work, meet him and his artist wife Jayasree and have a altogether pleasant time.

I have spent long years in the working world. Wherever I went I enjoyed myself to the full. Yet nothing can compare with the satisfaction I felt during my years as pro-vice chancellor. When I grow old and decrepit, when I can no longer write books or read because of my weakening eyes, I will sit in an easy chair and reminisce. And in my eyes glistening with tears of joy I will see reflected the faces of my past pupils—'a host of golden daffodils'.

ON THE POLITICAL FRONT

Straight after my eight-year stint as pro-vice chancellor of Calcutta University, I took charge of the newly formed West Bengal Council of Higher Education. Its mandate was to streamline issues of higher education throughout the state. As it turned out, I quit that post in a matter of months for an astonishing reason. The leading partner of the ruling Left Front government, the CPI(M), offered me a seat in the Rajya Sabha—the Upper House of the Indian parliament. I was stunned. I had nothing to do with the party, in fact, with any form of politics, and had never taken active part in any political movement. Why this totally unexpected offer from a political party arose, I had no idea. Jyoti Basu was chief minister of the state at the time. This must be his idea, I thought, so I talked it over with him. I asked whether it entailed my becoming a member of his party. 'Not if you don't wish to,' was his suave answer. No, I certainly did not wish to. Therefore, I went off to Delhi as a Member of Parliament (MP) with no party affiliation whatsoever.

I had studied political science at school and college and had a pretty good idea of how the Rajya Sabha was formed, what powers it had and what its relationship with the Lok Sabha was. But I had never imagined the setting to be so regal. Entering the parliament building, you first encounter the guards and security personnel, then a long red carpeted corridor at the end of which you find five or six marshals, all educated and experienced gentlemen. Then through an immense door to the lobby—that too red carpeted wall to wall. Leather upholstered sofas with elegant wooden tables in front allow members to hold informal discussions and make notes during presentations. Three doors lead from the lobby into the historic assembly hall with access restricted to sitting MPs. Rows of desks and benches are arranged in arcs, one behind the other, with expensive furniture gleaming with polish. Ten or twelve members can sit on each bench. MPs sit in groups party-wise—the ruling party on the left, the main opposition party on the right, while the others sit in the centre. Party leaders sit in the front rows while newcomers occupy the back rows. In the centre of the hall at one end is a slightly raised dais. The secretary general of the Rajya Sabha sits below it with a few members of his staff. On the dais sits the chairman who is the vice president of India.

When I joined the Rajya Sabha, K.R. Narayanan was its chairman, a polite and cultured man. He came from an indigent dalit family. On the second day I obtained permission to meet him and entered his room with some trepidation. I said, 'I'm very nervous, I don't know anything about politics. How should I conduct myself here.'

He laughed. 'You know where I received my best training in politics? When I was vice chancellor of Jawaharlal Nehru University.'

I forgot where I was and burst out laughing. He smiled reassuringly and said, 'You have managed Calcutta University for eight years. Just go ahead with confidence. You will do well.'

I proceeded, bursting with self-confidence. Just as I was about to step into the hall, I came across a good-looking, well-dressed, middle-aged woman with a sweet smile. I introduced myself. She said, 'Welcome. I am so happy to have you here.' She didn't give her own name, so I repeated my name and asked, 'And you, madam?' There was a minute's stony silence after which she gave her name haltingly, 'I am Vyjayanthimala Bali.' I shrunk in embarrassment. I should have recognized her; I'd seen her in a Hindi film called *Nagin*. When Shabana Azmi arrived as an MP, I had become somewhat smarter by then, thanks to having rubbed shoulders with politicians. I went straight up to her and said, 'You're Shabana Azmi. You look even prettier in the flesh than on screen.' Shabana was highly intelligent and politically conscious. She came regularly to the sessions—unlike Dilip Kumar or Raj Babbar—and prepared her arguments with a great deal of care. She spoke well. She and I held common views on many issues and we got on well. Her special area of interest was housing for the homeless. Mine was women's empowerment and the need for clean drinking water for all. We often discussed our points and worked together.

Our sessions at the Rajya Sabha started at 11 a.m. sharp. Ahead of that, at around 10.30 a.m., various party leaders would confer with the chairman. I was not supposed to be there but I often went along quite shamelessly because it held great attraction for me. They discussed the day's agenda. Would the programme printed in the bulletin be followed to the letter or would there be an adjournment? Would there be loud protests on any particular issue or would there be a quiet debate? Everything was discussed in advance at that meeting. The leaders would usually let one another know what their stand would be. I would sit in silence and observe how negotiations were made and bargains struck and how a leader managed to put forward his party's agenda or issues relating to his own state. It was a unique experience. As an outsider one can never make out how much the leaders actually know and what negotiations they have to make on an everyday basis. You have to attend the 10.30 meeting with the chairman to appreciate how deeply dependent on party politics our parliament really is and how deftly the leaders push their party's agendas.

The 10.30 meeting would end three to four minutes before 11 a.m., in time for everyone to take their seats and start the session at the stroke of the hour. That there are frequent disruptions during the session is a fact that everyone knows, thanks to television coverage. If there are no such incidents, the first hour is devoted to questions and answers. Members submit their questions in advance—these are printed in a thin red booklet. The relevant ministers answer the questions according to the serial number. If members are satisfied with the reply given, well and good. If not, further questions are allowed. This question hour ends at noon. It is now the turn for the ministers to submit their reports to parliament in writing—that is, lay the papers on the table of parliament. Then topics come up for special mention. (For example, it could be a train accident or a rape case.) Just three minutes are allowed for each topic to be raised. Sometimes the chairman allows a brief discussion on a topic considered extremely grave. Several members may voice their opinions on the subject. I once brought up the issue of a married woman's right to live in her marital home. A woman leaves her parents' home after marriage and goes to live with her husband and in-laws. If after a number of years living in the marital home, she is suddenly thrown out, where would she go? That day the discussion extended to an hour and forty-five minutes instead of the usual half-hour. Many members participated in this discussion but there was no mention of this in the next morning's papers. Our complaint against the media is precisely this: they often marginalize real day-to-day issues and ignore anything that is not sensational. However, it has to be said that they do manage, more or less, to cover political debates. I remember Dr Manmohan Singh had raised the issue of US intervention in Afghanistan. He was leader of the opposition then and he spoke very well. His argument was that it was an international issue therefore the USA should have consulted India, China and others. This gentleman, in his blue turban and spotless white kurta-pyjama, used to deliver his speeches in a soft, slow and calm manner. When he was not speaking, he would sit upright in his own seat and look straight ahead. He didn't look around nor did he speak with anyone unnecessarily. Not once did I see him in the lobby or central hall getting into huddles with any group or just chatting away with someone or the other. He came in with quick steps, walked out equally fast, his whole demeanour shining with integrity.

One o'clock was lunch break. The main business of the House was conducted from 2 to 5 p.m.—discussing bills and passing laws. Of course, on the day the budget was presented, the whole day would be devoted to debates on finance. On this particular topic, few could match Pranab Mukherjee. His brain is like a computer. Innumerable data—particularly on economic and foreign affairs—are stored in his memory bank. Exact dates, names, incidents, are all docketed systematically; just press a button and take a printout. Kapil Sibal's forte was his sharp, logical arguments delivered in lucid, impeccable English. He spoke at great length but thanks to his panache, he didn't give one a headache. Jayanti Natarajan, too, spoke very well. Dr Karan Singh from Kashmir was a man of few words but they were weighty ones. Listening to him was sheer pleasure—simply watching him too! Ambika Soni came during the last phase of my tenure; cerebral and capable.

Some happy memories during my days in parliament were of the special dinner hosted by the president of India in honour of eminent and distinguished guests, mostly heads of other countries. K.R. Narayanan, when he became president, invited me several times to these dinners and I accepted with pleasure. I didn't speak much—whom would I talk to anyway? I was more interested in watching the dignitaries, Indian and foreign, their dress and manners, the splendour of Rashtrapati Bhavan, the antique furniture, the priceless oil paintings, the interior décor and the management style.

As guests arrived in the reception room, fruit juice would be served to start with. Then a soft tinkling bell would announce it was time for dinner. The guests trooped into the banquet hall and took their seats as indicated by the name cards. The president entered last, accompanied by the chief guest. Rows of shining silver cutlery, butter dishes, salt and pepper and condiments, along with tiny silver vases with seasonal flowers decorated the table. Behind us the serving staff stood in white tunics, red cummerbunds and red turbans. The courses were served one at a time. The guests took up their knives and forks and picked on their food delicately. I will recall one menu here.

It was a lunch in honour of the Norwegian premier. First, fruit cocktails were served in silver tumblers. Next came leek soup. Then large plates were placed before us for the main courses. The serving men brought in tandoori fish, mutton seekh kabab, chicken biryani, mutton korma, dal bukhara, two kinds of vegetables, nan, roti, cucumber raita, papad and salad. Plates were changed again. Sweets arrived: jalebi and cake and a basket of fruits. And finally, tea and coffee. For vegetarians, there was paneer kabab, vegetable pancake, navratan korma, vegetable biryani. The menu was always north Indian. Perhaps Bengali delicacies like chingri machher malaikari, or rui machher doi-machh, or chitol machher muitha would not go well with such a menu. But in place of jalebis, chhanar payesh, rossogolla or that wonderful sweet called patisapta would not be so bad.

I attended all official dinners. On 15 August and 26 January we gathered on the lawns of Rashtrapati Bhavan for tea. The president would grace the occasion along with ministers and a host of distinguished guests. It was an excellent place to pick up bits of political news, gossip and rumour. I saw Sonia Gandhi for the first time at an Independence Day function. I was surprised. Slim, pretty, oozing intelligence, smart; photographs do not capture her charismatic personality. Perhaps she is not photogenic. She was not the consummate and astute politician that she is today but there was a quiet expression of determination and strong character even then. Some people say she is arrogant. I do not agree at all. When I sent her a copy of my book, *Women of India: Colonial and Post-colonial Periods* which had just been published, she immediately sent me a fine acknowledgement and letter of than us. Such politeness was not essential for an ordinary woman like me.

I did not attend private parties but made an exception in the case of Kartar Singh Duggal, the Punjabi writer. He didn't invite me, he practically ordered me to attend. In parliament, he sat upright and spoke on education, libraries and culture; he was completely secular though he ardently believed in Sikhism. A living example of the tenet that there is no antagonism between religious belief and secularism. He has translated the Guru Granth Sahib into English in his old age; listening to him read out from his translation is a delight.

One has so many different experiences in parliament. The day the parliament building came under terrorist attack, on 13 December 2001, I was in the central hall having coffee with General Sankar Ray Chaudhuri. I saw the deputy speaker P.M. Sayeed running with his slight limp. Before we could make out what was going on, all the doors in the hall were shut and the sound of gunfire reached us. A marshal ordered everyone to remain seated. 'Raiders are attacking this building.' That's great, I thought. All doors were closed and there was no way to get out and run. If they did come for us, we would all have to die together. I started laughing. One member asked me in an annoyed and serious voice, 'Why are you laughing, madam? It's a serious matter.' That's exactly why I was laughing. We were helpless. Death would certainly come to all of us one day. But who could have thought that it would come in this way?

Death did not come that day. The vice-president Krishna Kant used to go home for lunch at 1 p.m. The attackers knew there would be no armed guards on the grounds—parliamentary guards used to be unarmed those days—so they timed their entry. But they were out of luck, poor fellows. Krishna Kant was on his way out when one of the MPs approached him for some urgent business. Krishna Kant stopped. One of his bodyguards noticed the attackers and opened fire. A gun battle ensued which lasted for about twenty minutes. None of the attackers escaped alive. We were saved but an innocent staff member lost his life. That is how it always happens. Those who are not involved in any way, they're the ones who die. Wars, riots or terrorist attacks, it's always the same.

Some two hours later, Pramod Mahajan, then a minister, announced happily, 'Our cars are waiting outside. Please take those cars. You must report to the police station before you go home.' You should have seen Mahajan's triumphant look; as if he himself had rescued us! Pramod Mahajan, with his bright, intelligent face, used to walk around with a great

deal of authority. The Bharatiya Janata Party (BJP) was the
ruling party and the whole world was his. Arun Jaitley was
similarly inclined but his behaviour was polite and gentle.
Arun Shourie made no outward show of power but the very
expression on his face conveyed the message in a controlled
fashion. The BJP government was perhaps preparing these three
men to take over the reins of government in the future. If
their party had won the next elections, the plan might have
worked. They had the opportunity to learn how to govern
but not how to handle the situation when they lost. The BJP
has not experience enough to deal with the ups and downs
of political power, which is why the would-be new generation
leaders—alas, Pramod Mahajan has passed away—never got
their expected roles.

However, I won't say that my heart weeps for these people.
The one I feel sorry for is Najma Heptullah. As deputy
chairman of the Rajya Sabha, she conducted the proceedings
with a deft hand for fourteen years. She was on good terms
personally with most of the members irrespective of their
party affiliations. I have seen her at international forums too.
She was once contending for the post of the president of the
Inter-Parliamentary Union of world parliaments of democratic
nations. I was in London at the time in connection with an
academic conference. She requested me to go to Berlin to
canvass votes for her which was when I realized how popular
she was. She won by a huge margin. Najma was a member
of the Congress party then but she resigned suddenly. It was
her excessive ambition that caused her to do so. Fearing that
her own party would not nominate her for the post of vice-
president of India, she switched over to the BJP and she lost
everything. Thus a combination of high ambition and high
profile invariably spells doom in politics.

Someone else I remember is Purno A. Sangma from Meghalaya, a powerful orator with a vibrant personality. For some reason, he suddenly got into a tangle with Sonia Gandhi. When I became an MP he was speaker of the Lok Sabha. He would wave his arms, shake his head and vigorously put down any member for any unparliamentary language used. 'No, no, you can't say this. I won't allow you. Sit down. I say, please sit down.' I thought that this was exactly how a speaker should be. I have accompanied him on delegations to Mauritius and Indonesia. At the Inter-Parliamentary Union meet in Jakarta, he gave me the opportunity to speak on behalf of India. He did me one other big favour by inviting me to a dinner at his home one evening. The chief guest was Emika Aniyoko, secretary general of the Commonwealth Parliamentary Association. He was Nigerian and we became friends in a matter of minutes. Some months later, Aniyoko invited me to be a Commonwealth observer for the general elections in Guyana. Aniyoko had invited fourteen observers from as many countries, with Sir Anthony Siaguru of Papua New Guinea as the leader of the delegation. Guyana is about the size of Great Britain with a population of 8,00,000 people. Of this, 51 per cent were descendants of Indian labourers, 38 per cent were descendants of slaves from Africa, 4 per cent were Amerindians and the rest were from various other countries. There was great tension among the first three major groups—economic and political rivalries as well as cultural differences. Two candidates were competing for the highest post of the president. Mrs Janet Jagan was the Indian community's candidate; Desmond Hoyte was supported mainly by the Africans. After the delegation arrived in the capital, Georgetown, the fourteen observers were sent off to fourteen different provinces. I was sent to New Amsterdam, a seaside city beside the river Berbice, and was accompanied by Richard Nzerem of the Commonwealth secretariat. We reached there ten days before polling day.

We had to move from house to house and assess the soundness of polling arrangements. Would people be able to exercise their franchise free from fear? Had they received their identity cards? Were their names registered in the electoral rolls? Whichever house we visited, Richard an African and I an Indian, we were received with great excitement. People tried to speak to me in broken Hindi or Urdu, offered me a comfortable chair, served tea and asked me about India. Human sentiments can be so strange. Their ancestors had come from India many, many years ago; they themselves had never visited India. Yet there was a feeling of longing in their eyes, a feeling of pride for their Indian origins.

On the polling day we covered the city from dawn till late at night. Where there was controversy, I expressed my opinion clearly and never did I feel tired. The polls were conducted peacefully in our area but many were unable to vote because they didn't have identity cards. I was there for four days after the polls. Sadly, the final results had not been declared by then.

I had another opportunity to play a role in the international arena when Prime Minister I.K. Gujral sent me for a month as Indian representative to the 42nd session of the UN General Assembly. I was happy of course, but felt that at the UN relationships among people somehow did not get the prime focus. A place for building fellow feeling, sympathy and co-operation was being used for sharp politicking. I saw the palatial building, stunning décor, unique accoutrements and many important men. But the smiles on the lips never seemed to reach their eyes. All the symbols of modernity were meant to dazzle the viewer, no more than that. There is also a separate Indian embassy for the UN. People there are cordial enough but formal. India's re-election to the Economic and Social Council (ECOSOC) was the main topic that time. It was interesting to know which countries were to be approached, how and by whom. I also got an opportunity to understand the workings of the Indian embassy.

I had two responsibilities at the UN—to present India's viewpoint to the First and Third Committees; one was on foreign policy, the other was on women's empowerment. Funnily enough, both the speeches were written up for me in full by the external affairs office. All I had to do was read it out in my own way; nothing further.

As a member of the Rajya Sabha, I had the good fortune to visit many foreign lands, in fact I had fourteen fairly major trips in six years. Sometimes it was to deliver a lecture as a historian from India and sometimes to represent India as part of a delegation of parliamentarians. I will mention the very special ones. To me, there is some magic in the air in Paris. I have walked the spacious avenue of the Champs Élysées many a time by day or dusk. I had the rare fortune to be invited to the French senate. I was charmed by the building, its i(d) décor and its graceful ambience. In England I participated a number of times in conferences at the renowned Wilton Park—that charming old castle with a church that has a mention in the Domesday Book—and enjoyed meeting some of the world's leading thinkers there. Again, in Berlin a view of the demolished Berlin Wall brought to mind many historic events, as it would to almost all its visitors. My trip to Bali in Indonesia reminded me of our ancient cultural ties with that country and made me feel proud as an Indian. I have been enriched by the experience of coming face to face with the culture of ancient Arabia at Marrakesh in Morocco. The more I have seen of the world, the more I have learned.

Bellagio in Italy was an extraordinary experience. A prestigious study centre established by the Rockefeller Foundation, the house sits on top of a hill beside Lake Como near the borders of France and Switzerland. For every research scholar there is a separate room and a study. One has to be careful when touching anything in those rooms. It might be an antique French escritoire of the nineteenth century or an early twentieth-century Swiss armoire. Thank god, the bed at least was modern, so one could relax and sleep in peace. From the balcony one could see soft green grassland on one side and on the other an aquamarine body of water below a serene azure sky. The scholars who came from all over the world were of high international standing (I must have been a choice by fluke). One was a Nobel Laureate physicist, one was the chief composer of the Philadelphia Philharmonic Orchestra, one was a renowned biologist from Yale, one was an environmental scientist from Venezuela—such was the quality of people gathered there. One could not see them all day; they would remain confined to their separate studies in their dressing gowns or shorts, writing away on their computers. At seven in the evening the scene changed completely, as if at the touch of Alladin's lamp. They all emerged from hiding, dressed to the nines. Drinks were served for one hour followed by dinner. The style in which it was laid out, the variety of dishes and their taste, could make the London Savoy look like a village. The scholars forgot their professional standing and the importance of their work and met one another on an equal footing as friends. Laughter, conversation, jokes, arguments and general hilarity prevailed.

Though not as grand as Bellagio, Norway's Oslo was a lovely city too but the cost of living was extremely high. I think it must be the costliest place in the whole world. I could stay in Oslo because of the help I received from the Indian ambassador Nirupam Sen and his wife. An affable, highly educated couple, keen on good literature, they invited me for dinner and I spent a delightful evening at their place. In my view, the Sens are an exceptional couple among Indian diplomats abroad.

In Oslo, when I was presenting a paper at an international historians' conference, I could see that the workday lasted only till 3 p.m. After that people were free. What fun! Children could enjoy their fathers' company along with their mothers'. The residents of Oslo, who lived near the fjord, had a bathhouse by the sea, similar in design to their home. They went swimming in the sea and returned to the bathhouse for beer or some other drinks. After some completely relaxed moments they would be ready to go home. Indeed, for those who have the money, there is no lack of entertainment.

Oslo, London, Paris, New York, I love those places very much, but none can compare with Bangladesh. I go to Dhaka by bus, not by plane. When they load the bus on to the ferry on the river Padma, I come down and stand on the deck and my whole body quivers with excitement. I gaze spellbound at the water flowing gently like a languorous beauty resting her tired body in the midday sun. When I reach Dhaka, they ask me, 'An eight-hour bus journey, how could you take it? Wasn't it tedious?' Tedious? Not a bit. I was absolutely fine admiring the river, counting the fields, eating bananas, chewing peanuts and listening to people talking. Those who go to Bangladesh know how lavishly they entertain their guests. Five kinds of fish, three kinds of sweets are served straight on to your plate. And there is such pleading for you to eat more, as if they were begging you for a favour. Bangladesh has wonderful exponents of songs by Rabindranath Tagore, Dwijendralal Roy, Kazi Nazrul Islam and Atulprasad Sen—songs sung with such feeling, they reach deep within to touch your very heart.

Thanks to the Rajya Sabha, I not only travelled in foreign countries but also around our own vast country, which to me was surely more worthwhile. According to rule, MPs are organized into a number of parliamentary committees. When parliament is not in session, they travel around in India and inspect the work of the departments that come under their respective assigned committees. As a member of the Human Resource Development Standing Committee headed by the senior leader Shankar Chavan of Maharashtra, I went to the villages of Rajasthan and witnessed the farce that was then being enacted in the name of education. I examined the high standard of female education in Kerala and saw how the programme of non-formal education was falling apart in a number of states for lack of well-laid plans and adequate supervision. I was an enthusiastic member also of the Parliamentary Standing Committee on Science & Technology which Ramachandran of the Telugu Desam Party of Andhra Pradesh headed. When we visited the centre of environmental studies set up by the Bangalore Institute of Sciences under the able guidance of Professor Madhav Gadgil, we were so fascinated that we wished we could be students again. Meeting Madhav Gadgil was an experience in itself. He is a dedicated scientist, heart and soul. Such simplicity! Such modesty! Such humility! We were also impressed by the Institute of Management in Ahmedabad where Professor Anil Gupta and his team were working in remote hilly regions, interviewing elderly tribals and collecting valuable information about traditional herbal medicines orally transmitted from generation to generation. We saw the Indian Space Research Organisation's (ISRO's) main centre in Hassan, Karnataka. Observing, and vaguely understanding, how satellites in outer space are tracked from planet earth is awe inspiring. In Goa, we saw a videotape of our Antarctica expedition. Watching how the ship made its way cutting through thick ice, how our scientists were conducting experiments in that frozen land and speaking with the scientists stationed in the Antartica research centre via remote satellite was an equally thrilling experience. Again, as a member of the Joint Parliamentary Committee on Empowerment of Women led by Margaret Alva, I surveyed the status of women in Rajasthani villages, in the mountainous regions of Himachal Pradesh and in the strife-torn Kashmir valley. Family courts were yet to be established in Karnataka; the committee made a request to the chief minister S.M. Krishna and he readily agreed to expedite the process. He kept his word, so that was one successful intervention from the empowerment committee. We were not equally successful everywhere. In Mumbai, there were many under-trial women imprisoned for years waiting for their cases to come up in court. The committee recommended that one judge be sent to hold court within the prison premises. Either sentence them or let them go. Why should they rot in jail? It was a legitimate demand, but implementation was not feasible. I was happy working under Margaret Alva's leadership. In my opinion, Margaret is a leader of high stature. She began her training under no other than Indira Gandhi and has become a powerful orator, experienced and knowledgeable.

I remember another woman parliamentarian well—Phoolan Devi, the bandit queen. She was also a member of the empowerment committee. I had heard many defamatory remarks about her and many stories of her past. One day while we were taking one of our committee tours, I approached her on an impulse and said, 'We have been going around together in the same group for many days but we haven't really met. I don't know anything about you except through hearsay. I do research on the history of women. I would like to know about you.'

She answered with a dismissive shrug. 'You want to write? Plenty has been written already, read it.'

I said, 'If that's what I wanted, why would I wish to talk to you?' I explained to her that there was no guarantee that I would write. But if I did, it wouldn't be for a magazine or film world, but for a serious history journal. Not a biography, but an analysis of the events that could bring a sea change in the life of an Indian woman and turn her into a bandit. I wanted to hear her story from her own lips. 'Will you tell me, sister?'

'I will, but not here. Come and spend one night with me, or I could spend a night with you. You won't be frightened a woman dacoit, Didi?'

She put a hand on my arm. A woman dacoit's rough hand. There was a soft core hidden somewhere within her. I had planned to bring her home the next time I was in Delhi. 'I am very miserable, Didi,' she had told me then and I dearly wanted to hear what she had to say. That opportunity never came. She was shot dead in front of her own house by an unknown assailant. I still feel her touch on my arm.

My six years in the Rajya Sabha are over but I have a thirst for the elixir of joy. I continue to seek sustenance from the very source of this many-splendoured thing called life.

The journey leads from sunrise to sunset and back again from sunset to sunrise.

KHUKU

OUR DAUGHTERS

My first daughter's name is Isha but I call her Khuku. She was born in 1960 when I was going on twenty-six. Had Sundar-ma been alive then, she would have been almost a hundred and fifty years old. In this century and a half, how much has changed in the lives of middle-class Bengali women. Khuku is my first-born child. No conch shells sounded at her birth, there were no ululations. Shasuri-ma did not distribute sweets all around to show her joy. She forced a smile on her face and said, 'A girl, is it? Your first child. That's good, dear, the next one must be a boy.' She had examined the movement of the central vein in my stomach many times while I was pregnant, and was convinced that I would bear a son. I also wished for a boy since everyone else did the same. Yet, I had a girl. And worse, she was dark and plain, with tiny slits for eyes, a flat nose and hair all over. When I first saw her, I was quite distressed. How was this reaction any different from the way the birth of a girl-child was greeted a hundred and fifty years ago? How was it different from the attitudes of my grandmother or great-grandmother or the generations of women that had preceded them?

Yet, was there no change at all? To start with, the very procedure of childbirth has changed. For four generations of women, from Sundar-ma to me, babies were delivered at home by a midwife. My younger sister Pronoti was delivered at my

Didi-ma's home in Berhampore in the traditional way—by an old, established midwife of the locality. Our brother Abhijit arrived twelve years after Pronoti. Of course no one knew whether the baby would be a boy or a girl. Ma did not look for a midwife in Calcutta. She chose instead to go to the Calcutta Medical College, breaking family convention. Abhijit was delivered in a government hospital by a doctor, a woman trained in the Western medical system. For my first child I chose a private nursing home, having heard from specialists that the delivery procedure had advanced considerably. That is a fact, since science has come to supervise the birth of a human child. But not all doctors are equally experienced or conscientious. We three sisters were shown the light of day with natural simplicity by a midwife who had no knowledge of Western medical practices. My famous obstetrician—he was a man—opted for a forceps delivery. He dragged Khuku out of my womb ahead of time and considered that he had finished his duty. That I would have to suffer excruciating pain for days because of this was something he did not consider because it was not in his medical textbook.

Aching and exhausted, I brought Isha back with me to my mother's place, the place where new mothers traditionally bring their newborns to in India. A new mother finds relief in her own mother's care, with whom she can discuss physical problems without inhibition. I felt so relaxed in body and mind and so close to my mother emotionally. There was no quarantine in an atur ghar, the lying-in room used for all births, no puja rituals to be followed, nothing in excess. It felt like I was back in my own childhood, a state of utter bliss, worry free and untroubled, such as one can only have at one's mother's. Three months later, I went back to my in-laws' home in Lake Place, feeling a little worried. Khuku was my dark little baby girl; how would she be received by my mother-in-law?

Wonders would never cease! From the minute I placed my daughter in Shasuri-ma's lap, she didn't want to put her down again! In no time Isha became the apple of her grandparents' eyes. Under their infinite loving care Isha became lovelier and prettier by the day. And looks apart, it was her intelligence that became a matter of amazement for everyone in the house. At the age of two years and three months, Isha could breeze through the English alphabet (not Bengali though). Her ability to read was not confined to the printed page. If a car stopped at the gate, she would rattle off the number written on the licence plate. Her grandfather read an English-language paper in the morning. She sat opposite him and learnt how to read. I used to tell my Shasur moshai, 'It's no use teaching her at such a young age. She has to be six years old before she can be admitted to Class I—all schools have to follow this rule.' But I was thrilled inside—my daughter was going to be a brilliant student. In my subconscious mind I started feeling proud; a common weakness of parents all over the world.

My second daughter Tista was born when Isha was two years and three months old. This time I went to Woodlands Nursing Home under the care of Dr Kripa Mitra and his wife Bimala Bhattacharya. Bimala-di was a good doctor. She was the one who took charge of the actual delivery. Kripa-da said later that he stayed away out of fear because the umbilical cord twisted around Tista's throat while she was still in the womb. Yet, there was no problem. Bimala-di didn't use forceps though my birth pangs lasted a very long time. After the delivery, while I was still semi-conscious, I heard the nurse saying, 'Mrs Ray, you have another girl.' I was delighted; by then because of Isha we had all realized how glorious a daughter could be. Tista was a beauty at birth and all the nurses fussed over her. They said, 'What will you do with two daughters? Leave this one with us.'

Isha and Tista started growing up happily in the Lake Place house; spoilt by their grandparents, cuddled by their uncles, loved by the Sen Gupta family upstairs. Pahari's brother Kamu was their Kamu-mamu, his sister Usha, the exquisite singer, was named Gaan-pishi, her elder sister was their Gouri-pishi. They were no less dear to them than their real aunts. Thanks to Shasuri-ma, the house was frequented by relatives all the time; so the girls got to know the larger family circle quite well. They used to visit their Aparna kaki-ma and Mana-kaka at their 48 Rashbehari Avenue home quite often to be pampered by them and to play with Swati-di, their cousin, whom they dearly loved. Sundays were extra special. The whole family would gather at either Rashbehari Avenue or Lake Place and have a riotous time.

When we moved from Lake Place to King's Court, Isha was four and Tista nearly two. The bonds of the joint family loosened but Shasuri-ma visited us every day and Shasur-moshai came every Sunday, so the children were not at all cut off. They continued to confide their secrets and problems in their grandmother whom they called Namma and looked forward to Sundays to tell all their school stories to their grandfather who adoringly and untiringly listened.

When Isha was four years old, we started thinking about sending her to school. My mother said, 'Send her to Loreto House. I didn't send you there because we lived in a mofussil town. Besides, we were under British rule then. I didn't want to send you to a school run by them and have you chattering in English and listening to English songs all the time. Now the British are gone but the English language is increasing in

importance. You better send Isha to an English-medium school.'
I appreciated her logic and sent Isha to Loreto House.

The ambience there was different from the one we had at
home. Most of the students were from rich families, spoke
fluent English and some of them—though not all—had
substantial pocket money. I didn't give my daughter any
pocket money. I told her that she could ask for whatever she
needed. 'Don't forget your mother tongue or Bengali ways,'
I would often remind her. Fortunately, there were a few girls
in Isha's class who came from families like ours. One was
Sreemati Lal, daughter of Professor Purushottam Lal, and
Kisha who was a granddaughter of Ramananda Chattopadhyay,
the noted journalist and scholar. Another student in her class
was Madhabi Ray—naughty, ebullient, friendly, lovable and
generous. Soma Ray was quiet, gentle and sweet-natured. These
three girls were Isha's best friends and dear to me as my own
daughters. We share a warm relationship to this day.

As a school, Loreto House was excellent. The girls were not
under constant pressure to study and had plenty of opportunity
to play games. Children could breathe easily without the load
of bags full of textbooks and notebooks on their backs and
work at their own pace. Time and resources were put aside
for activities that were both educational and entertaining. Isha
joined the nursery class at age four and received a double
promotion to Class I. Uma Ahmed was her class teacher, and
Isha was lucky that she got a teacher of Uma's calibre. Under
her tutelage and inspiration, Isha's creativity and imagination
blossomed so well—in writing, drawing and craftwork—that I
became and remain an admirer of Uma. Another remarkable
teacher arrived while Isha was at Loreto House: Sister Cyril,
who is today a well-known educationist and social worker. Even
then I noticed the care with which she introduced children to

the natural world and how, through a series of entertaining games of questions and answers, she was able to impart to them important values and ethics. Tista joined Loreto House two years later.

Isha took art lessons at the Academy of Fine Arts. Classes were held on Sundays from 10 a.m. to 12 noon and Lady Ranu Mookerjee, a noted patron of art and culture, came regularly to supervise the classes. The teachers and their teaching methods were excellent. There were no strict rules or minute instructions and students were encouraged to learn on their own spontaneously. A flower or leaf or bird or toy was placed in front of them and they were told to draw whatever they pleased. The children happily played around with paints and brushes. They looked at each other's efforts and worked things out for themselves. Some very unusual artwork resulted, expressing a child's joy or her view of the world. When they grew a little older and seemed to be ready to take the next step, they were taught portraiture and given a little more guidance. Isha moved on to portrait painting of live models. Tista didn't attend these classes because her drawing skills were like her mother's—nil! Tista was immersed in the world of her friends and in looking after the needs of anyone with whom she came into contact—which still remains a dominant characteristic of hers.

Gradually, a change came over me. Isha became the central focus of my life. Whatever she did; drama, the sitar, elocution, debate, dancing and, certainly, studies, she came home with the first prize. I don't know when it was that I started identifying myself with her completely. I just thought that every prize she brought home was my prize. I shared her successes jubilantly, imagining that both of us were equally pleased. And then—well, I'll leave that for later.

Meanwhile Tista had become a problem. She was ill-tempered, badly behaved and a daredevil. She would throw tantrums if anything displeased her and yell if I asked her to study: 'Don't you understand that my chest hurts when I study? Why do you still insist?' In school, the teachers would say to her, 'Isha is such a wonderful girl, why are you like this?' Only her friends were very fond of her. Nusrat Gangjee, who was a little older, was especially protective about her. Tista would come back from school and run around the King's Court grounds with her wild uncombed hair in a mess. If I scolded her, she became more rebellious. I used to sit around and ponder with a heavy heart, 'Why are my two girls so different?' And then it struck me one day like a bolt of lightning—it was entirely my fault. Tista was just a child. It is a mother's duty to pay equal attention to her children and I had failed. From the time they were newborn babies, Isha had been in my Shasuri-ma's care while Tista was tended by their ayah, Narayani. For their grandfather, the entire world was on one side of the weighing scale and Isha on the other, and the scales tipped on Isha's side. I myself was obsessed with Isha. I delighted in the success of one daughter and was displeased by the other's naughtiness. It was not right, not right at all. I realized I had to make amends immediately. I turned my attention to Tista and sure enough, her temper vanished, her behaviour changed and we heard no more about chest pains. Where did this laughing, vivacious, compassionate sparkling being come from? Did someone from heaven above give me a wake-up call and bring me this rare gift called Tista?

Isha and Tista left Loreto House after passing their secondary examinations with glowing results and joined the La Martinière Girls' School for their Indian School Certificate exams. There Isha was taught English by John Mason. At that time John Mason was a young man from an ordinary family, raised by his widowed mother, studying for his B.Ed. degree. The future really is inscrutable. John Mason climbed higher and higher up the ladder of success till he became principal of the renowned Doon School at Dehradun and gained acclaim as a respected educationist. He was an excellent teacher with a tremendous ability to inspire his students. He was very fond of Isha and as well as directing and acting with her in school plays, he taught her how to debate. Unfortunately, Tista missed out on him.

Isha completed her Class XII and sat for her Oxford-Cambridge entrance exam. Following the principle of the Senior Cambridge examination system at that time, students were permitted to take the Oxbridge exam after twelve years of schooling. That is no longer possible. I made personal enquiries at Oxford University, brought copies of the syllabi and question papers and then arranged for Isha to sit for the examination through the British Council. We preferred Somerville the most, a college that former prime minister Indira Gandhi had briefly attended. To our delight, Isha was not only selected by Somerville, but was also awarded the Mary Ewart scholarship—which they said was given for the first time in nineteen years to a student without an interview.

The time came for Isha to leave us and go to Oxford. We saw her off at Calcutta airport. Isha was a home-loving girl who had till then never spent a night away. She flew off, alone, to an unknown, foreign land where other than one single English couple we knew no one. Looking relaxed and full of self-confidence, Isha walked away, stood for a moment, turned back and waved at us. These children of the 1960s—their self-perception and their world view are not like ours.

Some months later, absolutely unexpectedly, the principal of

Somerville College sent me a hand-written letter singing Isha's praises. I was euphoric and felt vindicated. My assessment of her was correct—not one of an obsessed mother's but of a teacher's. She was sure to graduate with a first-class degree.

After that joyful letter came another a few months later, this time from Isha. She was not interested in a first class, she wrote. A second would do well enough. She didn't have much time for studies because she had joined a social service network called 'Night Line'—Good Samaritans—where they took turns being on duty all night. I wrote back—you have all your life to do as much social service as you like but you have just three years in Oxford. Be a good girl and work hard at your studies for just two more years, come back home with a fabulous degree, then you can join any social work organization here. Her response, couched in beautiful, polite language, conveyed this message: What I do with my life is for me to decide. Do not interfere.

What was Khuku trying to tell me? Did she think that her life was hers alone and that the right to make decisions about her life was solely hers? Were the eighteen years I had spent as an integral part of her life of no value? I ran' into my bedroom and shut the door. I entered the bathroom and opened two taps so that the sound of water would drown any other sound. Then I wept out loud. I do not know for how long I cried. How can one measure time when one's hopes and dreams are shattered? But life's losses and heartaches, however severe, can be borne; it only takes time. Time taught me that this was Khuku's revolt against me. For eighteen years she had given me exactly what I had wanted—success, praise and medals. In my utter blindness and thoughtlessness I had believed that this was what we both desired. What had she given up in order to bring a smile to my face? How tired she must have become of suppressing her own wishes for my sake. Khuku, I promise you, I had not realized this. Why didn't you ever tell me?

Was I the only one who had committed such a mistake? Having been jolted into awareness, I opened my ears to people all around me. I heard the same echo from innumerable other middle-class homes. 'It's my life.' 'I will do what I think is best.' 'I'll do what I like, what is it to you?' 'Mother, don't interfere!' I saw how differences between parents and children were increasing in each home. A generation gap had appeared in every middle-class family. Why should it be so? Why do we have such misunderstandings with the children whom we cherish and love so much that it keeps us awake at night? Why do feelings of mutual recrimination and hurt constantly raise their ugly heads in this relationship?

It is inevitable. Two generations nurtured in different and changing social and political environments must perforce develop different ideas and consciousnesses. It is true that children's lives are their own. We may want to help them avoid the mistakes we made in our own lives but that cannot be. Each one's experience is one's own, as is his or her life. Our children's ideals will be based on their changed environment. They will dream new dreams, tread different paths. They will walk, sit, stand and rest in their own ways. They will even eat differently. It cannot be helped. Old notions and ideals are being crushed under the rapidly moving wheels of time. I now realize the truth in what Isha had said. At that time, however, I decided that since my daughter wished to be independent, I too would distance myself. I was wrong. A few years later, when I fell ill and had to undergo surgery, I saw that my two daughters were still the same as before. Their love, tenderness and care for me had not lessened at all. It is just that they lived their own lives.

I wish I could be a mother all over again. Then I wouldn't repeat the mistakes I made earlier. In my son's case, for instance. His proper name is Jishnu Pratap Ray but I call him Khokon. He arrived suddenly five years after Tista's birth. I believe that of my three children, the youngest is the brightest. I didn't realize this when he was growing up. I was so busy—and enamoured—with Isha and Tista, I didn't pay much attention to him. And yet Khokon, without any help from us, sailed through his graduation with a first class first in economics, went to the Indian Institute of Management, Bangalore, for his MBA and made a successful career, having started a company of his own along with two other friends. He has excellent relationships with people and is immensely loved and admired by his colleagues, and almost anyone who comes in contact with him. He doesn't talk much or socialize, yet he's always there for his friends and relatives whenever they need help in any crisis. Thoroughly dependable and unpretentious, he is our mainstay today. Khokon does not speak about it but surely deep in his heart there must be a sense of hurt. Childhood memories of care or neglect, of lessons good or bad, have a lifelong effect on one's psyche. We often act unthinkingly and utter words that hurt a child's tender heart. We often do not understand the aches of their sensitive souls. We don't even try. If I could be a mother once again, I would make a much greater effort to understand my children. Then again, perhaps as a new mother I might make new mistakes.

'Mistake' perhaps is not the right word. A difference in perspective and lack of thought would be more correct. I had a disagreement once with Lopa, my unofficially adopted daughter. I first met her when she was fifteen; she was a school friend of Tista's. Today she introduces me to strangers as 'my mother'. I don't know how her mother feels about this! Lopa had come first in the entrance exam for admission to English honours in Presidency College but showed no sign of joining classes. 'What's the matter?' I asked her.

'I'm not doing English honours in Presidency. I'll do a BA pass course at St Xavier's College,' she said.

'Whatever for?'

'I want to work in advertising. You need just a BA degree for that. It takes two years to finish an ordinary pass course. Why should I do a three-year honours course and waste one whole year?'

I was displeased. 'Is it only for the degree that you do your BA? You learn so much more when you do honours. You will meet so many bright students at Presidency and you will learn a lot from them. We had to wage a minor battle at home to join a co-ed college. Today your paths are open. Don't you wish to make good use of opportunities?'

She did not listen to me. She did her BA from St Xavier's and moved to Delhi to join Tara Sinha's advertising agency as a trainee. Then she moved further and further up the career ladder, acquired one qualification after another necessary for her profession and now she works as an adviser for a UN agency. She lives in Pretoria, South Africa, in a large bungalow with a big lawn. She married someone she loved from her schooldays—Shivaji Bhattacharya, a gem of a boy. They have one child, a daughter named Disha—born when Lopa was thirty-one—sweet-looking, equally sweet-natured and bright. The two of them have brought Disha up with infinite care. How can I now say that ignoring my advice and choosing her own way of life was a mistake Lopa made?

Sreemati Lal was with Isha at Loreto House. Both were the same age, born in 1960. Sreemati studied English honours at Presidency College and married a fine boy. Their marriage didn't last. Today Sreemati is an artist and holds exhibitions in Delhi, London, Paris and New York. Why should we judge the generation of the '60s by the values and norms of our generation? Their life is theirs—they move to a different rhythm.

Isha and Tista have married. When Isha came back from Oxford I knew by the expression on her face that she was ready to fall in love. She went in September to Stanford University, California, with a handsome fellowship to do her Ph.D. By October she had plunged into a sea of love. Indeed, it appeared not to be a mere sea but more like the Atlantic Ocean! The fortunate fellow was Jitendra Malik. He had graduated from the Indian Institute of Technology, Kanpur, with flying colours and was doing his Ph.D. in computer science at Stanford University. I don't believe in the caste system but I was worried about the fact that the boy was from a Jat family whose original home was in Mathura, Uttar Pradesh. Perhaps there would be a lot of arguments about marriage rituals. Would the question of dowry be raised? So I told Isha, 'You have chosen extremely well. A brilliant as well as a solid boy, dependable and decent. We have no problems at all in giving our consent. Have a civil ceremony at Stanford. Your father and I will come.'

Isha's face fell. 'Will just the two of you attend my wedding? What about my uncles and aunts—Kaku, Aparna-kaki, Swati-didi, Ronnie, my school friends? Won't they be there?'

There was nothing I could say to that so we decided to hold the wedding in Calcutta. The date was fixed as 15 July 1985—Isha would be just twenty-five then and Jitendra twenty-six.

For the wedding, Jitendra's father, Dr Brahma Singh Malik, a scientist and dean at a university in Jabalpur, came with sixteen friends and relatives at their own expense and never mentioned dowry or any gift for anybody, not even the bridegroom. They were my guests in Calcutta. We did not do a sampradan, the giving away of the bride, because I don't believe it is possible to give away a human being. But we did follow the sapatapadi, the walking of the seven steps together, which is the essential feature of a Hindu wedding. The ceremony was concluded without any problem, indeed very pleasantly and affably. After the wedding, Isha spent a few days with her in-laws in Jabalpur and then went to the University of California at Berkeley, where Jitendra had accepted a professorial post.

After her Ph.D., Isha secured a prestigious assignment with the International Irrigation Management Institute. Her research was on water resources. They sent her to Turkey, where she stayed for six to eight months. She learnt the Turkish language, socialized, worked, made friends and enjoyed herself. And then, to my surprise, she quit. Seeing me displeased, she explained, 'I don't want to live away from Jitendra for six months in the year. I will do what I can, living together.' Thus it was that Isha became a professor at the University of California at Berkeley. And, I will add, is still in the Atlantic Ocean of love!

Tista is at Berkeley too. She didn't go to Oxford like Isha. Instead she went to Bryn Mawr College in the USA. I learnt about the place from my friend Professor Krishna Bose who had sent her daughter Sharmila to Bryn Mawr. Once I received all the details from Krishna, I decided to send Tista there. She obtained a full scholarship so finances were not a problem. Bryn Mawr is an extraordinary place. A girl's college more than a century old; and long may it live! It turned my daughter, whom once the very thought of books made ill, into a super academic. She picked up rare qualities of leadership there. Tista is well known among academics as Raka Ray—which is her proper name—a professor of sociology, and the director of the Centre for South Asian Studies at the University of California at Berkeley. Half of my family seems to be at Berkeley!!

From Bryn Mawr, Tista went to the University of Madison in Wisconsin to do research in sociology. The climate is very cold there but one adjusts quickly when one is young. In Wisconsin Tista received tremendous affection from her professors and classmates. And there she found Eric Parker whom she wanted to marry. Sukhendu said, 'I hope it lasts.'

I said, 'There's no use asking her not to, she won't listen. Her life is her own.' Besides, I'd seen several young women around Isha's and Tista's age marrying foreigners. Krishna Bose's daughter Sharmila married an Englishman. So did Tista's classmate Nandini Gooptu. My brother's wife Janice is from America. They all seem to be happy and so would Tista be, I argued. I liked Eric. He was pleasant-looking, soft-spoken and a book lover. Tista was twenty-eight, Eric twenty-nine. They registered their marriage abroad. Sukhendu and I were unable to attend. I sent her a deep pink zari-bordered Benarasi sari for the wedding day and a set of navaratan ornaments. She wore them and sent lovely pictures of the two of them smiling happily. Both looked radiant.

Tista's research was based in Mumbai and Kolkata. She came for a few weeks every year to do fieldwork. The year she was writing her thesis, she came to India for a couple of months to double check on her data. Ten days after her return, she wrote to me. 'Ma, before you read the rest of this letter, I want you to remember that you have raised very strong girls. You have always known of my ability to survive—and now is the time to believe it. Eric and I are separating. It was his decision, not mine. I have tried to talk to him but to no avail.

And now, I have to move on and continue my life.' Isha's letter arrived a few days later. 'Just as you have always taught us, Ma, to keep our brain steady in our heads during any crisis, I have kept myself together, and to a remarkable—really remarkable—extent, Tista has too. Of course I was able to think about precious little since this happened, but I thank god that I was readily available to her during the day or the night. We covered a lot of ground together—re-examining all our assumptions about life, about marriage, about what makes sustainable relationships.' Eric, I was told, had been weeping all day and yet saying that he didn't want to stay together with Raka. I got extremely annoyed. Why was he putting on this ridiculous show? If he didn't wish to stay, then he should simply leave. Perhaps he wanted to soften Tista's heart or show that he was really a good man. Put on a show that his heart was breaking but there was nothing else he could do. Tista had no clue why he wanted to end the marriage. There did not seem to be another woman in the picture. My own conviction is—although Tista doesn't agree to this day—that the real reason was his inferiority complex. Both of them were in the same field. As a man and as a husband, how could he bear her scoring over him repeatedly in every single area of academics, from grades to the coveted editorial assistant's position in prestigious journals?

Tista left Eric, left Wisconsin and moved off to the west coast, armed with her new Ph.D. She took a teaching job as an assistant professor at the University of California at Berkeley. The two sisters came together in the same city after many years. They are, happily, as close—if not more—as ever. They have there also Godhuli, an old friend, who had studied with Isha in La Martiniére School in Calcutta.

At Berkeley Tista met Ashok Bardhan, the son of

A.B. Bardhan, a politician of all-India standing. Ashok is Bengali in name; raised in Nagpur, his mother tongue is Marathi. Sukhendu and I were present at their wedding, a registered wedding with a few Hindu rites and rituals that were conducted by Ved Vatuk, a Sanskrit scholar. That was over twelve years ago. Tista has no children but she is deeply attached to her husband and the affection is reciprocated. A beautiful partnership!

Isha had conceived twins. Unfortunately, her womb, after a surgery, was unable to carry two babies. Within six months she gave birth prematurely to a girl and a boy. They didn't survive. There are few things in the world as painful as the loss of a child. I could not go to Isha or share her profound sorrow. That is something which will give me pain all my life. Isha and Jitendra's desire for a child was fulfilled when Kabir arrived on 26 April 2005. Isha was forty-four, by which age my Didi-ma had had three grandchildren and my mother was about to become a grandmother. Kabir was born by a totally modern method. The doctors stitched up Isha's womb so the baby would stay safely inside; after nine months, they opened the stitches, and Kabir was born immediately.

Times change. In my time, I was cared for by my Shasuri-ma and Ma both before and after I gave birth. Isha did not ask me or her mother-in-law to come to Berkeley. She followed her doctor's advice and looked after herself. I was naturally worried after the last unfortunate experience. I asked her, 'Shall I come, Isha?' She said, 'Don't worry, Ma. I'm being very careful. If there's any problem, I'll let you know.' I didn't worry because I'd seen Lopa. Before Lopa's daughter Disha was born, she followed the doctor's advice about diet, walking, exercises and yoga so strictly that three days after delivery, Lopa didn't even look like a new mother. She was perfectly fit. She nursed the baby and did everything around the house without any help from her mother or mother-in-law. Isha was the same; she adopted modern techniques, took assistance from professionals and managed the baby and herself, looking slim and beautiful, ten years younger than her age. Jitendra was in the delivery room with his camera, taking pictures. When I saw those pictures, I could hardly believe what I saw. Tista said, 'Don't be surprised, Ma. These days doctors say that the father's presence during delivery is a good thing. He should see for himself the pain a mother goes through to give birth.'

Tista also says, 'You know, Ma, we want to decide for ourselves whether we wish to become mothers or not, or if we do, what would be the convenient age for motherhood, or should we give birth or adopt. Look at our friends.'

So I looked. Sreemati Lal has no children. Madhabi has no children either. She and her husband both work full time and enjoy life in their spare time. Shoma has one son—she was thirty-plus when he was born. Lopa has only Disha. Another of my dearly loved 'daughters', Dolly, and her husband are bringing up with great care and love a little girl they adopted. I love her too as my granddaughter. I see that though women of this generation have little time for bearing children, when they do have children, they are vigilant in rearing and nurturing them. They bring up their one child or, at the most, two children with expert care and attention.

The young women whose stories I have been relating so far were all born in the 1960s. I have seen the generation of the '70s from a little distance, some as students, some as younger colleagues, some as the daughters and daughters-in-law of friends and relatives. Of the generation of the '80s, I know little, except for Kumar's daughter Ritika. It takes eighteen years for children to finish school. Those who were born in the late '80s or '90s are still in school or college. I see them when I'm invited to their school and college functions to distribute prizes or to inaugurate some programme. I enjoy watching them. They are in their teens and twenties, have hardly any inhibitions, and chatter away with bright eyes and happy faces. Few wear the long, swinging plaits of our youth; most have short hair, or ponytails. Girls look more graceful in saris but only a few still wear them—the salwar offers so much more freedom of movement. These young girls seek new things not just outwardly but also inwardly. In matters of love, they are freer and more transparent. They are interested in romance and equally curious about sex. More than the songs of Rabindra, Nazrul, Dwijendra, Atulprasad, they prefer the Backstreet Boys, or in Bengali, the bands Chandrabindu and Bhoomi. Rather than Kathak and Bharatanatyam dance recitals they prefer to watch what they call 'fusion'—a sort of hybrid mixture of Western and oriental music and dance forms. In place of *Thakurmar Jhuli* they read Harry Potter or English and Bengali comics. Instead of memorizing poetry, they prefer polishing their computer skills. Instead of Nelson Mandela, their heroes are Sachin Tendulkar and Shah Rukh Khan. This new culture is no longer restricted to children from the upper middle class studying in English-medium schools; it is on the rise at every level of middle-class society. Over and above everything else, what is most evident is their ambition both in terms of their marriage and their career. What one notices also is how middle-class girls view the world outside once they step out of their homes. There can be criticism or praise of their attitudes; they are simply natural. Each age fashions itself in its own image. But there is little fundamental difference between the generation of the '60s, the generation of the '80s or even the '90s. I wonder whether the big changes had set in sometime after independence from the 1960s onwards. Or did it start even earlier—without manifesting clearly?

Kabir's arrival has brought my matrilineal story of five generations to a close. The sixth generation has brought a son and there is little chance that another girl will be born. But daughters continue to arrive in other homes, if not in mine. What will they be like, these daughters of the twenty-first century? What will their food habits be, how will they dress? How will they conduct themselves at home as homemakers, and in the wider world in their working lives?

The future does not speak. It signals to us but we don't comprehend. And is it really necessary for us to know? The new generation will tell it's own story in its own way, or perhaps it won't. The generation that follows will listen, or it may not. Perhaps it will value the tradition handed down by our grandmothers and great-grandmothers; then again, it may not. It is its decision, because its life will be its own.

AND SO I THINK

Our story has come to an end but I'm not done yet. I still have something left to say.

In the beginning, I said that this would be a story about one particular family—mine. Reading through it makes me think about the changes that have taken place in the private lives of middle-class urban women as a group over five generations. Their lives have been tossed around by so many mighty waves.

They have seen two devastating world wars, fearful famine, violent and non-violent struggles against a colonial power, the coming of independence and the curse of partition. The economic map has been re-drawn in unimaginable ways; new industries and new towns have come up and the most current technologies introduced. Countless artistes in music, dance, drama and painting have provided inspiration for the nation. Thousands of novels, plays and poems have reflected fresh ideas and their impact on the ever-flowing stream of life. Women's lives—husband centred, soaked in maternal love and filled with the cooking of rice, fish and vegetables—have also taken on a different shape and rhythm. The call of romance is more persuasive, homes are decorated in novel ways and daily living seeks out a newer tempo.

Nevertheless, I look back and realize that there were really no basic changes within the home-centred lives of our first three generations, apart from girls being married at a later age (and having children at an older age) and that too only in the third generation—that of my mother's. Sundar-ma and Didi-ma were both educated women—Didi-ma's exposition of Bankimchandra's novels used to amaze me—they were self-taught within the confines of their homes; they never had the opportunity to attend school or college. My mother did, though she was restricted to girls' schools and colleges. She was highly educated by the standards of those days—BA and a gold medallist—yet it never occurred to her to earn her own living. She sought fulfilment within her home. She accompanied her husband wherever he was posted within Bengal and travelled with him to many parts of India. The wider world outside did attract her but her heart was occupied by her husband. Her children came next. She fed them, clothed them and educated them, built and maintained relationships with the wider family circle and did some social work as well. All in all, she was a happy woman.

Of the five generations in this story, mine was the first to undergo major modifications. Let us consider Presidency College first. In other words, co-education and the chance to interact with men, discuss ideas, converse freely, make friends, become intimate, fall in love and marry. This was a clear and perceptible change. Less apparent at the time were the inner changes. Walking side by side with men was a consciousness-raising experience; it enabled us to raise our sights and increase our self-confidence. We began dreaming of the same career paths as those of men and achieving similar successes. The long-shut doors, that had started opening little by little as women's education became widespread, were now swung wide open by a sudden whirlwind that reached right into the innermost recesses of our homes. This happened in the 1950s.

It was in the 1950s that middle-class women started joining the workforce in earnest. It is not as if no woman had worked outside the home before. Chandramukhi Basu and Kamini Ray were teachers, Kadambini Ganguly and Jamini Sen were doctors. But there were just a handful of them. After the Second World War, the pressure of spiralling prices forced a few middle-class women to take up jobs—they worked in ration shops, telephone offices, schools and hospitals. After independence, taking advantage of equal rights granted by the Indian constitution, many a woman from the middle class entered the workforce. I was one of them. I was the first 'working girl' on my father's side of the family and the first 'working wife' on my in-laws'. My working life was a product of my times and circumstances. Ma, Didi-ma and Sundar-ma were not given those times and those circumstances within which to live their lives.

How can working women possibly devote their lives wholly to their spouse and progeny? While husbands and children do not have to be pushed to the periphery, women's singular focus of the past is now certainly split in two spheres—and both spheres remain perforce somewhat incomplete. Moreover, earning an income brings with it an unspoken power which is evident in every aspect of a woman's life. Families are smaller, there are fewer children, the aged and the ailing get less hands-on care (for lack of time) and husband worship has given way to friendship.

In the fifth generation again, there have been tremendous transformations. My own two daughters studied abroad, as did many others. Both have married according to their own choice, ignoring differences of race, religion, nationality, as have many of their generation. One of my two daughters has gone through a divorce. But her world did not come to an end. Her work didn't suffer and she is now remarried. They reside, these daughters, in places far away. Women living here in India have also witnessed a sea change in their lives. Since the Hindu Code Bill passed into law, marriages are no longer said to be made in heaven; they are subject to law, and can be made or broken. Divorces are taking place. In other words, the main tenet of Hindu marriage, that it is a sacrament for life (and, indeed, extends into the afterlife) has been shaken at its root.

I do not mean to imply that all marriages are breaking up. Most of them do not. It is companionship that best enables marriages to survive and thrive. I see my own daughters and their friends who reside abroad. Husbands and wives there both work outside the home and work together to maintain their home. I see the same thing in our own country where double incomes make for a better lifestyle. If one comes home late, the other helps with household work. If the wife has to travel abroad for research or office work, the husband steps in to look after the children. This I see in my niece Sangeeta Das Gupta's or my student Suparna Gooptu's homes, as well as in many others. This is what 'love' looks like in modern times. It involves a mutuality of understanding, working together and equality in companionship.

Domestic life is not domestic in the same way. Women who do not step out of the house to earn a living, now run boutiques from homes, design jewellery, deal in precious stones, or run or work in social service organizations. Those who have not yet found their calling search eagerly for some kind of outlet for their energies. Therefore, the only thing to do is follow the example of Sunanda Ghosh of Bethune College. Make your lifestyle simple within the home and make time to work outside the home.

Has life indeed become simpler? The fifth generation is at the eye of the storm of globalization. My Ma and Didi-ma would think twice before spending ten rupees (of course ten rupees meant much more than it does now). So did I. This generation understands money differently. Their notions of spending are poles apart from ours. They have a different philosophy of life and different values.

They think of and want things that we did not and could not think of or want. They run companies as Anuradha Ray (a friend of my children's) does, while supervising the needs of their husband and children and wearing saris they themselves have designed. They keep one eye on the family, the other on work. They have an inner drive towards self-improvement—at work, in their looks and in their dress. The daughters of this generation are truly multifaceted. They wear salwar-kameez instead of saris; saris are reserved for special occasions. It is well known that one's clothes communicate unspoken messages. Their salwar-kameez is indicative of their sense of liberation and a desire for freedom of movement.

They are on the move. In the process the home and the outside world are fusing together. Home is no longer confined to four walls. Life at home has become one with life in the world.

ACKNOWLEDGEMENTS

Countless friends and relatives have inspired me to write this book. I am indebted to them all. Many of the people who feature in my story have related their life stories without reservation and provided me with factual details. It is impossible for me to repay their generosity. I am grateful to Professor Rajat Kanta Ray, the present vice chancellor of Visvabharati, who was kind enough to read through and make valuable comments on the entire manuscript. I was able to recover some old and tattered diaries written by the first two generations in my story. They serve as mirrors of their minds. Unfortunately, all I can do now is to remember them with gratitude. There are a number of authors to whom I have referred directly or indirectly in order to enrich my own thoughts. They are: Hemachandra Bandhopadhyay, Michael Madhusudan Dutt, Chandidas, Kabikankan Mukundaram, Krisnachandra Mazumdar, Debendranath Sen, Saratchandra Chattopadhyay, Kailasabasini Devi (Gupta), Kailasabasini Devi (Mitra), Prasannamoyee Devi, Saratkumari Chaudhurani, Ashapurna Devi, Amartya Sen, Pratul Bandopadhyay, Virginia Woolfe and Rabindranath Tagore. Others have helped me in numerous ways—Pronoti Deb, Suranjan Das, Gautam Bhadra, Sulata Chaudhuri, Monobina Das Gupta, Soumyendu Ray, Ajitkumar Sen, Ashok Das Gupta, Bijan Sen and Abhijit Sen

Gupta. I owe a debt to all of them. I thank Madhuchhanda Karlekar for her translation from the original Bengali and Sukhendu Ray and Anurag Basnet for competent editing.